# Visualforce in Practice

Michael Floyd

Don Robins

Matt Lacey

Michael Topalovich

Dan Appleman and Lior Gotersman

Ryan Sieve

Peter Gruhl

# Copyrights

Written by Michael Floyd, Don Robins, Michael Topalovich, Dan Appleman and Lior Gotersman, Ryan Sieve and Peter Gruhl.

Contributions by Pat Patterson, Sandeep Bhanot, Raja Rao DV, and Michael Alderete.

Cover by Domenique Sillett.

Special Thanks to Nick Tran, Adam Seligman, Quinton Wall, Andrew Waite, Chris Wall, and Lesley Schneiderman.

# Introduction

The making of this book is an interesting story. The seed of its inspiration came from developers like you. Following one of our ELEVATE Workshops, an attendee was asked what he would like to see next. He simply replied "A book about Visualforce."

Then my colleague Mario Korf spoke up, saying that "We have an Advanced Apex book," authored by Dan Appleman to compliment our Introductory Apex Developer's Guide. "We should do an Advanced Visualforce." And that's how this book was born.

But rather than follow the Beginner-Advanced documentation model, I wanted a book that shows developers how to do real things while learning through actual apps that have been deployed and are in practice. This is Visualforce in Practice.

I also wanted readers to get the opportunity to learn from Force.com practitioners, developers in the trenches that are earnestly building enterprise applications and deploying them to the cloud. I wanted to share the experience of those who have gone before you.

And so I recruited Don Robins, a veteran Force.com Certified Salesforce Trainer and Salesforce MVP—the only developer to hold both titles. With Don's help we recruited Matt Lacey, Michael Topalovich, Dan Appleman, Lior Gotesman, Ryan Sieve and Peter Gruhl.

Together we've assembled a collection of Visualforce example apps that you can use in your own practice. This is not documentation, and it is not intended to document every feature built into Visualforce. This book is intended to share the experience and expertise of our authors.

## About the Book

Visualforce in Practice is intended for intermediate Force.com developers. The book assumes you have walked through the Visualforce Workbook tutorial, and know the basics of creating a Visualforce page.

Chapter 1, Thinking in Visualforce lays the groundwork by discussing the MVC design Pattern, when you should use Visualforce and alternatives for using Visualforce under various use cases.

The Standard Controller is an amazingly versatile component that changes behavior based on the objects it's working on. In that sense it is a polymorphic component that can do an amazing amount of work without having to write code. In Chapter 2, Don Robins walks you through the Standard Controller and sheds light on mysterious components like URLFOR().

Because you'll need to write custom controllers or controller extensions at some point, Chapter 4 introduces you to "Just Enough Code." Rather than providing introductions to Apex and SOQL, this chapter gives you the basics so you can get started writing controllers and extensions immediately.

In Part II the rubber meets the road with chapters that will show you how to work with and paginate lists using the StandardSetController (Chapter 4), and how to create wizards that walk users through a process (Chapter 5). Chapter 6 shows how to create amazing looking charts to display data using the Analytics API, and Chapter 7 walks through the process for creating dashboards.

Chapter 8 uses the Streaming API to stream live data into Visualforce pages, while Chapter 9 shows how to build Visualforce page templates like those in the Salesforce Mobile Templates. Chapter 10 shows you how to add JavaScript and HTML5 to your Visualforce pages, which sets up Part III covering mobile development.

Chapter 11 walks you through the process of refactoring existing Force.com apps, then extends to mobile the Warehouse App used in the Force.com Workbook. Chapter 12 introduces you to the Salesforce Mobile Templates, the brainchild of Developer Evangelist Sandeep Bhanot. And Finally Chapter 13 presents readers with tips and tricks for optimizing Visualforce pages to ensure peek performance.

Looking back, there are many topics we would like to have covered in this book, and with the introduction of Salesforce1 there are many new topics we would like to include in the future. Indeed, I'm looking forward to creating a second edition of Visualforce in Pracice. In the meantime, it is my sincerest hope that you find this book not only educational, but useful in your everyday practice.


Sincerely,


Michael Floyd

Editor in Chief, Developer Force

Salesforce.com

# Contents

# Chapter 3—Just Enough Code Introduction to Controllers and Extensions

# Chapter 1
# Thinking in Visualforce

The Salesforce Platform tool chest is brimming with tools that enable you to build your database, add field validation, embed workflow rules and business logic, create custom UI's, query database objects, run reports and retrieve analytics. Aside from the standard platform tools, Salesforce Platform provides mobile packs, open-source SDKs and tools, SOAP and REST APIs so you can integrate with other platforms like Heroku, APIs to access Chatter feeds, tools for building web sites, and well, you get the idea.

For the new developer, it can be overwhelming. But just who is this new developer? In fact, Salesforce developers as a group come from diverse backgrounds. But whatever their roles I believe that many of these developers are looking for more than a quick start. I believe many are looking for a deeper understanding in the hopes of achieving some level of unconscious competence. I also believe these developers are looking at Salesforce Platform as a general-purpose tool for building data-driven applications in the cloud, not just a tool for building or extending CRM apps.

So before you dive into Visualforce, you should gain some experience with the Salesforce Platform. The final section in this chapter addresses the five things you should know before getting started with Visualforce.

Since this book is about Visualforce in practice, I'm not going to spend a great deal of time introducing you to the language. After all, there's a wealth of tutorial walkthrough's, getting started guides and the Visualforce Developer's Guide to get you up to speed using Visualforce. Later in this chapter I'll share the resources that will give you the foundations you'll need for mastering not only Visualforce, but the entire Salesforce Platform.

So with that said, this chapter will give you a brief introduction, then provide pointers to where you can learn the basics. What's more interesting is what you can (and can't) do with Visualforce. So we'll start with the what, when and why before jumping into the how. This chapter presents the things you should know about Visualforce before diving in.

## What is Visualforce

Visuaforce is an interesting tool. If I were to define it in a nutshell I'd say "Visualforce is a markup language that allows you to describe the user interface components that live on your Force.com pages."

Visualforce pages consist of two elements: Visualforce markup, and a controller. That is, you use markup language to define the components that will live on your page and tie it to a controller (either standard or custom) to execute the logic behind those components. Visualforce lives on the server. So any code you write will be generated and run on the server. Let's start by understanding the need for view state.

As you'll learn in Chapter 3, a developer can either use a standard controller provided by the Force.com platform, or add custom controller logic with a class written in Apex.

## Controllers and Extensions

A **standard controller** consists of the same functionality and logic that is used for a standard Salesforce page. For example, if you use the standard `Accounts` controller, clicking a **Save** button in a Visualforce page results in the same behavior as clicking **Save** on a standard Account edit page. If you use a standard controller on a page and the user doesn't have access to the object, the page will display an insufficient privileges error message. You can avoid this by checking the user's accessibility for an object and displaying components appropriately.

A **standard list controller** enables you to create Visualforce pages that can display or act on a set of records. Examples of existing Salesforce pages that work with sets of records include list pages, related lists, and mass action pages.

A **custom controller** is a class written in Apex that implements all of a page's logic, without leveraging a standard controller. If you use a custom controller, you can define new navigation elements or behaviors, but you must also reimplement any functionality that was already provided in a standard controller. Like other Apex classes, custom controllers execute entirely in system mode, in which the object and field-level permissions of the current user are ignored. You can specify whether a user can execute methods in a custom controller based on the user's profile.

A **controller extension** is a class written in Apex that adds to or overrides behavior in a standard or custom controller. Extensions allow you to leverage the functionality of another controller while adding your own custom logic.

# About the Markup

If you know anything about XML, you know that it allows you to create other markup languages using DTD's or XML Schema. Visualforce syntax is essentially another markup language. Markup elements are overloaded with components, and attributes are used to configure these components, making it a powerful language that's super easy to use. Visualforce is used for creating forms, presenting lists and rollups from the database, and creating UI elements. You can embed XHTML in a Visualforce page, making it versatile for creating web pages and mobile-optimized pages with responsive design.

To give you a quick taste, here's a Visualforce fragment that will display an article from Article database:

```
<apex:page standardController="Article__c" >
        <apex:form >
            <apex:pageBlock mode="detail" >
                <apex:pageBlockButtons location="top">
                    <apex:commandButton action="{!edit}" value="Edit"/>
                <apex:commandButton action="{!delete}" value="Delete"/>
                </apex:pageBlockButtons>
                <apex:pageBlockSection columns="1" title="Article
Information">
                    <apex:outputField value="{!Article__c.Name}"/>
                    <apex:outputField value="{!Article__c.Author__c}"/>
                    <apex:outputField value="{!Article__c.Status__c}"/>
                <apex:outputField value="{!Article__c.Publish_Date__c}"/>
            <apex:outputField value="{!Article__c.Link_to_Article__c}"/>
                </apex:pageBlockSection>
            </apex:pageBlock>
        </apex:form>
</apex:page>
```

In terms of the MVC model, a Visualforce page involves both the View and the Controller.

# About View State

To maintain state in a Visualforce page, the Force.com platform includes the state of components, field values, and controller state in a hidden form element. This encrypted string is referred to as the view state  and has a limit of 135KB. Large view states require longer processing times for each request, including serializing and de-serializing, and encryption and decryption. By reducing your view state size, your pages can load quicker and stall less often.

Consider a user request for a web page with a simple form on it. The user fills out the form and submits it. If the user's input fails the validation rules for the form, the server responds with an error message - the user corrects the error and resubmits it successfully. Behind the scenes the browser is issuing HTTP requests.

The page is initially retrieved with a GET request and form submissions happen via POST requests. These POST requests are also called postbacks since the data on the form is being posted back to the same page. From the user perspective, this is a stateful interaction since the page state is changing based on its previous state. However HTTP is a stateless protocol, which means that the initial GET and the two subsequent POSTs are treated as independent requests for the page. As a result, some other mechanism is needed to persist state information across HTTP requests.

In Visualforce, page state is persisted as a hidden form field that is automatically inserted into a form when the page gets generated. We call this the view state of the page. The view state captures the state of the page -- state of its associated controllers and extensions and the component tree on the page. The view state is posted back along with the other form data, which gives the server enough information to recreate the page state to which new changes can be applied. Please consult this section in the Visualforce documentation to understand the order of execution for a Visualforce page.

## What is Contained in the View State?

The data in the view state should be sufficient to recreate the state of the page when the postback is received. To do this, it stores the following data:

- All non-transient data members in the associated controller (either standard or custom) and the controller extensions.

- Objects that are reachable from a non-transient data member in a controller or controller extension.

- The component tree for that page, which represents the page's component structure and the associated state, which are the values applied to those components.

- A small amount of data for Visualforce to do housekeeping.

View state data is encrypted and cannot be viewed with tools like Firebug. The view state inspector described below lets you look at the contents of view state.

## Examining the View State

Developer environments have a view state inspector, which lets you view the contents of the view state. This information can help you in optimizing the view state size. Once enabled, it shows up as a tab in Development Mode, as follows.

| Name ▲ | Type | Value | Size (KB) | % Of Parent |
|---|---|---|---|---|
| ▲ ▢ View State | | | | |
| ▲ ▢ State | | | 5.65 | 100 |
| ▲ ▢ NewAndExistingController | Page vf6 Controller | | 5.18 | 92 |
| ▢ account | Account | | 1.02 | 18 |
| ▢ ApexPage.pagemessagecomponentcontroller | Component pagemessage.apexc Controller | | 0.18 | 3 |
| ▢ ApexPage.PageMessagesComponentController | Component pagemessages.apexc Controller | | 0.77 | 14 |
| ▢ Internal | | | 0.77 | 14 |
| ▢ Component Tree | | | 2.62 | 51 |
| | | | 0.48 | 9 |

*Figure 1-1. Examining view state with the inspector, available when Development Mode is enabled.*

## View State in Action

In the previous sections, we looked at what is contained in the view state and how the view state inspector lets you view its contents. To make the concepts around view state a little more concrete, this section looks at a few sample pages and their associated view state

```
<apex:page standardController="Account">
    <apex:form >
        <apex:pageBlock title="My Content" mode="edit">
            <apex:pageBlockButtons >
                <apex:commandButton action="{!save}" value="Save"/>
            </apex:pageBlockButtons>
            <apex:pageBlockSection title="My Content Section"
columns="2">
                <apex:inputField value="{!account.name}"/>
            </apex:pageBlockSection>
        </apex:pageBlock>
    </apex:form>
</apex:page>
```

### VIEWING STATE WITH A CUSTOM CONTROLLER

The following listing shows a Visualforce page with a custom controller and a single field. Figure 1-2 shows the associated view state which contains an account instance since it has been declared as a non transient member variable in our controller. Notice how simple our controller code for updating the account is.

```
<apex:page controller="MyController1" >
    <apex:form >
        <apex:pageBlock title="My Content" mode="edit">
            <apex:pageBlockButtons >
                <apex:commandButton action="{!save}" value="Save"/>
            </apex:pageBlockButtons>
            <apex:pageBlockSection title="My Content Section"
columns="2">
                <apex:inputField value="{!account.name}"/>
            </apex:pageBlockSection>
        </apex:pageBlock>
    </apex:form>
</apex:page>
```

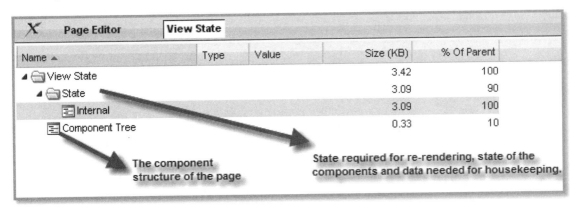

*Figure 1-2. States include component tree, rerendering, components and other housekeeping data*

```
public with sharing class myController1 {
    public final Account account {get; set;}

    public myController1() {
        account = [select name from Account where id
= :ApexPages.currentPage().getParameters().get('id')];
    }
    public PageReference save() {
        update account;
        return null;
    }
}
```

## EXTENDING THE EXAMPLE

Let's modify the previous example by making the account name and ID controller member variables. We'll make the account name member transient so that only the record ID is being saved in the view state. The page and the controller code is shown below. When this page is posted back, we'll need to retrieve the record again, apply the new values and then update the database. This highlights the main benefit of view state - making the job of a developer easier by automatically maintaining state between postbacks.

```
<apex:page controller="myController" >
    <apex:form >
        <apex:pageBlock title="My Content" mode="edit">
            <apex:pageBlockButtons >
                <apex:commandButton action="{!save}" value="Save"/>
            </apex:pageBlockButtons>
            <apex:pageBlockSection title="My Content Section"
columns="2">
                <apex:outputLabel for="aName">Account Name:</
apex:outputLabel>
                <apex:inputText value="{!accountName}"/>
            </apex:pageBlockSection>
        </apex:pageBlock>
    </apex:form>
</apex:page>
```

| X    Page Editor    Controller | View State | | | |
|---|---|---|---|---|
| Name ▲ | Type | Value | Size (KB) | % Of Parent |
| ▲ View State | | | 3.72 | 100 |
| ▲ State | | | 3.39 | 91 |
| ▲ myController | Page vf8 Controller | | 1.19 | 32 |
| ▲ account | Account | | 0.16 | 4 |
| Name | String | Burlington Northern Railways | 0.11 | 3 |
| Id | String | 001t0000008MB00A,AG | 0.09 | 3 |
| Internal | | | 2.2 | 65 |
| Component Tree | | | 0.33 | 9 |

*Figure 1-3. State for the extended example.*

```
public with sharing class myController {

    private final Id accountId ;
    transient public final String accountName {get; set; }

    public myController() {
        Account account = [select Id, Name from Account where id
= :ApexPages.currentPage().getParameters().get('id')];
        accountId = account.Id ;
        accountName = account.Name ;
    }

    public PageReference save() {
        Account myAccount = [select name from Account where id
= :accountId];
        myAccount.name = accountName ;
        update myAccount;
        return null;
    }

}
```

## ADDING A NEW COMPONENT

Finally, let's add a new component to the page and observe the effect on view state. We will add a standard `pageMessages` component - the resulting view state now shows the controller state associated with this component.

```
<apex:page controller="myController1" >
    <apex:form >
        <apex:pageBlock title="My Content" mode="edit">
            <apex:pageMessages/>
            <apex:pageBlockButtons >
                <apex:commandButton action="{!save}" value="Save"/>
            </apex:pageBlockButtons>
            <apex:pageBlockSection title="My Content Section"
columns="2">
                <apex:inputField value="{!account.name}"/>
            </apex:pageBlockSection>
        </apex:pageBlock>
    </apex:form>
</apex:page>
```

Optimizing your view state can improvethe performance of your pages. Understanding how view state is affected by components is the first step. Chapter 13 provides tips and techniques for optimizing View State for better performance.

## New Additions to Visualforce

Visualforce is constantly evolving, and the latest release (Winter '14 at the time of this writing) is no different. Visualforce enhancements in Winter '14 are focused on improving the experience of developing HTML5 apps, along with some additional development tool improvements and other changes. Notably, the new `<apex:input>` and related elements provide an HTML 5-friendly, general-purpose input component that adapts to the data expected by a form field. These elements use the HTML `type` attribute, particularly values new in HTML5, to allow client browsers to display type-appropriate user input widgets, such as a date picker or range slider, or use a type-specific keyboard on touch devices, or to perform client-side formatting or validation, such as with a numeric range or a telephone number. Additional UI components support "pass-through" attributes that let you add arbitrary attributes to many Visualforce components that will be "passed through" to the rendered HTML. In addition, components can generate an HTML 5 `<datalist>` block for associated input fields.

Other Visualforce enhancements include:

- Deferred Loading of JavaScript Resources
- Server-Side View State
- Accessibility improvements
- Preview Page Button for Visualforce Pages
- Available for Touch Checkbox Renamed
- New `<apex:milestoneTracker>` Component
- Other minor fixes, updates and deprecations

## Salesforce1 and Visualforce

The recently announced Salesforce1 Platform includes the Salesforce1 app, a flexible mobile app that instantly transforms existing custom Salesforce apps, and delivers a mobile-ready solution. Records, driven by metadata that provides context to the user experience, deliver information that takes advantage of mobile device features. For example, address fields can be plotted on maps and phone numbers can be dialed with a simple tap. Designed for scale, Salesforce1 also provides open APIs for extensibility and integration.

While you could take an existing Visualforce page and surface it in Salesforce1, you'll want to consider how that page will look and function on a mobile device. Most likely, you'll want to create a new page designed especially for a mobile experience. We didn't have time to include Salesforce1 in this book. For more information about where Visualforce pages can appear in the user interface, See the set of Salesforce1 guides including the Developer's Guide, Admin Guide and API guide.

## Five Things You Should Master Before Getting Started with Visualforce

1. **Develop a solid understanding of the platform.** The basic learning path is to follow the tutorial in the Force.com Workbook, which walks you through the construction of the Warehouse app, an inventory management system. Not only does the tutorial guide you through and provide hands-on experience with every major component of the platform, the solution you create is a near-ubiquitous solution that can be adapted to numerous use cases. Also:

Read Force.com Platform Fundamentals. This guide provides thorough coverage of the platform and will fill in the gaps left by the Force.com Workbook. Likewise, check out "the multitenant white paper" on Developer Force.

2. **Learn and know your tools.** It sounds simple but the best developers (on any platform) know their tools right down to that last 10% of the feature set. The fact is, you will be living in your development environment. You'll be more productive, and in the beginning you will find that you will fumble less for answers. Salesforce Platform offers numerous tools. Choose the tool that's right for you and learn how to use it well. Here's a list of the tools:

**The Developer Edition (DE) environment.** More than just a tool, the DE environment is a browser-based development workspace that gives you access to Apex Code, Visualforce, Chatter, SOAP and REST integration APIs, and well, this just scratches the surface. Later when you deploy to a production environment, you'll see that the Developer Edition environment allows you to continue development without affecting your production deployment. Since this is where you will be developing apps, installing packages, setting up administrative access, configuring and customizing your experience, you will want to take the time to learn the environment and become comfortable with it's most prominent features.

The DE Environment is pretty cool but as a long-time Java hack, I like to use Eclipse. It so happens that the Eclipse-based Force.com IDE is a powerful client application for creating, modifying, testing and deploying Force.com applications. As a plugin to Eclipse, it provides a comfortable environment for programmers familiar with integrated development environments, allowing you to code, compile, test, and deploy all from within the IDE itself.

The Developer Console. The Developer Console is a versatile tool that lets you create, edit, debug and test your applications directly from your Salesforce org. Many developers work exclusively in the Developer Console, but where it shines is testing and debugging. You can step through the execution path of your app, set checkpoints, inspect variables and retrieve their values. The Developer Console also gives you access to debug logs so you can look at your Apex and Visualforce source, as well as callouts, validation rules and workflow rules. The Developer Console also allows you to execute SOQL queries directly in the tool, and there's also a performance tree that allows you to look at memory usage and processing time. You can run Apex tests and view code coverage, set checkpoints and more.

3. **Learn some code: SOQL, Visualforce, and Apex.** As I mentioned, this technically isn't a requirement for building basic apps. In fact, you can do a lot with formulas, approval processes and workflow rules. But if you plan to use Salesforce Platform as a general-purpose tool for building cloud applications, you will, in practice, want to write some code.

Apex Code. Apex is a strongly typed, object-oriented language that is syntactically similar to languages like Java and C#. However, the language is platform aware and contains constructs that make it easy to work with relational data. If you are familiar with other programming languages, you'll still need to learn about execution contexts, bulk patterns, query optimization and limits. Beyond the basics you'll find on the Apex Code page, I would point you to Dan Appleman's Advanced Apex book.

SOQL. If you're familiar with SQL, you'll feel right at home with SOQL. To get a quick comparison of the two, check out Dan Appleman's From SQL to SOQL.

4. **Choose Apps that are well-suited to Salesforce Platform**. As a general purpose development tool, Salesforce Platform is really good for building data-driven cloud apps that require security, identity management and OAuth authentication. So first, you'll want to choose a problem that calls for these requirements. Spend time learning everything you can about both the Database and Security models.

5. **Learn from the pro's**. Read a lot of code. You can learn a lot from others. And finally, test as you go. Salesforce already incorporates unit testing. But you'll still need to write code to test your Apex. This is where the developer console really comes in handy.

Follow the Community Boards. The best place to find Salesforce practitioners, MVPs and your peers is on the discussion boards. Along with some of the Developer Evangelists, you'll find Salesforce MVP's, other developers and enthusiast, and of course, me. It's a great place to pose your questions and learn from others in a practical setting. And as Samantha Ready pointed out, "hang out on Stack Exchange, and remember to Google."

Employ the principles of good design. Learn about the Salesforce MVC model. Then employ the principles of abstraction, separation of concerns, and other practices of good object-oriented design.

## Parting Words

Once you get to the point where you're building your own apps I would add "Plan your design before you begin." Salesforce Platform utilizes the classic model-view-controller model. You don't need to follow formal design patterns, but you should map out your app and decide where you want to implement features. And "Factor in Refactoring." In my own development I've discovered that once you've set up your objects, added field validation, workflow rules and business logic, and get to the user interface, there's always more logic required. Sometimes this logic finds its way into a Visualforce button.

Now let's go learn about the Standard Controller.

# Chapter 2
# The Standard Controller—
# Pushing the Envelope

Many developers first learning the Force.com platform, as well as many working with it for years, often don't understand just how the Model View Controller (MVC) software pattern applies to the basic functionality of the standard Salesforce applications. Or, it can be assumed that the MVC pattern only applies to Visualforce and the standard or custom Apex controllers developers choose to bind them to when building custom pages.

However, all familiar Home Page, List Views, Detail Page displays and dialogs are managed by means of built-in or 'standard' controller capabilities that manipulate the presentation and user interaction with the data of both standard and custom sObjects.

For those of you new to Salesforce, sObject, (AKA Salesforce object,) is the technical term used for both an entity type as well as a data record in Salesforce. We will use the term record when discussing an sObject instance in the database or in memory, and sObject as a type of standard or custom entity.

The user interface for the Salesforce Sales and Service cloud applications, as well as any custom Force.com business applications, is materialized at runtime by the Force.com platform, which is designed and built using an MVC software pattern.

The metadata-driven engine provides for the configurable display of screens and dialogs (the Views) containing business data (Models) and for the management of user interaction with the primary data operations as well as navigation across all views (Controllers.)

Before delving into the details of building Visualforce custom pages, it is beneficial to understand this built-in and ever-present controller instruction set and its capabilities.

Mechanisms are available to developers to programmatically access it when implementing custom Visualforce pages, with or without a custom Apex controller. However, the variety of mechanisms often overlap in capability and function, requiring developers to choose which approach or mechanism to utilize based on particular development requirements.

These mechanisms include the following:

- sObject view-related metadata controlling the configuration and presentation of list, page and dialog views.

- sObject interaction-related metadata such as actions, buttons and links defining the common, yet potentially disparate actions across both standard and custom sObjects.

- A StandardController object that is automatically provided for most standard and all custom sObjects, bindable to a Visualforce page component with the `standardController` attribute. It provides a reference to a single record, (or list of records,) as well as to a set of common actions for data processing and default navigation.

- An Apex system-delivered `StandardController` class for use from within an Apex class, such as custom controllers, controller extensions, or unit tests. This system delivered class can be used as a reference to the StandardController object bound to a Visualforce page through the attribute standardController, and provides programmatic access to the associated data and related actions. While a custom Apex custom controller can completely replace a StandardController, an Apex controller extension class can reference the StandardController bound to a page by use of a StandardController instance injected as a parameter to the constructor of the Apex extension class. This allows leverage of all the standard controller capabilities, while providing additional functionality from the custom extension.

- The `URLFOR()` function allows dynamic generation of relative URLs though pages can be accessed, actions performed, and processes executed. Operations result in page redirection, and multiple arguments can be added to provide URL parameters, additional record and sObject context, and configurable action override control.

- The `$Action` Global Variable can be used with the `URLFOR()` function to invoke dozens of different kinds of actions available to both standard and custom sObjects, independent of any StandardController and its associated sObject.

- The `$ObjectType` global variable allows programmatic access to metadata describe information for sObject and field schema, including security context for accessibility based on the current logged in user, in accordance with their particular profile sObject CRUD and field-level security permissions.

Visualforce page navigation and command components, such as `apex:commandButton`, `apex:commandLink`, and `apex:outputLink` can interact with the above mechanisms which can be used in combination to deliver complex controller capabilities.

This chapter will focus on the standard controller mechanisms provided, as well as the configurable actions and navigation capabilities that developers can leverage programmatically.

## What Is a Standard Controller?

While it is generally understood that a standard controller provides management of views, data, and actions in Salesforce, there is often confusion regarding exactly what a standard controller is.

It might appear that a standard controller is a component or class, pre-existing for standard sObjects and auto-generated for newly created custom sObjects at design time. Some might speculate from some of the formal documentation (ie. "Every standard controller includes a getter method that returns the record specified by the id...") that they exist as classes in Apex or Java not visible to developers.

It is probably more accurate to represent a standard controller, not as a component or class, but rather as a consistent set of user interface and data operation instructions. It is automatically provided by the Force.com engine, and available at design and runtime for most standard and all custom sObjects.

It is tightly integrated with sObject metadata, configurable for each sObject, and it drives the runtime page materialization, record management and action processing of most of the built-in user interface. This includes dialogs, search layouts, record detail page layouts, as well as record list views and the associated actions and behavior.

Focusing on how a standard controller is implemented and delivered by the Force.com platform is far less important than focusing on what it provides. What is most important to understand is how central it is to managing the user interface, navigation and data operations on sObjects, regardless of whether or not a developer chooses to implement custom Visualforce pages, with or without Apex logic.

## What Does a Standard Controller Do?

The interaction between a user and their business data can be simple or complex, but nonetheless requires a detailed set of instructions and rules to be managed. It is the controller that provides such management, while preserving a clean separation between the view layer and the data model.

In the MVC pattern, Views know how to present their data and accept input from the user, but know nothing about how to actually fetch that data or process it.

Data Models know how to perform various operations such as Save, Delete or Merge, but need to be told when to operate, and need to be provided with the data to operate on.

It is the Controller's job to marshal both data and action selection, as initiated by the user from within the View, to the Model. Controllers are also responsible for responding accordingly with navigation redirection based on the results of any particular action.

In the Salesforce MVC paradigm, it is the standard controller that facilitates the ability of users to access and interact with the structured business data contained in records and displayed in the materialized user interface.

A standard controller's tasks are as follows:

- **Controlling Data:** Standard controllers fetch data and provide it to the page, list, dialog or form, all referred to here as views. While it is the view's task to manage the presentation of its data, the controller gathers the data from the view as entered or changed by a user, and passes it to the data model for processing.

- **Controlling Actions**: Standard controllers respond to user or programmatic commands initiated from a view. Such commands, referred to as Actions, might be associated with processing the data gathered from the view, or simply to respond to a navigation link.

- **Controlling Navigation**: Standard controllers navigate the user to any specific view associated with an action. They also handle redirection to subsequent views, based on the specific outcome of various actions and data operations.

Developers might assume that they must resort to the implementation of custom Apex logic to provide complex functionality that their applications require, yet might be unaware that such functionality might already be available to them in Visualforce via standard controller mechanisms.

It is a best practice to make sure you understand what is available to leverage in the standard controller layer before you begin to design and build your own custom pages and controllers to avoid 'reinventing the wheel.'

Let's break down the standard controller into its core parts, focusing on both the common and less obvious aspects to clarify what is automatically available in the Force.com standard controller instruction set.

# CONTROLLING VIEWS

## Materializing a User Interface

The metadata-driven user interface is one of the most powerful aspects of the Force.com platform, making development of business applications both rapid and cost effective.

Using no code, complex relational database applications can be configured and deployed in short order because the standard user interface for each sObject, including the Home Page, List Views, Search Dialogs, Detail and Edit pages, are all materialized by the Force.com engine at runtime, and managed by standard controller functionality.

- The controller mechanism utilizes each sObject's default or customized metadata, field configuration, and other various settings available on the detail setup page.

- There is a minimum metadata configuration provided by default for each standard sObject delivered with a new org, and for each custom sObject created that includes the following:

- Inclusion of a hyperlinked standard Name field in all list views and dialogs. These views can be further configured to display additional fields.

- A default page layout including all standard fields, (other than the record ID,) pre-existing for standard sObjects and initially generated and configured for each new custom sObject.

- Custom fields added to any sObject are added to page layouts by default at design time, although the user can choose to exclude them.

- During the creation of relationships on child sObjects, users can choose to include related lists on page layouts of the related parent sObject.

- During the creation of custom fields, profile-based, field-level security is defaulted to allow read/write access to all new fields to all users of all profiles, but the user can customized access as needed.

All of this related metadata is used by the standard controller engine to auto-render a basic user interface with the appropriate data display or input controls, whether 'out of the box' or customized by a developer.

## Standard User Interface Flow

The typical standard User Experience (UX) is as follows for any standard or custom data management in Salesforce:

- A user logs into their Salesforce org and is presented with those applications to which they have rights. Once an application has been selected, the associated tabs are displayed. Developers should realize that Apps and Tabs are in themselves a configurable view.

- Selecting any tab (our focus will be on sObject Tabs rather than Visualforce or Web tabs), directs the user to a set of views managed by the standard controller, (for the selected sObject,) that follows a consistent navigation path.

- The initial tab displayed is the Home Tab for that sObject, displaying a dropbox selector of available list views, and a list of any recently viewed records. Various standard sObject Home Tabs also display additional information, such as reports or tools, etc.

- A user can select one of the available list views from the dropbox, the All view is present by default. Or they can select to navigate to one of the listed 'Recent' links which will direct them to the detail view of the selected record.

- Selection of a list view displays all records matching the filter and column configuration, the default **All* view displays all records with just the hyperlinked Name field. List views may be added or customized, allowing users to select column display configuration and list filtering. These mechanisms are managed by the standard controller instruction set. You might also note that this same set of list views are available to leverage with programmatic access within a Visualforce page.

- Selection of any record will navigate to its detail view, which is rendered based on the associated sObject page layout metadata. The user's access to buttons and links will be mitigated by the standard controller based on the user's permissions, or as configured in the page layout. If there are page layout and record type assignments configured, the appropriate layout will be used based on the user's profile assignment.

- The various buttons invoke the associated actions, associated navigation and processing, again all managed by the standard controller instruction set.

This user experience flow might seem obvious for any user who is familiar to Salesforce. However, our purpose is to make it clear that the control of the navigation path, the management of the data components displayed on each view, the rendered controls, links and their associated actions, the configuration of the display and filtering criteria of the list views; all are delivered by the standard controller instruction set working behind the scenes as driven by the Force.com engine.

This configurable behavior, whether default or customized, is persisted in the metadata of the associated sObject, and might also be affected by other means, such as user profile permission configuration.

Each of the primary data views associated with a set of standard actions on any sObject can be overridden with a custom Visualforce page. Page layouts, which are also configurable, can contain nested Visualforce pages as well.

The best part is that the greater majority of the controller instruction set capabilities are available to developers to access programmatically from their Visualforce pages, with or without underlying Apex controller or extension logic.

This foundation-level understanding of what the Force.com engine does is beneficial to guiding your development effort when building custom functionality, so let's take a closer look.

## CONTROLLING DATA

### Referencing a Single Record

No page, standard or custom, would be of much use to a user without some data to operate on. One of the key tasks of the standard controller is to provide that data, and to facilitate binding a view's controls to the record's fields, for either display or input.

Data binding to Visualforce components is relatively straight forward, but there is an aspect of managing field data that is a bit more obscure.

As most developers know, we can associate a standard controller with a Visualforce page by use of the standardController attribute on the component. We simply identify the standard or custom sObject for the controller as follows:

```
<apex:page standardController="Account" >
```

Once bound, the page associates within the context of the specified sObject. The standard controller will provide the data from an associated record and allow the record's fields to be bound to the page's various components using merge expression syntax. This is the same merge syntax used in formula expressions, email templates, and anywhere that field values need to be merged for expression evaluation:

```
<apex:inputField value={"!Account.name"} />
```

Values of any specified fields associated with the controller's sObject are accessed using standard dot notation. The name of the sObject is used to represent the record instance. Fields on related parent sObjects, (whether a lookup or master-detail relationship,) can also be referenced and bound:

```
<apex:inputField value={"!Account.Owner.Firstname"} />
```

Lists of records from child sObjects can be referenced and bound to components that render collections. Note that the value of the list attribute is the literal name of the field representing the child relationship:

```
<apex:relatedList list="Contacts" />
```

The standard controller requires record context that can be provided by including a URL parameter named 'id' and assigned with a valid 15- or 18-digit record ID. The record specified by the ID must match the sObject type associated with the StandardController on the page, or an error will be thrown when the page attempts to render:

```
https://naX.salesforce.com/apex/CustomAccountPage?id=001A0000005HjZL
```

This is slightly different than the URL pattern to access a standard detail page for any record, which simply requires that the record id follow the Salesforce server instance name:

```
https://naX.salesforce.com/001A0000005HjZL
```

This standard URL pattern is referred to as a 'Frontdoor URL', and is available to invoke a view, edit and insert of a record, as well as some other actions. We'll take a closer look at this syntax a bit later in the chapter, but for now just note that both of the above approaches require the record id to be present in the URL.

This allows the standard controller to fetch the data for the referenced record, and makes the values of all referenced fields available through the sObject reference for binding.

## Loading Field Values

The key in the sentence above is *referenced fields*. What might not be obvious is that the standard controller will automatically populate the underlying sObject instance with only those fields explicitly bound to components included in the page.

In other words, while all fields in the schema of the referenced sObject are available for binding to Visualforce page components, only those fields explicitly bound to components on the Visualforce page will have their values fetched by the underlying query managed by the standard controller; excluded field values will not be available for reference.

This is not unlike how a developer must explicitly include fields in a SELECT clause of a SOQL query in Apex on any target sObject in order to obtain their values and be able to programmatically manage them.

Just as in the Apex scenario when runtime code attempts to access a field not explicitly specified in a SOQL query, if code in a Visualforce page attempts to reference a field that has not been explicitly bound on the page, an error will be thrown at runtime and presented to the user.

This can also occur when the StandardController instance is passed into an Apex custom controller extension as a parameter on the class constructor. If the record is retrieved by use of the getRecord() method on the StandardController instance, and some Apex code attempts to reference a field not bound on the page, an exception will be thrown.

An error will also occur during page rendering if such an excluded field is referenced elsewhere in the Visualforce page. This can be in a formula function bound to a component, perhaps built into a link component, or referenced somewhere in a block of Javascript. Regardless, in any such scenario, if the field value is not available, an error will occur.

One simple solution to extend the set of fetched field values is to add a hidden, non-visual or un-rendered Visualforce component to the page and bind the necessary field to the component's value attribute. This will cause the field's value to be included when populating the sObject instance.

For example, if you want the lookup ID value of a Contact's parent Account available for a navigation link, including only a reference to the field value when constructing the link, or including it as a parameter in a URLFOR() function, will not cause the field's value to be fetched by the standard controller from the database.

You will have to explicitly bind the field as a value attribute to some other Visualforce component, and if you don't want the value displayed, you will need to set the rendered attribute to false:

```
<apex:outputText value="{!contact.accountId}" rendered="false"/>
```

To make your code a bit less confusing to other developers who might wonder why the component exists if never being rendered, binding the field to a variable component will also work:

```
<apex:variable value="{!contact.accountId}" var="accountId" />
```

Once bound it will be available for reference elsewhere on the page.

## Loading Field Values in Apex

We won't go into too much detail regarding custom controllers and Apex, but it's worthwhile to simply note that this same issue might occur when using an Apex controller extension class with a referenced StandardController when your code needs to access fields on the sObject that have not been bound in the Visualforce page.

You can programmatically add additional fields in Apex using the addFields() and reset() instance methods on the referenced StandardController instance passed into the extension class constructor. The addFields() method takes a single argument of a String[] collection containing a list of those field you wish to populate.

There are some important considerations however when using these methods.

- The addFields() method must be called before referencing the sObject with the getRecord() method.

- Any pending changes to the record will be lost when the addFields() method is called.

The following example shows where the method is called in the constructor just before getting the record:

```
public class DemoControllerExt {
    public DemoControllerExt(ApexPages.StandardController
controller){
        controller.addFields(new List<String>{'accountId'});
Contact contact=(Contact) controller.getRecord();        ...
{
        ... }
```

You can add more fields to the list later in code and call the reset() method to refetch the record which will include all of the desired field values specified.

A word of caution when unit testing your controller extension classes. Documentation on these methods tells us that they are only for use with "controllers used by dynamicVisualforce bindings," suggesting that `reset()` and `addFields()` only work when the standard controller on a Visualforce page is responsible for loading the data.

The implication is that if your Apex unit test code is responsible for setting up an sObject, explicitly instantiating a standard controller instance with that sObject, and then passing that `standardController` instance into a controller extension class for testing purposes, these methods won't function as expected.

You will need to have your test sObject completely loaded with all desired field values before instantiating a `StandardController` instance to pass to the constructor when instantiating the Apex controller extension class for your tests. In addition, you will likely want to conditionally execute your `addFields()` code only if not in a testing context:

```
if( !Test.isRunningTest() ){
        controller.addFields(new List<String>{'accountId'});
Contact contact=(Contact) controller.getRecord();
    }
```

## Referencing a List of Records

The standard controller instruction set also manages lists of records, such as in standard list view pages where users can configure both the fields displayed in columns, as well as filters on the records displayed.

The StandardController as bound to a Visualforce page is also capable of fetching a list of records and managing paging through the list. Its behavior as a set controller is activated by adding an additional parameter named `recordSetVar` on the `apex:page` component.

```
<apex:page standardController="Account" recordSetVar="accounts" >
```

Leveraging this mechanism allows your page to operate on a collection of the specified sObject bound to the controller.

The `recordsSetVar` specified becomes a reference to a List of the sObjects, and the controller will now have the following additional actions available to be directly bound to command controls, (in addition to the primary set of actions available on a bound StandardController managing only one sObject):

- first displays the first page of records in the set.

- last displays the last page of records in the set.

- next displays the next page of records in the set.

- previous displays the previous page of records in the set.

You also have access to two new attributes, `filterId` and `listViewOptions` for managing list view selection and applying filters.

There are quite a few instance methods available on the Apex system-delivered class `ApexPages.StandardSetController`, and a variety of practical development patterns to use when managing lists of records in Visualforce.

You'll want to dig into the standard Visualforce documentation for details on the instance class methods, and we will revisit the standard set controller for some of these concepts in Chapter 5.

# CONTROLLING ACTIONS AND NAVIGATION

## Actions as Navigation

A controller's primary functions include responding to and processing user actions as initiated from any associated view. The Salesforce standard controller is no exception, and in the Force.com platform, actions are primarily navigation based.

Actions are processed by the standard controller instruction set on the server, they may or may not result in the processing of data, and are responsible for determining subsequent navigation to the next appropriate page, often depending on the result of the action.

There are two ways to bind Visualforce components to actions made available on sObjects through the standard controller instruction set.

1. Stateful Actions: direct binding to a standard controller instance referenced by the page.

2. Stateless Actions: indirect binding to the standard controller instruction set of the Force.com engine.

## Stateful Actions

Stateful actions are those available to be bound to Visualforce components directly from the standard controller as referenced on the page by its `standardController` attribute, and are dependent upon a form submission. Actions can also be submitted with AJAX calls from JavaScript, and in both cases subsequent navigation redirection will be dependent upon the action invoked and its outcome.

Such actions are most commonly bound to either an `apex:commandLink` or `apex:commandButton` component, and invoked by a user clicking the control. Because these command components are always associated with a form submission, they must always be nested in an apex:form component or the Visualforce page will not compile at design time.

These same controls can also call AJAX processes by setting their `rerender` attribute to reference the ID of some other component on the page. In this scenario, they will execute an asyncronous call behind the scenes via JavaScript, and are typically used to render a partial page refresh.

While AJAX is discussed in detail elsewhere in this book, suffice to say that these processes all typically result in some form of HTTP request back to the Force.com server and are managed by the standard controller. These requests may also contain additional URL parameters, added by use of the apex:param component.

Developers can also construct their own URLs to execute actions or expose links to any desired web page. We'll discuss the use of the `URLFOR()` function that allows this programmatic navigation when we discuss stateless actions.

## Stateful Action Mechanisms

The Visualforce stateful action components are most typically bound to a common set of standard controller actions available for all sObjects associated with any standard controller as referenced on the page.

The most commonly used action components include:

- `apex:commandButton` which renders a button that calls an action.
- `apex:commandLink` which renders a link that calls an action.
- apex:page can call an action upon load with its action attribute.

Additional components are available specifically designed for AJAX processing:

- `apex:actionPoller` which calls an action on a timer.
- `apex:actionSupport` which binds to a JavaScript 'on' event on a referenced component to call an action.
- `apex:actionFunction` that generates code for a JavaScript function to call an action.

The following are the common actions which can be invoked in the context of the sObject associated with the referenced standard controller:

- **List**: navigates the user to the default list view.
- **View**: navigates to the default detail page.
- **Cancel**: aborts an edit operation, and returns the user to the page where the user originally invoked an edit or insert.
- **Save**: inserts a new record or updates an existing record in context, and then returns the user to the default detail page for the saved record.
- **QuickSave**: inserts a new record or updates an existing record in context, but unlike the save it does not redirect the user to another page but leaves the user on the page where the action was initiated from.
- **Edit**: navigates to the edit page for the record in context, and then whether saved or cancelled, returns the user to the page where the action was originally invoked.
- **Delete**: deletes the record in context, and then navigates the user to the Home Tab of the associated sObject.

Here is an example of the direct binding syntax for each with an apex:commandButton component:

```
<apex:commandButton action="{!list}" value="List" />
<apex:commandButton action="{!view}" value="View" />
<apex:commandButton action="{!cancel}" value="Cancel" />
<apex:commandButton action="{!save}" value="Save" />
<apex:commandButton action="{!quickSave}" value="Quick Save" />
<apex:commandButton action="{!edit}" value="Edit" />
<apex:commandButton action="{!delete}" value="Delete" />
```

It is important to note that the subsequent navigation of the user following the action invocation is dependent upon the outcome of the action, as well as the original location of the user when the action was initially invoked, and there can be many permutations.

You may also note the conspicuous absence of a few important and very common sObject standard actions such as New, Share, and Clone. There are many more specific actions that may also be available on different standard sObjects.

If you take a look at the detail setup views of any standard sObjects, in the related list 'Buttons, Links and Actions' you will see that each may have its own additional set of specific actions, like Close on Cases, Accept on Leads, or Advanced Setup on Campaigns.

| Action | Label | Name | Description | Type | Content Source | Icon | Overridden |
|--------|-------|------|-------------|------|----------------|------|------------|
| Edit | Add to Campaign | AddToCampaign | | | Standard Salesforce.com Page | | |
| Edit | Clone | Clone | | | Standard Salesforce.com Page | | |
| Edit | Contacts Tab | Tab | | | Standard Salesforce.com Page | | |
| Edit | Delete | Delete | | | Standard Salesforce.com Page | | |
| Edit | Edit | Edit | | | Standard Salesforce.com Page | | |
| Edit | Enable Customer User | EnableCustomerPortal | | | Standard Salesforce.com Page | | |
| Edit | Enable Self-Service | EnableSelfService | | | Standard Salesforce.com Page | | |
| Edit | List | List | | | Standard Salesforce.com Page | | |
| Edit | Merge Contacts | Merge | | | Standard Salesforce.com Page | | |
| Edit | New | NewContact | | | Standard Salesforce.com Page | | |
| Edit | Request Update | RequestUpdate | | | Standard Salesforce.com Page | | |
| Edit | View | View | | | Standard Salesforce.com Page | | |
| Edit | View Customer User | ViewCustomerPortal | | | Standard Salesforce.com Page | | |
| Edit | View Self-Service | ViewSelfService | | | Standard Salesforce.com Page | | |

*Figure 2-1: Contact Actions*

| Action | Label | Name | Description | Type | Content Source | Icon | Overridden |
|--------|-------|------|-------------|------|----------------|------|------------|
| Edit | Accounts Tab | Tab | | | Standard Salesforce.com Page | | |
| Edit | Del | Billing | Billing | | Detail Page Link | URL | |
| Edit | Delete | Delete | | | Standard Salesforce.com Page | | |
| Edit | Edit | Edit | | | Standard Salesforce.com Page | | |
| Edit | List | List | | | Standard Salesforce.com Page | | |
| Edit | New | New | | | Standard Salesforce.com Page | | |
| Edit | View | View | | | Standard Salesforce.com Page | | |

*Figure 2-2: Account Actions:*

## Demo Custom sObject Actions:

These actions, and dozens more, are certainly managed by the standard controller in the materialized user interface. So how can they be called programmatically if they can not be directly bound to stateful Visualforce action components?

| Action | Label | Name | Description | Type | Content Source | Icon | Overridden |
|---|---|---|---|---|---|---|---|
| Edit | Accept | Accept | | | Standard Salesforce.com Page | | ☐ |
| Edit | Cases Tab | Tab | | | Standard Salesforce.com Page | | ☐ |
| Edit | Change Status | ChangeStatus | | | Standard Salesforce.com Page | | ☐ |
| Edit | Clone | Clone | | | Standard Salesforce.com Page | | ☐ |
| Edit | Close | MassClose | | | Standard Salesforce.com Page | | ☐ |
| Edit | Close Case | CloseCase | | | Standard Salesforce.com Page | | ☐ |
| Edit | Delete | Delete | | | Standard Salesforce.com Page | | ☐ |
| Edit | Edit | Edit | | | Standard Salesforce.com Page | | ☐ |
| Edit | List | List | | | Standard Salesforce.com Page | | ☐ |
| Edit | New | NewCase | | | Standard Salesforce.com Page | | ☐ |
| Edit | Related Case: Copy Parent Details | CloneAsChild | | | Standard Salesforce.com Page | | ☐ |
| Edit \| Del | Up-sell / Cross-sell Opportunity | UpsellCrosssellOpportunity | | Detail Page Link | URL | | ☐ |
| Edit | View | View | | | Standard Salesforce.com Page | | ☐ |

**Buttons, Links, and Actions** — New Action | New Button or Link | Default Custom Links — Buttons, Links, and Actions Help (?)

*Figure 2-3: Case Actions:*

## Stateless Actions

There is an alternative mechanism available to developers for binding standard and custom sObject actions to both stateful and stateless Visualforce components, (those requiring a form submission or not,) as well as invoking them from custom buttons and links on standard page layouts.

This mechanism is based on the creation of a relative URL for an HTTP request, with expression evaluation based on the use of the URLFOR() function.

As defined in the Visualforce documentation:

This function returns a relative URL for an action, s-control, Visualforce page, or a file in a static resource archive in a Visualforce page. This can be used to return a reference to a file contained in a static resource archive (such as a .zip or .jar file).

This function can be leveraged to create URLs that support a variety of usage as identified above. For our purposes here, we will focus solely on the usage to invoke actions. The key to this usage is how we leverage the function parameters when declared.

| Action | Label | Name | Description | Type | Content Source | Icon | Overridden |
|--------|-------|------|-------------|------|----------------|------|------------|
| Edit | Accept | Accept | | | Standard Salesforce.com Page | | ☐ |
| Edit | Add to Campaign | AddToCampaign | | | Standard Salesforce.com Page | | ☐ |
| Edit | Change Status | ChangeStatus | | | Standard Salesforce.com Page | | ☐ |
| Edit | Clone | Clone | | | Standard Salesforce.com Page | | ☐ |
| Edit | Convert | Convert | | | Standard Salesforce.com Page | | ☐ |
| Edit | Delete | Delete | | | Standard Salesforce.com Page | | ☐ |
| Edit | Edit | Edit | | | Standard Salesforce.com Page | | ☐ |
| Edit | Find Duplicates | FindDup | | | Standard Salesforce.com Page | | ☐ |
| Edit | Leads Tab | Tab | | | Standard Salesforce.com Page | | ☐ |
| Edit | List | List | | | Standard Salesforce.com Page | | ☐ |
| Edit | New | New | | | Standard Salesforce.com Page | | ☐ |
| Edit | View | View | | | Standard Salesforce.com Page | | ☐ |

*Figure 2-4: Lead Actions:*

| Action | Label | Name | Description | Type | Content Source | Icon | Overridden |
|--------|-------|------|-------------|------|----------------|------|------------|
| Edit | Add to Campaign | AddToCampaign | | | Standard Salesforce.com Page | | ☐ |
| Edit | Clone | Clone | | | Standard Salesforce.com Page | | ☐ |
| Edit | Contacts Tab | Tab | | | Standard Salesforce.com Page | | ☐ |
| Edit | Delete | Delete | | | Standard Salesforce.com Page | | ☐ |
| Edit | Edit | Edit | | | Standard Salesforce.com Page | | ☐ |
| Edit | Enable Customer User | EnableCustomerPortal | | | Standard Salesforce.com Page | | ☐ |
| Edit | Enable Self-Service | EnableSelfService | | | Standard Salesforce.com Page | | ☐ |
| Edit | List | List | | | Standard Salesforce.com Page | | ☐ |
| Edit | Merge Contacts | Merge | | | Standard Salesforce.com Page | | ☐ |
| Edit | New | NewContact | | | Standard Salesforce.com Page | | ☐ |
| Edit | Request Update | RequestUpdate | | | Standard Salesforce.com Page | | ☐ |
| Edit | View | View | | | Standard Salesforce.com Page | | ☐ |
| Edit | View Customer User | ViewCustomerPortal | | | Standard Salesforce.com Page | | ☐ |
| Edit | View Self-Service | ViewSelfService | | | Standard Salesforce.com Page | | ☐ |

*Figure 2-5 Campaign Actions:*

## Stateless Action Mechanisms

Below is an example usage of creating a link to invoke an action. Note that no standard controller needs to be declared on the Visualforce page, nor does the apex:outputLink component need to be nested in an apex:form component.

Usage is as follows:

```
<apex:outputLink value="{!URLFOR(target, id or $ObjectType, [inputs],
[no override])}" >
    <!-- Do Something -->
</apex:outputLink>
```

An example of a New action on the Account sObject declared as an outputLink:

```
<apex:outputLink value="{!URLFOR(Action.Account.New)}" >New
Account</apex:outputLink>
```

The same action bound to a stateful command control, (which must be nested in an apex:form component):

```
<apex:commandButton value="New Account" action="{!URLFOR($Action.
Account.New)}" />
```

So to invoke a stateless action:

- Replace target with a specified $Action, (or a hardcoded full or partial URL for simple redirection.)

- Replace id with a reference to the record to act upon, or set as null if no record context. Take note that for some actions, (like Tab and List,) the second parameter is a $ObjectType and not an ID, yet this is not well documented.

- Inputs are optional, but can be replaced with a collection of parameter key value pairs that need to be passed to the target action, (we'll look at some useful examples below.)

- The optional no override argument defaults to 'false.' You can replace no override with 'true' when you want to display the standard Salesforce page, regardless of whether there is an override defined to launch a Visualforce page for the action in the sObject setup detail.

## $Action Global Variable

The target action in this usage is represented by the global variable $Action, which can access dozens of different kinds of actions that are available to both standard and custom sObjects. Many actions are specific to a particular sObject, and others are applicable to many sObjects such as $Action.Account.New or $Action.MyObject__c.List.

Using this mechanism, actions can be executed with or without the declaration of a standard controller on the Visualforce page. It requires only the evaluation of the URLFOR() function with the $Action global variable and any additional parameter values necessary for the specific action.

You can also declare actions by embedding the URFOR() function call in expressions persisted behind custom buttons and links declared on the detail setup pages for both standard and custom sObjects.

Some of the common sObject actions listed above that are available with direct binding to a standard controller on a page, (such as **List**, **View**, **Edit** and **Delete**,) are also accessible with this mechanism. But actions that are stateful by nature, (such as **Save**, **QuickSave** and **Cancel**), are not available as they require a form submission.

Many additional specific actions for standard Salesforce sObjects can only be invoked programmatically in this manner, and are not available with direct binding to the standard controller. This mechanism also provides some additional flexibility over stateful actions.

To summarize the features included in stateless actions:

- There is no dependency for any standard controller on the page.

- There is no dependency for a form component and form submission.

- Because there is no form, there is no view state on the page, reducing page size.

- You can include URL parameter key/value collections when invoking the action.

- You can configure the no-override parameter to bypass an action's pre-existing override.

- You can declare and invoke actions on multiple unrelated sObjects from the same page, such as invoking actions against related parent sObjects or even sObjects not related to the one referenced by the page's standard controller.

All of these actions leverage the built-in standard controller instruction set. Although not accessed directly from a page's standard controller instance, they can and should still be considered standard controller functionality.

The StatelessActionDemo Visualforce page demonstrates stateless links for a variety of `$Actions` on the Account and Contact standard objects. See the comments in the page that will direct you to assign a valid `Account Id` and `Contact Id` to two apex:variable components so you can experiment with the actions. The page will also display the URLs generated by the `URLFOR()` function for each `$Action` for your inspection.

## URLFOR() Directing to a Visualforce page

In addition to invoking actions, you can also use the `URLFOR()` function for simple navigation to redirect a user to any web page, including any Visualforce page, by specifying the target as the name of your page prepended with *apex/* to create the partial URL.

For example, to redirect to our Visualforce page named CustomAccountPage we would use the following syntax:

```
<apex:outputLink value="{!URLFOR('apex/CustomAccountPage')}" >
    Goto My Custom Account Page
</apex:outputLink>
```

In addition, you can also construct links referencing any Frontdoor URL pattern to directly launch an insert, edit or view action on any sObject by simple URL navigation.

```
<apex:outputLink value="{!URLFOR('/'+Contact.accountId)}" >
    View My Parent Account
</apex:outputLink>
```

In actuality, the resulting URL would have the same result as executing the view with the $Action syntax:

```
<apex:outputLink value="{!URLFOR($Action.Account.View, Contact.
accountId)}" >
     View My Parent Account
</apex:outputLink>
```

This same syntax can also be used to access documents or attachments stored in Salesforce by constructing the appropriate URL containing the record ID of the desired target.

You will want to learn the usage for these common $Actions that you may need to execute from a custom Visualforce page CommandButton or CommandLink, but that are not included in the common set of directly bindable actions:

**Share:**
```
<apex:commandButton value="Share" action="{!URLFOR($Action.Account.
Share, Account.id)}"/>
```

**Clone:**
```
<apex:commandButton value="Clone" action="{!URLFOR($Action.Account.
Clone, Account.id)}"/>
```

**New:**
```
<apex:commandButton value="New" action="{!URLFOR($Action.Account.
New)}"/>
```

**Tab:**
```
<apex:commandButton value="Tab" action="{!URLFOR($Action.Account.Tab,
$ObjectType.Account)}"/>
```

# URLFOR() and $Action Considerations

Some important considerations regarding URLFOR() and $Action are as follows:

- There are dozens of $Actions available on standard sObjects, many specific to just one sObject type. While there is available Visualforce documentation on both the URLFOR() function and the $Action variable, it is not comprehensive, specifically with regard to declaring parameters when invoking each $Action. Some actions are not identified in the documentation as applicable to custom sObjects, but in fact they are - such as Tab and Share. Others may be attributed to certain sObjects where in reality they do not work - such as New on Contact, (the equivalent is NewContact.)

- Many $Actions are fairly simple to use, and typically only require one additional argument for the target record ID. However, required parameter syntax is not documented in detail, and it is difficult to know just how to set parameter values. For example, when invoking the Tab or List actions, there's little to tell you that the second parameter of the URLFOR() function requires a $ObjectType or you will get an error message Invalid parameter for function URLFOR.

- Actions or attributes available on the standard controller for binding to Visualforce components are not discoverable through the code complete in any development environment as of Winter '14; you have to get to know them.

- You can't access URLFOR() and the $Action global variable in Apex – they are for client-side navigation processing only. The closest equivalent in Apex is the construction of URLs when instantiating a PageReference instance as a return value of an action method.

- The syntax and usage of the URLFOR() function and it's parameters can be fragile, and some actions accessed with this mechanism have various dependencies conditionally based on the state of the associated record's data, the context of the page, or the configuration of the associated sObject. For example, with the Share action, the associated sObject's Organization Wide Default (OWD) settings must be set to either ReadOnly or Private, or an error will occur when invoked. This does makes sense when OWDs are configured as Public ReadWrite, as no sharing is necessary, therefore you would expect an error. However, the wording of the error indicates that the user does not have appropriate permissions, so the message to the user is ambiguous at best.

- $Actions bound to stateful command components have variable presentation behavior based on the provided record context. For example, if the page has no ID parameter value provided in the URL, the Edit and Delete actions simply won't render a visible button, and selecting View will simply refresh the existing page rather than navigate the user to the default view page. There is also some default behavior built in that will redirect the user to the sObjects Home page if the standard controller can not determine a specified record context.

All in all, when required conditions are in order, the selected $Action will perform the associated data processing and navigation on the record referenced by the page. If an sObjects standard action has an override configured in its metadata, the appropriate override will be performed when the action is called.

## Adding URL parameters on Actions with URLFOR()

The standard controller is very smart when it comes to redirection after an action has completed, often with alternate behavior based on the outcome of the action. It manages the redirection by automatically embedding a URL parameter named retURL.

If you navigate to a Visualforce page from anywhere, and look carefully in the URL, you will likely see this embedded parameter with an encoded value containing a URL reference to the page upon which the original action was invoked to launch the page. This allows a redirection back to the originating page when a user has completed their action, such as executing a **Save** or a **Cancel** operation on an editable page. You should note that not all $Actions embed this parameter.

You can take advantage of this parameter if you want to explicitly redirect the user to an alternate page following completion of your action. You simply need to add the parameter and it's properly encoded URL value in the parameter collection on the function call. Here's an example of invoking a New Contact action, which will return to a custom Account page for the current **Account** record:

```
<apex:commandButton
    value="New"
    action="{!URLFOR($Action.Contact.NewContact, null, [ "retURL"="\
apex\MyAccountPage?id=" + accountId ]} />
```

Some considerations:

- You can put additional parameters on the stateful command components using apex:param components, so you can also leverage `retURL` with `apex:commandButton` and apex:commandLink.

- You are free to load up the parameters on your URL by passing a collection of value pairs, so you may choose to use other parameters including `saveURL` or `cancelURL`.

- You may embed field values to be used when defaulting values in a `New` action, but you will need to research and include the field Ids which can be a bit tricky.

You can use expression evaluation to create parameter values in your collections, and there is also a parameter that can auto-invoke a `save` action when New or Edit pages are invoked. You simply add an encoded `save=1` at the end of your parameter list.

A word of caution - we are stepping into the realm of what is often referred to as URL Hacking, and you must tread carefully as there is no guarantee that the parameter values you hardcode today will continue to be supported by the Force.com platform tomorrow. So carefully weigh the risks of unpredictable code breakage down the road!

# STANDARD CONTROLLERS IN APEX

## Injecting an ApexPages.StandardController Instance

No chapter on the standard controller would be complete without a discussion of how it can be leveraged when extended by a custom Apex controller extension.

The syntax for extending the standard controller with a controller extension is well documented in the Apex Developer's Guide. A reference to an instance of the page's standard controller is simply injected as a parameter on the constructor of Apex controller extension class.

Typically, in order to persist the instance, the reference in the class's constructor is copied to a private class attribute so that it will be available for access in various methods in the extension class.

## Fetching the ID or record

A primary usage is to fetch the sObject instance or its ID from the passed standard controller, which is done with these instance methods:

**getId()**: Returns the ID of the record that is currently in context, based on the value of the ID query string parameter in the Visualforce page URL.

**getRecord()**: Returns an instance of an sObject that can then be cast into a concrete sObject to represents the record currently in context, based on the value of the ID query parameter in the Visualforce page URL.

Remember from the loading section above, that the values available will include only those for fields directly bound to components in the Visualforce page. If additional fields are required in your Apex, you can apply the `addFields()` and `reset()` methods as discussed above.

## Leveraging Standard Controller Actions in Apex

While you will not have access to the comprehensive collection of sObject `$Actions` available from within your Visualforce page, the stateful common actions on the page's standard controller are available as methods on the standard controller instance passed into the class constructor.

It is often useful to leverage these common actions from within Apex action methods for their existing action behavior as well as their default navigation or overrides. Each will properly redirect the user to the default page location following the completion of the associated operation.

The return type of each of these instance methods is an `ApexPages.PageReference`, which can be used to control subsequent navigation upon completion of the action. Remember that you can also override default behavior for each action by setting an override in the sObject detail setup page.

Here are the available actions available as instance methods on the StandardController class:

`view()`: Returns the `PageReference` associated with the sObject's `view` action (standard detail page by default) for the designated record.

`edit()`: Returns the `PageReference` associated with the sObject's `edit` action (by default standard edit page) for the designated record.

`save()`: Saves changes and returns the `PageReference` associated with the sObject's `view` action (by default standard detail page) for the updated record refreshed with the updated data.

`cancel()`: Abandon's any changes and returns the `PageReference` associated with the `cancel` action (by default the standard detail page) for the designated record refreshed with the original data.

`delete()`: Deletes the record and returns the `PageReference` associated with the `delete` action (by default the sObjects Home page).

Take note that there are a few other Apex classes available that extend the StandardController class:

- `ApexPages.IdeaStandardController`
- `ApexPages.IdeaStandardSetController`
- `ApexPages.KnowledgeArticleVersionStandardController`

Each provides the same base functionality of the StandardController or StandardSetController class, but adds specific methods to support additional actions or functionality required by the associated standard sObjects.

We simply want to call your attention to them as they represent an example of where the Apex language has been extended to provide additional system delivered standard controller functionality.

## Concurrency Considerations

There is an important distinction to note with regard to user concurrency between a standard page and a Visualforce page dependent upon a standard controller.

Here is the standard page scenario. Two users, (we'll call them Frank and Sally,) concurrently attempt to edit the same record. Frank saves his changes first, and when Sally attempts to save her changes, (which could overwrite Frank's saved changes,) Sally will be directed to an error page that will display the following message:

Your Changes Cannot Be Saved The record you were editing was modified by Frank during your edit session.

Please re-display the record before editing again.

The 're-display the record' text is hyperlinked, and when clicked will navigate Sally back to the edit page of the record. However, this will also force a refresh so that the page will now show the newly updated fields from Frank's save operation.

Here's the distinction mentioned above. If the same scenario is played out with a Visualforce page bound to a standard controller, the concurrency behavior will be different. If Frank and Sally both launch an edit on the same record, and Frank saves his changes first, Sally's subsequent save operation will result in an overwrite of Frank's newly saved data. No error or warning will be displayed to her or anyone else, and no one will know that Frank's changes were silently overwritten.

Take note that there are ways to code logic in an Apex controller extension class to check for and manage such concurrency conflicts. We will not go into further detail here, but this is an important inconsistency to be aware of.

## Action Method Navigation with ApexPages.PageReference

If you need to override an override as set in a setup page for an sObject, Apex controller extension methods allow you to define the final redirection with a returned `ApexPages.PageReference` instance from each action method.

You can dynamically construct full or partial URLs to direct the user to a desired page. You can also leverage the Frontdoor URL syntax mentioned earlier, or the return value of the standard controller instance methods for the appropriate redirection.

The key point here is that you have many, many options including adding parameter values on the `PageReference`, even those derived from standard controller instance methods.

# CONTROLLING SECURITY

## Security Context Variables - Standard vs. Custom

Unlike Apex code in custom controllers, standard controller behavior in Visualforce pages is consistent with the default behavior of the standard Salesforce user experience with regard to user CRUD permissions on sObjects, field-level security, and record sharing.

This simply means that the user will only have access to what is appropriate based on how their administrator configured their permissions, and whatever record data their particular sharing settings should expose to them.

This includes actions as well as records, so if you decide to move to a fully customized controller, you will have to carefully manage what gets exposed to which user. You will need to provide logic for sObject CRUD operations, field-level security and all other actions necessary to manage functionality—all of which can be a substantial task. This is one of the greatest benefits of leveraging a standard controller in Visualforce.

## Summary

The purpose of this chapter was to provide a foundation-level perspective on just how pervasive the standard controller instruction set is in your Salesforce implementation, and how a developer can leverage its numerous and flexible mechanisms when building custom Visualforce pages, with or without Apex.

The key is to fully understand what its capabilities and benefits are before digging in too deeply building custom Apex solutions.

# Chapter 3
# Just Enough Code
# Introduction to Controllers and Extensions

- Overriding Built-in Functionality

- Controller Extensions & Custom Controller Anatomy

- View State

- The Transient Keyword

- Inner Classes

- Collections

- Sharing

- Unit Testing

Visualforce markup can include HTML and CSS to control the visual appearance of your page. It can include Javascript to control the client-side functionality of your page. But if you want to access Force.com data or implement any server-side logic, you need to use Apex tags that communicate with code residing on the platform. Apex classes that contain this code are referred to as Visualforce controllers. These can be standard controllers that are provided by the platform and contain built-in functionality, extension controllers you build to add functionality to a Visualforce page using a different controller, and standalone controllers that are completely customized for a page or set of pages.

Standard controllers offer the same familiar functionality you've seen and used before on standard Salesforce pages, such as save, edit, delete, and cancel. Associating your Visualforce page with a standard controller lets you create interactive components that call these actions without any additional code. Convenient, and easy-to-use as it sounds, standard controllers have a major disadvantage – the functionality available to your Visualforce page is limited to that implemented in the standard controller. Custom controllers and extension controllers allow you to overcome these limits, allowing you to override standard controller actions or create your own functionality.

## Overriding Built-in Functionality

Say you have a Visualforce page that creates an opportunity, and you want to set the Opportunity close date to one month after today's date. Your page can use an Opportunity standard controller and include a button that calls the standard save action. Creating a standard controller extension that overwrites the built-in save action makes it possible to modify the close date before inserting the record.

## Creating New Functionality

Say you want an action on your Visualforce page that calls an external service that validates an Account's billing address. There are multiple ways to implement this functionality. A good start is to write a method on an extension controller that validates a user-inputted address by sending it to a postal address validation service with an HTTP request.

You can then create a button on your Visualforce page that directly calls your validation method. Or you can override the built-in save action and call the service as part of a new saving process. Another option is to implement the address validation method in a custom controller.

## Overriding Permissions

Every Apex class can use the "with sharing" or "without sharing" attributes to regulate enforcement of the sharing rules that apply to the current user. You can thus define a Visualforce page that calls some methods that respect sharing rules and some that don't. You can do this by creating an inner class on your custom controller (inner classes do not inherit sharing settings from container class) or by creating an extension with different sharing settings.

> **Concepts covered:** Custom Controllers, Standard Controllers, Extensions, With Sharing, and Without Sharing keywords.

## Basic Extension and Custom Controller Anatomy

The basic structure behind extensions and custom controllers is fairly straightforward and familiar to anyone who has implemented a class in Apex, or for that matter, C#, Java or any other modern block-structured language. The challenge is in finding the best architecture for the problem you're trying solve. To illustrate this, let's define an objective and then explore the tradeoffs between different solutions.

## Objective

Create a Visualforce page that allows users to edit an Account's Rating field value, and to see a table of all the open- and closed-won child Opportunities (to help users decide on a rating). The table will have four columns: Name, Amount, Stage, and close date. If the user submits the Rating value "Hot," create a Task on all open child Opportunities. Next, assign the Task to the Opportunity owner, set its Status field value to "Not Started," and set its Subject field value to "Send follow-up email to primary contact."

## Extension Class Solution

One approach is to create an extension controller for a Visualforce page associated with an Account standard controller. Extension controllers always have a reference to the main controller passed as an argument to their constructor. In this example, the constructor receives an instance of an `ApexPages.StandardController` object (If the Visualforce page is using a custom controller, it will receive an instance of an ApexPages.`CustomControllerName`).

```
public class StandardControllerExtension {
public StandardControllerExtension(ApexPages.standardController std)
{
}
}
```

A common design pattern is to set an instance variable to the Account record you want to rate – the one defined by the parameter passed to the constructor. This variable will be useful in the rest of your controller's code.

```
Account acct;

public StandardControllerExtension(ApexPages.standardController std)
{
    acct = (Account)std.getRecord();
}
```

Standard controllers include a `getRecord()` method that returns the record specified in the ID parameter in the page URL. If the URL has no ID parameter, `getRecord()` returns an initialized object of whichever object type the standard controller references. In this example, the objective is to set the rating field on existing Account records, especially those with child Opportunities. In this case, you must make sure your Visualforce page's URL contains an ID parameter that's set with the ID of the Account record you want to rate. If you find that the account referenced has an ID property of null, you can assume the account is being inserted, and you can either disable the functionality, or display an error message.

Standard controllers allow Visualforce page markup to reference their associated object using the `{!object}` syntax. This lets you reference the Account's `Rating` field by writing `{!Account.Rating}`, as shown in Listing 3-1. You can also use the standard controller's built-in save method to save the new Rating value to the database.

*LISTING 3-1. REFERENCING THE ACCOUNT'S RATING FIELD*

```
<apex:page standardController="Account"
extensions="StandardControllerExtension">
    <apex:form>
        <apex:pageblockButtons >
            <apex:commandButton action="{!save}" value="save" />
        </apex:pageblockButtons>
        <apex:inputField value="{!Account.Rating}" />
    </apex:form>
</apex:page>
```

So far, your Visualforce page enables users to modify and save an Account's Rating field.

In order to display a table containing the Account's child Opportunities, you can use a `<apex:pageblocktable>` tag that references a list of Opportunities.

LISTING 3-2. VISUALFORCE PAGEBLOCKTABLE ELEMENT IS USED TO DISPLAY THE ACCOUNT'S CHILD OPPORTUNITIES.

```
<apex:pageblocktable value="{!childOpps}" var="co">
  <apex:column value="{!co.Name}"/>
  <apex:column value="{!co.Amount}"/>
  <apex:column value="{!co.StageName}"/>
  <apex:column value="{!co.CloseDate}"/>
</apex:pageblocktable>
```

When your Visualforce page loads, it will expect your extension controller to have a property called childOpps with a getter method -- otherwise, when you try saving your Visualforce page's markup, you'll see the following error:

```
Error: Unknown property 'AccountStandardController.childOpps'
```

Here is one way to implement the childOpps property:

LISTING 3-3. IMPLEMENTING THE CHILDOPPS PROPERTY.

```
public List<Opportunity> getChildOpps() {
    return [Select Name, Amount, StageName, CloseDate
        From Opportunity
        Where AccountId = :acct.Id
            and (IsWon = true or IsClosed = false)];
}
```

This method implements a property using a special syntax. Naming a method using the syntax `getIdentifier` or `setIdentifier` creates a getter and setter method. It's up to the method to retrieve or set the data. The code in Listing 3-3 is essentially creating an Apex property named childOpps with a getter method, allowing the Visualforce page to evaluate `{!childOpps}`.

The final piece of functionality for this extension controller creates a Task associated with any open child Opportunities after the user selects the "Hot" rating and clicks the save button. By default, the save button invokes the standard controller's save method when clicked. The save button in this example will need to either invoke a new method or an overridden save method containing code that implements the new functionality.

LISTING 3-4. APEX METHOD THAT CREATES THE TASK ASSOCIATED WITH OPEN CHILD OPPORTUNITIES.

```
private void createTaskOnChildOpps() {
    List<Task> tasksToInsert = new List<Task>();
    for (Opportunity opp : childOpps) {
        if (!opp.isClosed) {
            tasksToInsert.add(
                new Task(
                    WhatId = opp.Id,
                    OwnerId = opp.OwnerId,
                    ActivityDate = Date.today() + 3,
                    Status = 'Not Started',
                    Subject = 'Send follow-up email to primary contact'
```

```
                    )
                );
            }
        }
        if (tasksToInsert.size() > 0) insert tasksToInsert;
    }

    public PageReference save() {
        if (acct.Rating == 'Hot') {
            createTaskOnChildOpps();
        }
        update acct;
        return new PageReference('/' + acct.Id);
    }
```

In the code shown in Listing 3-4, if the Account's Rating field is set to "Hot," the createTaskOnChildOpps() function is called to perform the Task creation.

## Custom Controller Solution

Custom controllers cannot have any arguments passed to their constructor. In the extension controller example, an instance of ApexPages.StandardController is passed to the constructor, allowing you to call getRecord() and magically obtain the Account record with the ID referenced in the URL. In a custom controller, you'll have to implement this functionality yourself as shown in Listing 3-5.

LISTING 3-5. CALLING A CUSTOM CONTROLLER FROM A VISUALFORCE PAGE.

```
public class CustomController {

    public Account acct {get;set;}

    public CustomController() {
        String acctId = ApexPages.currentPage().getParameters().
get('id');
      acct = [Select Rating From Account Where Id = :acctId];
        }

    public PageReference save() {
        update acct;
        return new PageReference('/' + acct.Id);
    }
}

<apex:page controller="CustomController" >
  <apex:form>
    <apex:pageBlock >
      <apex:inputField value="{!acct.Rating}" />
      <apex:commandButton action="{!save}" value="Save">
    </apex:pageBlock>
  </apex:form>
</apex:page>
```

Since you're not using a standard controller, your Visualforce page's `<apex:inputField>` tag won't be able to evaluate `{!Account.Rating}`. Instead, you need to define a public property that your page can reference in order to use the `{!PropertyName.Rating}` syntax. There's a property declaration above the constructor in the form:

```
public Account acct {get;set;}
```

The property, named 'acct' returns the current account. It must be declared as public to be referenced from your Visualforce page. The `{get;set;}` syntax is a shortcut for creating getter and setter methods for the acct property, and automatically handles the storage and retrieval of the object.

To set the acct value, first grab the key value of the id parameter in the page URL using `ApexPages.currentPage().getParameters().get('id')`. Then query for an Account record where the ID equals the ID in the URL. Make sure you're querying all the fields your controller or Visualforce page will reference—otherwise you'll see an error, such as:

```
System.SObjectException: SObject row was retrieved via SOQL without
querying the requested field: Account.Rating
```

You can implement the childOpps property in the custom controller the same way as in the extension example, but Listing 6 shows a more powerful and elegant alternative.

LISTING 3-6. IMPLEMENTING THE CHILDOPPS PROPERTY IN A CUSTOM CONTROLLER.

```
public List<Opportunity> childOpps {
    get {
        if (childOpps == null)
        {
            childOpps = [Select Name, Amount, StageName, CloseDate,
OwnerId, IsClosed
                From Opportunity
                Where AccountId = :acct.Id
            and (IsWon = true or IsClosed = false)];
        }
        return childOpps;
    }
    set;
}
```

This approach uses the `{get;set;}` shortcut to implement its getter and setter methods, and define a property called `childOpps`. The shortcut improves your code's organization and readability.

This example uses a design pattern known as "*lazy loading.*" By only fetching the Account's child Opportunities when the childOpps property is null, you prevent the accessor code from running each time your controller references the property. Lazy loading makes your Visualforce page run more efficiently. (See Chapter 14, "*Performance and Best Practices*" for more information on Lazy Loading.)

Your controller's code might reference the same property more than once in the same running context, invoking the property's getter method each time it's referenced. A property's getter method might contain accessor code that uses a lot of processing power, making redundant calls inefficient. You also increase your risk of breaking governor limits if the accessor code contains SOQL queries or describe calls. Lazy loading helps avoid these issues by keeping the bulk of your accessor code from running whenever a property is referenced more than once.

Here are several other ways you can improve the efficiency of your code on page load and reload:

- When making a SOQL query without adding a LIMIT clause, your code runs the risk of exceeding governor limits. Add a LIMIT clause that's higher than the record count you expect the query to return and lower than the governor limit of 50,000.

- If you're displaying multiple records in a Visualforce page, add pagination. Pagination allows you to cut down the number of records retrieved on a given page. Without pagination, you might end up displaying a collection of possibly tens of thousands of records, putting you at risk for slow page loads, an over-sized view state and a dizzying visual experience.

- Use custom objects or custom fields on sObjects to aggregate data and allow queries to fetch fewer records. Say you have a Visualforce page that renders a line chart of the average Tasks created per day for the past year. Making a SOQL query that fetches all of these Tasks is likely to exceed limits. You can create a custom object named Daily_Data__c that contains aggregated data per day. You can schedule a daily batch process that populates a custom field on the Daily_Data__c, object called Tasks_Created__c, with the number of tasks created that day. Now your controller can query the new custom object and only have to fetch a maximum of 365 records per year.

## When and How To Use Standard, Custom, and Extension Controllers

When deciding whether to use a standard controller, consider whether you'll find standard controller actions useful. Standard actions are useful in Visualforce pages that handle single records, but not multiple records of the same or different object types. For example, if you have a Visualforce page with an action that resets the Rating field on a collection of Accounts, a custom controller is more appropriate. In some cases, you might wish to use a standard set controller when handling multiple records of the same object type.

If you make a Visualforce application with multiple pages that mostly use the same functionality, you should associate each page with the same standard or custom controller. This allows you to avoid creating custom controllers or extensions with duplicate functionality. For example, your custom Knowledge Base application might have a navigation bar and keyword search box on every page. These components use the same functionality and can be written on a shared controller. Remember, the same controller can be used by multiple pages or Visualforce components.

Extension controllers can be built to extend your controller's functionality. For standard controllers, extensions are required for adding new functionality. For custom controllers, extensions aren't necessary for new functionality, but can still be useful. Large multi-page Visualforce applications that use one custom controller can improve their controller's modularity and readability by moving some functionality into extension controllers. For example, if only one of your application's pages allows users to heavily interact with an external web service, you can move all the code that supports the interaction into an extension controller that's only used by that page. This reduces your custom controller's size and makes a more explicit connection between your pages and functionality.

**Review of Concepts Covered:** Constructors, Initializing custom controllers and Extensions, Instance Variables, Apex Properties, Getter and Setter Methods, Access Modifiers, SOQL Limits, Lazy Loading, Overriding standard controller actions, ApexPages uses, How to select controller type.

## The View State

Most Visualforce pages you'll build will be interactive. You'll want your users and your application to pass information from one to the other, possibly multiple times per session. The view state is what keeps this interaction alive—by magically keeping the data in your controller synced with the data on the user's client.

You can think of the view state as a set of information that captures the state of the page. As the user modifies the state by changing a field value or clicking a button, the view state updates to incorporate the change.

If it wasn't for the view state, the controller wouldn't know which data was modified by a user upon form submission. Take, for example, a controller with one Integer property called clickCount (that's set to 0 in the constructor) and a method called buttonClicked() that increments clickCount by 1. Say you wanted to display clickCount in a Visualforce page with a button that invoked buttonClicked(). This is illustrated in Listing 3-7.

*LISTING 3-7. EXAMPLE SHOWING HOW VIEW STATE TRACKS DATA AND VALUES FROM ONE PAGE TO ANOTHER.*

```
public class CustomController {

    public CustomController() {
        clickCount = 0;
    }

    public Integer clickCount {get;set;}

    public void buttonClicked() {
        clickCount++;
    }
}

<apex:page controller="CustomController">
  <apex:form>
    <apex:commandButton action="{!buttonClicked}" value="Click
Here"/>
    {!clickCount}
  </apex:form>
</apex:page>
```

Without view state, clicking the button will never increment clickCount and will instead raise a NullPointerException error because clickCount will be reinitialized to null each time the controller is created. The view state keeps track of the value of clickCount in a hidden form field that's automatically inserted into a form when the page gets generated. So when buttonClicked() is invoked, the controller "remembers" the previous value and increments the property.

## The Transient Keyword

Because the view state is data serialized and stored on your user's client, it can affect your Visualforce page's performance, and thus, your user's experience. Not only can a large view state slow down your Visualforce page's load time, it's subject to a maximum view state size governor limit of 135K.

Fortunately, you can add the transient keyword to your properties to prevent them from being included in the view state, as shown here:

```
transient public List<Lead> allLeadsCreatedThisYear = [Select Name,
Id From Lead Limit 50000];
```

Properties loaded with large collections in your controller not directly referenced by your Visualforce page are good candidates for the transient modifier. Consider whether you'll need to recreate the property every time the page reloads, say, when a user invokes a method by clicking a button. Including the property in the view state eliminates the need for your controller to re-create it on every page load. You'll have to decide whether it's better for your application to have a larger view state or have more processing done on each page load.

The Salesforce Winter '14 Release is piloting (at the time of this writing) a new feature that allows a Visualforce page's view state to be stored on the server rather than the client, eliminating the need to send the view state back and forth between the two. This feature resolves some of the issues raised in this section by reducing the amount of data transferred with each page request.

The new feature is especially useful for mobile apps. These apps run on devices that are more likely to have low bandwidth or high latency. Because the view state currently gets sent back and forth between the server and client, bandwidth and latency can affect the speed of this interaction. (See Chapter 14 for more details.) When the view state is only stored on Salesforce's server, no back-and-forth is required, freeing up bandwidth for other functions.

**Concepts Covered:** View State, Form tags, Transient keyword

## Inner Classes

Inner classes play a large role in Visualforce development, perhaps more than in any other area of Salesforce development. Besides improving the organization of your code, inner classes let you display a collection of regular objects (non-sObjects) in standard list components and make it easy to support more flexible sharing settings.

## Collections of Objects

Say you want to add a new column to the table in the example code that displays an Account's child Opportunities. This new column will indicate the number of closed Tasks per Opportunity. The problem is that this value is not a field on the Opportunity object. Nor can you create a roll-up field counting closed Tasks. Without inner classes, the solution to this problem would be rather complex.

In the previous example, `childOpps`, a list of Opportunities, was associated with the value attribute on an `<apex:pageblockTable>` tag. Instead of passing a list of Opportunities, you can pass a collection of objects created from an inner class defined in your controller. This object will function as a wrapper class for Opportunities and contain an additional property that holds the closed Task count, as shown in Listings 3-8 and 3-9.

LISTING 3-8. THIS APEX CONTROLLER ACTS AS A WRAPPER CLASS FOR OPPORTUNITIES.

```
public List<OppWrapper> childOppWrappers {
    get {
        // Accessor code here
    }
    set;
}

public class OppWrapper {

    public Integer closedTaskCount {get;set;}
    Opportunity opp {get;set;}

    public class OppWrapper(Integer p_closedTaskCount, Opportunity
p_opp)
        closedTaskCount = p_closedTaskCount;
        opp = p_opp;
    }
}
```

On the Visualforce page, we can now use `childOppWrappers` instead of `childOpps`:

LISTING 3-9. THE ASSOCIATED VISUALFORCE PAGE.

```
<apex:pageblocktable value="{!childOppWrappers}" var="cw">
  <apex:column value="{!cw.opp.Name}"/>
  <apex:column value="{!cw.opp.Amount}"/>
  <apex:column value="{!cw.opp.StageName}"/>
  <apex:column value="{!cw.opp.CloseDate}"/>
  <apex:column value="{!cw.closedTaskCount}"/>
</apex:pageblocktable>
```

## Sharing Settings

Inner classes do not inherit sharing settings from their container class. This means you don't have to create a new extension controller with a different sharing mode in order to add functionality with different sharing settings.

Say you have a Visualforce page that's associated with a controller that doesn't enforce sharing rules. You define the class using the "without sharing" attribute, as follows:

```
public without sharing class CustomController {
  }
```

You want the page to implement functionality that everyone in the organization, regardless of permissions, should be able to use. But let's say there's one method that creates an Opportunity on an Account and you want to enforce DML insert permissions when it's invoked. You can do this using an inner class, as shown in Listing 3-10.

*LISTING 3-10*

```
public without sharing class CustomController {

    public CustomController(){
    }

    public with sharing class withSharingClass {

        public void insertOpp() {
            // Code that inserts Opportunity
        }

    }
}
```

The same pattern can be used for any case where you want to control where sharing rules apply. Use caution–careless use of the "without sharing" attribute can lead you to revealing data that you really want to keep secure. In most cases, you'll use the inverse of this example—defining your outer class as "with sharing," while using an inner "without sharing" class to allow access to selected data.

**Concepts Covered:** Inner Classes, Sharing Settings, Wrapper Class, Overriding standard controller actions

## Unit Testing

Custom controllers and extensions, like any Apex classes, need to be covered by unit tests. Don't approach unit test design with the sole goal of meeting the code coverage requirement. Your goal should be to create testing scripts that interact with your code the same way users or other programs will interact with your code when it's live on a production organization. For controllers, this means you should think about all the different ways you expect users to interact with your Visualforce page. Test your expectations about what the controller should output based on the kind of data users will submit or methods they'll call. Try having each of your test methods test for one specific function that your controllers provide. If you write these kinds of functional unit tests, code coverage will be almost always be a non-issue.

## Writing Unit Tests For Extensions

Listing 3-11 shows an example code for testing the example extension above.

LISTING 3-11. UNIT TEST FOR TESTING THE EXAMPLE ABOVE.

```
@isTest
public class StandardControllerExtensionTest {

    public static testMethod void testRatingChangeAndSave() {
        Account acct = new Account(name='Test');
        insert acct;
        List<Opportunity> childOpps = new List<Opportunity>();
        for (Integer i = 0; i < 4; i++) {
            childOpps.add(
                new Opportunity(
                    AccountId=acct.Id,
                    Name='Test Opp' + i,
                    StageName='Prospecting',
                    CloseDate=Date.Today()
                )
            );
        }
        childOpps[0].StageName = 'Closed Won';
        childOpps[1].StageName = 'Closed Lost';
        insert childOpps;

        Test.startTest();
        ApexPages.StandardController std = new ApexPages.
standardController(acct);
        StandardControllerExtension sce = new
StandardControllerExtension(std);

        // Change rating, then save
        sce.acct.Rating = 'Hot';
        sce.save();
        Test.stopTest();

        // getChildOpps returns the right amount of child Opps
        System.assertEquals(3, sce.getChildOpps().size());

        // Fetch Tasks that were added to open Opportunities
        Set<Id> childOppsIds = new Set<Id>();
        for (Opportunity opp : sce.getChildOpps()) childOppsIds.
add(opp.Id);
        List<Task> addedTasks = [Select Id From Task Where WhatId IN
:childOppsIds];

        // The right amount of Tasks were inserted
        System.assertEquals(2, addedTasks.size());

    }
}
```

First, create and insert an sObject of the type your extension is expecting, which in this case is Account. To test the extension's `childOpps` getter method, insert four Opportunities under the Account, one of them set to a StageName that will close the Opportunity. In order to instantiate your extension class, you need to create an instance of an `ApexPages.StandardController` object associated with the test account you created, and pass it to the extension controller's constructor.

Use `system.AssertEquals` on childOpps to verify your expectation that only closed won and open child Opportunities will be returned. After the save method is called, query for Tasks associated with the child Opportunities and use `system.AssertEquals` to verify your verify expectation again, that the right number of Tasks were created. Since two of the four Opportunities created are open, there should only be two Task records returned.

Use `Test.StartTest()` and `Test.StopTest()` to mark the point where your test begins and ends. Code run between these methods runs with its own governor limits. Code initializing variables should be included before `Test.StartTest()` is called. Code verifying results should be placed after `Test.StopTest()` is called. This simulates practice in the real world, ensuring that the governor limits with the test measure only the controller functionality, and not the test initialization and validation code.

## Writing Unit Tests For Custom Controllers

Here is how the example code might be written to support a custom controller:

*LISTING 3-12. A UNIT TEST FOR A CUSTOM CONTROLLER.*

```
public class StandardControllerExtensionTest {

    public static testMethod void testRatingChangeAndSave() {

        // sObject intialization code

        Test.startTest();
        PageReference pr = Page.MyVisualforcePage;
        Test.setCurrentPageReference(pr);
        pr.getParameters().put('id', acct.Id);
        CustomController cc = new CustomController();

        // Change rating then save
        cc.acct.Rating = 'Hot';
        cc.save();
        Test.stopTest();

        // getChildOpps returns the right amount of child Opps
        System.assertEquals(3, cc.childOpps.size());

    // Fetch Tasks that were added to open Opportunities
        Set<Id> childOppsIds = new Set<Id>();
        for (Opportunity opp : cc.childOpps) childOppsIds.add(opp.Id);
```

```
        List<Task> addedTasks = [Select Id From Task Where WhatId IN
    :childOppsIds];

        // The right amount of Tasks were inserted
        System.assertEquals(2, addedTasks.size());
    }
}
```

Custom controllers don't have any arguments passed in their constructor. The custom controller in the example code uses the id parameter in the page URL to fetch the Account record. This means that in order to test the custom controller, you need to set the current page to the controlled Visualforce page, set the id parameter, using `setCurrentPageReference()` to set the page reference, and the `getParameters` method to access the page's parameter collection. After creating Account records and child Opportunities, set the page's `ID` parameter to the Account's `ID`. The rest of the testing code is the same as the extension controller unit test code.

> **Concepts Covered:** Unit tests for custom controllers and extensions, `Test.startTest()` and `Test.stopTest()`, `System.assertEquals()`, Setting Current Page, Setting page URL parameters.

## Conclusion

Visualforce makes it easy to create interfaces for users to interact with the Force.com platform. In this example, you learned that with less than 100 lines of code, you can make a Visualforce page that allows users to edit an Account's rating, saw a table of child Opportunities, and created Tasks on the open child Opportunities.

As long as your code handles few records, users, and UI components, Visualforce development isn't hard. However, poorly designed controllers can easily exceed governor limits or slow down your application's performance. Just referencing a property more than once, not adding a `LIMIT` clause in a SOQL query, or not managing your view state size can cause your application to slow down, or fail. Governor limits force developers to optimize their custom controllers and extensions at design time. Designing a sound architecture that scales will keep your application performing well when handling edge cases you might not have expected. One of the best tools for optimizing your controllers is to write unit tests that handle all the likely states your program might find itself in.

The Apex language is very similar to other block-structured languages. With an understanding of a few concepts and keywords, along with basic optimization techniques and unit testing, you'll be able to implement virtually any functionality you need, for both desktop and mobile applications.

# Chapter 4
# The Standard List Controller

- Displaying Standard Lists of Records
- Customized List Displays
- Adding Pagination
- Filtering with List Views
- Mass Updates of Records
- Providing Feedback

Like many areas of developing on the Salesforce platform, building an effective Visualforce page requires a developer to know and understand what can be done with the components already in place. Just as a developer needs to know about declarative features such as workflows and roll-up summaries lest they recreate the wheel in a trigger, knowledge of the Standard List Controllers and the corresponding `StandardSetController` Apex class are vital when you want to work with lists of records.

Something about Visualforce that is all too easy to overlook is the fact that a lot can be done without ever writing an Apex class or a SOQL query. Before diving headlong into the use of StandardSetControllers within custom controllers using Apex and other more advanced scenarios, we'll take a look at some of the results that can be achieved through the use of Visualforce mark-up alone.

## Displaying Standard Lists of Records

First of all we need to know how to display lists of records in Visualforce, and there are multiple elements capable of doing this. If you're simply looking to show the standard list view for any particular object then you need not look further than the `<apex:listViews>` tag, it's by far the easiest and fastest way to embed this functionality within a page, though if you want an accurate match for the view displayed when a user clicks on a tab (including the title icon, selection checkboxes, pagination, etc.) then `<apex:enhancedList>` should be used.

```
<apex:page>
  <apex:listViews type="Account"/>
  <apex:enhancedList type="Account" height="500"/>
</apex:page>
```

If you're looking for a standard-style list of related records for a parent record, then the easiest route is to use, unsurprisingly, <apex:relatedList>. At this point we're dealing with a specific record, i.e. the parent of the children we want to display, and as such a StandardController must be used and a suitable record ID provided in the URL. If a record ID is not provided then nothing will be displayed as the StandardController will provide a new record that necessarily has no children.

```
<apex:page standardController="Account">
  <!--This page must be accessed with an ID parameter
    e.g. /apex/RelatedList?id=001i000000McLJl -->
  <apex:relatedList list="Contacts"/>
</apex:page>
```

## Customized List Displays

While it's great to know how to display these standard views as part of a page, the chances are high that if you're creating a Visualforce page in the first place that you're looking for a better solution.

Access to general lists of records (as opposed to related lists) requires the use of a List Controller, and they're enabled for a page simply by specifying the recordSetVar parameter in the opening <apex:page> tag along with a regular standardController. This parameter specifies the name that will be used to access the list in the rest of the page.

The first port of call is the humble <apex:repeat> tag, which does nothing but iterate over a list of items, giving you fine control over the mark-up generated. The important parameters involved are value, which is the name of the list itself, and var (short for variable) that defines the identifier used to access the current record in each loop iteration.

```
<apex:page standardController="Contact" recordSetVar="contacts">
  <apex:repeat value="{!contacts}" var="c">
    <div class="name">
      <apex:outputText value="{!c.FirstName + ' ' + c.LastName}"/>
    </div>
  </apex:repeat>
</apex:page>
```

Building everything from scratch can prove a little tiresome, so if you don't need such a detailed level of customization, it makes more sense to use Visualforce components that do some of the job for you. When it comes to displaying lists of records, the usual suspects are <apex:dataList>, <apex:dataTable> and their styled sibling <apex:pageBlockTable>.

<apex:dataList> is the most basic of the offerings, it simply generates a standard HTML unordered list, with a list item for each record encountered; the upshot of this is that it's great when working on pages with custom styling, but looks somewhat shabby when used in a page built with standard UI components.

In a similar fashion, `<apex:dataTable>` generates basic HTML table output without applying any styling to it, displaying the data without any borders or styling making it great for customisation with CSS. Its counterpart `<apex:pageBlockTable>` is intended for pages that leverage the standard look and feel of the system, immediately stretching the table to fill the width of the containing block, adding borders, highlighting on mouse over and shading for column headers.

The following complete page presents a list of contacts to the user, in a standard table with their ID, name and email address.

```
<apex:page standardController="Contact" recordSetVar="contacts">
  <apex:pageBlock title="Simple Contact List">
    <apex:pageBlockTable value="{!contacts}" var="c">
      <apex:column value="{!c.Id}"/>
      <apex:column value="{!c.FirstName}"/>
      <apex:column value="{!c.LastName}"/>
      <apex:column value="{!c.Email}"/>
    </apex:pageBlockTable>
  </apex:pageBlock>
</apex:page>
```

This creates an attractive table of the information and if there are enough contacts in the org, then it will display the first 20 records by default. Since we're outputting fields from an object and using `<apex:pageBlockTable>`, the column headers are automatically created using the labels for the fields in question.

Finally, be aware that these Visualforce tags work just as effectively for displaying related records, so if we wanted to display an Account's basic information with the related Contacts below we might do the following:

```
<apex:page standardController="Account">
  <apex:detail subject="{!Account.Id}"/>
  <apex:dataTable value="{!Account.Contacts}" var="c" rows="2">
    <apex:column value="{!c.FirstName}"/>
    <apex:column value="{!c.LastName}"/>
  </apex:dataTable>
</apex:page>
```

## Adding Pagination

When working with general lists there is no filtering by default, meaning the page will have access to every record in the system. As noted, the default size of the list displayed is 20 records. This can be increased (using the rows parameter on `<apex:dataTable>` and `<apex:pageBlockTable>`), but to provide the user with a sensible interface it's important to add pagination controls. Pagination is easy to implement using List Controllers and the documentation for its Apex equivalent, the `standardSetController` class, provides some insight into how it works. The controller methods include `GetNext()` and `GetPrevious()` that allow jumping between pages, and the methods `GetHasNext()` and `GetHasPrevious()` that let you quickly determine whether there is a page available either side of the current one.

Now we're heading into the realm of user interaction through <apex:commandLink> elements, the page needs to also include <apex:form> tags, if you omit these you will see an error to that effect. The full source for the previous <apex:pageBlockTable> demonstration with pagination added is below.

```
<apex:page standardController="Contact" recordSetVar="contacts">
  <apex:form>
    <apex:pageBlock title="Simple Contact List">
      <apex:pageBlockTable value="{!contacts}" var="c">
        <apex:column value="{!c.Id}"/>
        <apex:column value="{!c.FirstName}"/>
        <apex:column value="{!c.LastName}"/>
        <apex:column value="{!c.Email}"/>
      </apex:pageBlockTable>
      <apex:commandLink action="{!Previous}" value="Previous Page"
rendered="{!HasPrevious}"/>
      <apex:commandLink action="{!Next}" value="Next Page"
rendered="{!HasNext}"/>
    </apex:pageBlock>
  </apex:form>
</apex:page>
```

It's important to note that although we can control the number of rows displayed with <apex:pageBlockTable> and other tags, the size specified does not carry over to the effective page size of the controller. In other words, if you specify rows="5" then your table will initially display rows 1 through 5 of the 20 in the controller's current page. Clicking the **Next** link (assuming there are more than 20 relevant records in the system) would then refresh the table and show records 21 through 25 from the next page of 20.

The documentation states that a custom controller extension is needed to change the size of pages displayed, however that is not the case! In order to change the number of records per controller page we must alter the PageSize member variable of the controller. We can extend page size as an option to the end user by providing them with a picklist of various values, and by adding an <apex:commandButton> with a NULL action to force the controller to update. The code below demonstrates this technique, and replaces the two <apex:commandLink> lines in the previous example. Note the addition of an <apex:panelGrid> to help keep everything spaced out, and an <apex:outputPanel> to group together the label, picklist and button in the third column of the grid.

```
<apex:panelGrid columns="3" cellspacing="16">
  <apex:commandLink action="{!Previous}" value="Previous Page    "
rendered="{!HasPrevious}"/>
  <apex:commandLink action="{!Next}" value="Next Page    "
rendered="{!HasNext}"/>
  <apex:outputPanel>
    <apex:outputText value="Records per page: "/>
      <apex:selectList value="{!PageSize}" size="1">
        <apex:selectOption itemValue="{!10}" itemLabel="10"/>
```

```
        <apex:selectOption itemValue="{!20}" itemLabel="20"/>
      </apex:selectList>
    <apex:commandButton action="{!NULL}" value="Update"/>
  </apex:outputPanel>
</apex:panelGrid>
```

Last but not least, another nice feature that's trivial to add is an indication to the user of which page they're viewing and how many there are in total. The first part is trivial: the variable `PageNumber` represents the page the user is currently viewing.

The `ResultSize` member variable indicates how many records are in the list in total, and as we know `PageSize` indicates the number of records displayed per page, so we can divide one by the other in order to obtain the number of pages available. There is one potential issue with this division however: if there are 10 records to a page and 16 to display, we wouldn't want to tell the user that they're on page 1 of 1.6, or worse yet, 2 of 1.6! This can be addressed by use of the `CEILING()` Visualforce function, which ensures any fractional parts are rounded up.

```
<apex:outputText value="Page {!PageNumber} of {!CEILING(ResultSize /
PageSize)}"/>
```

## Simple Filtering - Leveraging Standard List Views

So far our pages have taken little effort and include a couple of features that make them user-friendly, however one drawback is that we have no control over which records are displayed, we're only controlling which fields are displayed. All object tabs in Salesforce include a list view: You get some out of the box but an administrator can easily define new views, specifying which records should be presented based on simple field criteria.

These views can also be made visible to all users or controlled using groups and user roles, so that users are presented options relevant to them. With all this fine tuning available and easily accessible through the standard user interface, recreating such control through custom development would definitely qualify as a recreating-the-wheel scenario, so using them is a good choice. The best part is that using them is trivial.

Once more we use `<apex:selectList>` to present a picklist to the user, though this time we will be using options predefined by the list controller rather than specifying our own. The next code snippet can be inserted anywhere inside the `<apex:form>` tags.

```
<apex:selectList value="{!filterId}" size="1">
  <apex:selectOptions value="{!listViewOptions}"/>
</apex:selectList>
<apex:commandButton value="Go" action="{!NULL}"/>
```

## Mass Updating of Records Using Visualforce

Depending on the path you've taken to become a developer on the platform, this technique might surprise you; it certainly surprised me when I first came across it as until then I'd been building similar functionality using custom controllers. It's another prime example of why learning what's supported out of the box can save you a lot of time and make your life as a developer a lot easier.

List controllers actually maintain two lists of records, the main list which we've been using up until now, and a second list which specifies a subset of the main list, comprising records that have been manually selected by the user. Since in our page tags we're still specifying a StandardController, we also have a master record available to us—if we're using StandardController="Account" in the page tag then we know we can display the Account name using {!Account.Name}—this is the record that we can manipulate in order to bulk update the list of selected records.

Once again we can fall back on the standard user interface to provide the user with a way to select records to work with—why fix what isn't broken?—but before we get to that we'll create a new page named "ContactAccountUpdate" that displays a list of selected Contact records.

```
<apex:page standardController="Contact" recordSetVar="contacts">
  <apex:form>
    <apex:pageBlock>
      <apex:pageBlockTable value="{!selected}" var="c">
        <apex:column value="{!c.FirstName}"/>
        <apex:column value="{!c.LastName}"/>
        <apex:column value="{!c.Account.Name}"/>
      </apex:pageBlockTable>
    </apex:pageBlock>
  </apex:form>
</apex:page>
```

When you view this page in the browser, the first thing you'll notice (and hopefully expect) is that the table is empty; we haven't selected any records anywhere. So the list of selected records in the controller is empty. The first step is to go to **Setup** and navigate to **Customize > Contacts > Buttons, Links and Actions**.

**Tip: You can quickly find links using the Search box at the top of the navigation panel.**

Click **New Button or Link,** which will open a window similar to Figure 5-1 and enter sensible values for the label and name; "Change Account" would make a good label for this page, the name will be populated with a default value automatically after typing the label. Choose **List Button** as the Display Type, and then **Visualforce Page** for the Content Source. Now choose the page you just created from the **Content** picklist. The only pages available for selection will be those that use the Contact StandardController and a recordSetVar parameter to indicate that they support lists of data. See Figure 5-1 for a completed form.

Once the button is created we want to ensure that we have a list of Contacts to work with somewhere within the standard user interface, and a one way to do this is to add the Contacts related list to the Account page layout. When the section has been added (and before the page editor has been closed) we can then add our new button to the related list, which in turn modifies the list so that users can select the records that they want to work with.

With the button added and the layout saved, select a few checkboxes alongside some Contacts on an Account, and then click the button added to return to the Visualforce page once more. Now the list should contain the selected contact records and we can consider how to update them.

As already mentioned, we are still using the StandardController and that provides a master record for us to work with: all we have to do in order to update our list of selected records is specify the desired values on that record and then call the `Save` action to update them. You may have guessed from the table and the name of the page, but the field we'll be updating is the `Account` field, allowing us to move multiple Contact records from one Account to

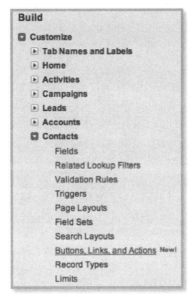

*Figure 5-1: Filling in values for the **New Button or Link** form.*

another at once. Above the list of records we will insert a single input field and two buttons: one to call the `Save` action and another to call the `Cancel` action which will let the user back out if they decide they don't want to update the records after all.

```
<apex:page standardController="Contact" recordSetVar="contacts">
  <apex:form>
    <apex:pageBlock title="Account Update">
      <apex:pageBlockButtons location="bottom">
        <apex:commandButton action="{!Save}" value="Update
Contacts"/>
        <apex:commandButton action="{!Cancel}" value="Cancel"/>
      </apex:pageBlockButtons>
      <apex:pageBlockSection>
        <apex:inputField value="{!Contact.AccountId}"/>
      </apex:pageBlockSection>
    </apex:pageBlock>
    <apex:pageBlock>
      <apex:pageBlockTable value="{!selected}" var="c">
        <apex:column value="{!c.FirstName}"/>
        <apex:column value="{!c.LastName}"/>
        <apex:column value="{!c.Account.Name}"/>
      </apex:pageBlockTable>
    </apex:pageBlock>
  </apex:form>
</apex:page>
```

That's all there is to it! In this particular scenario our use of `<apex:inputField>` to get obtain a standard lookup field means that there's little chance of error, though one addition that's always worth adding to pages that gather input is the venerable `<apex:pageMessages/>` tag.

As soon as a page starts reading user input there's a chance that an error will be encountered due to bad input, and without adding such a tag the user will simply see the screen refresh when they press the Save button and be none the wiser to the problem encountered.

## Advanced Filtering—Using Standard Set Controllers Inside Custom Controllers

List controllers are extremely useful for working with sets of records in Visualforce, but filtering data through the use of standard views is not always ideal. In these scenarios one solution is to make use of the List Controller's Apex counterpart, `StadardSetController`, and put it to work in a custom controller. StandardSetControllers are initialized using a list of records, and we can obtain such a list using a SOQL query, allowing us to only grab the records relevant to the current use case. Here's a bare-bones controller for working with a list of Accounts.

```
public with sharing class CustomAccountListController
{
    public ApexPages.StandardSetController ssc {get; private set;}

    public CustomAccountListController()
    {
        ssc = new ApexPages.StandardSetController([select Id, Name,
Rating, NumberOfEmployees from Account limit 500]);
    }
}
```

To use this controller in a page we need to use the controller parameter, as opposed to the `standardController,` which we've been using up until now. The list of records can be accessed using `{!ssc.records}`, but there is a catch: the list of records returned is a list of generic SObjects (the base type for other objects) so if you attempt to reference a field directly, such as with `{!a.Name}` you'll receive a compiler error. There are two ways around this; the first is to add a controller method that casts the list to the correct type:

```
public List<Account> GetAccounts()
{
    return (List<Account>)ssc.GetRecords();
}
```

The second method is to use dynamic binding in the Visualforce page, whereby the name of the field is referenced using a string, e.g. `{!a['Name']}`.

Regardless of the method you choose, if you try to output a field that's not been queried for, you will receive an error at run time (when you try to view the page), so it pays to be careful about which fields you're using.

By making the member variable for the `StandardSetController` public accessing it's various properties in the corresponding Visualforce page is trivial, so pagination etc. works exactly the same way as it did in the first part of this chapter, you just have to prefix all of the references with "ssc.".

Recall that Apex getter methods that are called from Visualforce pages must start with "get" even though that prefix is discarded inside the page mark-up itself; because our set controller is public we call its getter methods directly as shown in the pagination links in the code below.

```
<apex:page controller="CustomAccountListController">
  <apex:form>
    <apex:pageBlock>
      <apex:pageBlockTable value="{!ssc.Records}" var="a">
        <apex:column value="{!a['Name']}"/>
        <apex:column value="{!a['Rating']}"/>
        <apex:column value="{!a['NumberOfEmployees']}"/>
      </apex:pageBlockTable>
      <apex:commandLink action="{!ssc.Previous}" value="Previous
Page" rendered="{!ssc.HasPrevious}"/>
      <apex:commandLink action="{!ssc.Next}" value="Next Page"
rendered="{!ssc.HasNext}"/>
    </apex:pageBlock>
  </apex:form>
</apex:page>
```

When you view this page you should see a list of up to 500 accounts, and the next step is to gather input that we can use to filter the records selected from the Database. As in the bulk update example we'll place a form above the list of records to gather the user's input. To filter according to specific field values, a public Account member variable facilitates input since it allows the use of <apex:inputField>, but since we're using a custom controller there are other options available.

If, for example, the goal of the page were to allow the user to view Accounts according to their headcount, instead of asking the user to type in a number, and potentially receiving bad input as part of the process, it would make better sense to provide pre-defined options that align with the company's definitions of Account size; as you may well have guessed the tag to use in the page is <apex:selectList> and it can be populated with options directly in the page as seen previously, or the options can be provided by our controller.

Since we're taking action in code based on the value selected, it would be wiser in this case to have the available options listed in the controller so that when it comes to maintaining the page we only have to look in one place, not two. So, first add two member variables for storing the list of options and the chosen value:

```
public List<SelectOption> sizeOptions {get; private set;}
public String chosenSize {get; set;}
```

Then add the following code to the constructor in order to initialise the list of options and default the selected value when the controller is instantiated:

```
sizeOptions = new List<SelectOption>
{
    new SelectOption('small', 'Small'),
    new SelectOption('medium', 'Medium'),
    new SelectOption('large', 'Large')
};

chosenSize = 'small';
```

Insert the following mark-up into the page above the `<apex:pageBlockTable>` to display the custom picklist to the user:

```
<apex:pageBlockSection>
  <apex:selectList value="{!chosenSize}" size="1">
    <apex:selectOptions value="{!sizeOptions}"/>
  </apex:selectList>
</apex:pageBlockSection>
```

Next we need to create a new custom action that the Visualforce page can call to actually change the filter being used, as right now we're simply providing a mechanism for gathering input but not doing anything with it. The controller method to do this is simple; it simply builds a new SQOL query and creates a new instance of the `StandardSetController` class. The reasoning behind building up the query as a string, as opposed to having three if statements that each create a new controller, is that should the page require another filter in the future it'll be far easier to add in.

```
public PageReference ApplyFilter()
{
    String query = 'Select Id, Name, Rating, NumberOfEmployees from
Account where ';

    if(chosenSize =   = 'small')
    {
        query += ' Employees <= 100 ';
    }
    else if(chosenSize == 'medium')
    {
        query += ' Employees > 100 and Employees <= 500 ';
    }
    else
    {
        query += ' Employees > 500 ';
    }

    query += ' limit 500 ';

    ssc = new ApexPages.StandardSetController(Database.Query(query));
    return null;
}
```

The last step is to fire this action from the page, and rather than using an `<apex:commandButton>` or `<apex:commandLink>` as we have done in previous pages, we'll utilize the `<apex:actionSupport>` element so that the page will automatically refresh when the user changes the selected value. This tag supports the `action` parameter as you'd expect, but another required parameter is called event, and the value it takes should be the name of the JavaScript event that we want to hook an action to. (For more details see Chapter 10, "*Using JavaScript and Visualforce*.") For this scenario we'll be using the `OnChange` event, so the `<selectList>` should updated accordingly to reflect the next code snippet.

```
<apex:selectList value="{!chosenSize}" size="1">
  <apex:actionSupport action="{!ApplyFilter}" event="onchange"/>
  <apex:selectOptions value="{!sizeOptions}"/>
</apex:selectList>
```

Now if you test the page out you should find when you change the value in the picklist the table will update to reflect the matching accounts. You may have noticed that the initial view shows all accounts, and doesn't match the preselected filter option. The fastest solution is to modify our constructor and call the `ApplyFilter()` inside it so that we're showing accurate data from the offset.

```
public CustomAccountListController()
{
    sizeOptions = new List<SelectOption>
    {
        new SelectOption('small', 'Small'),
        new SelectOption('medium', 'Medium'),
        new SelectOption('large', 'Large')
    };

    chosenSize = 'small';
    ApplyFilter();
}
```

## Providing Useful Feedback

Before we finish up with this page, let's add a couple of extra features to make it that bit nicer to use for the user. First we'll provide some on-screen feedback when the list is being updated; because the page changes dynamically when the picklist is changed it'd be useful to let the user know that something is going on. To this end we'll use <apex:actionSupport> which provides a way to toggle content display according to whether an action is being invoked or not. It uses two facets, one named start and the other named stop, with (slightly confusingly) the start facet being shown when the action is triggered. The stop facet is displayed when the page first loads and once actions have been completed.

If you just want to display text for one of the facets then you can also use the startText and/or stopText parameters, in the example we'll use both to demonstrate how both options work.

The <apex:actionSupport> tag itself is given an ID, and that ID is used in the <apex:actionSuppport> in the status parameter. Furthermore, in order for the status to update correctly we need to specify a rerender target for the action, and to that end the <apex:pageBlock> now has an ID which is used for that. The upshot of all this that when the user chooses a new value, we can hide the picklist, show something else (the text "Please wait…" in the next example) while the action is in progress, and then switch back after. Additionally, because we're now using a rerender target the experience is less jarring as the page no longer refreshes in its entirety.

```
<apex:pageBlock id="theList">
  <apex:pageBlockSection>
<apex:actionStatus id="filterStatus" startText=
"Please wait...">
```

```
            <apex:facet name="stop">
              <apex:selectList value="{!chosenSize}" size="1">
                <apex:actionSupport action="{!ApplyFilter}"
      event="onchange" status="filterStatus" rerender="theList"/>
                <apex:selectOptions value="{!sizeOptions}"/>
              </apex:selectList>
            </apex:facet>
          </apex:actionStatus>
        </apex:pageBlockSection>
        <!-- etc. -->
```

One other area in which our page is lacking is in providing useful feedback when there are no records to display. You may or may not have seen this depending on the data in your org, but with the bundled data in a Developer Edition org you should find there are no accounts to be seen when choosing "Small" from the picklist. Displaying an empty table isn't much use, and due to the fact that the headers also go missing it does give the impression that there was an error when there wasn't.

To alleviate such symptoms we'll hide the table when there's no data to display through the use of the rendered parameter. This parameter takes a boolean value and that can be the result of an expression, so all we need to do is check whether the list exists by comparing it to null.

```
<apex:pageBlockTable value="{!ssc.Records}" var="a" rendered="{!ssc.
Records != null}">
```

In addition to hiding the empty table we can put a message onto the page to inform the user that no matching records were found, this could be a static message but it can also be controlled by the custom controller; we'll take this option as it'll be more flexible should we want to display other messages in the future. The first step is to insert an `<apex:pageMessages>` element inside the `<apex:pageBlock>`:

```
<apex:pageBlock id="theList">
  <apex:pageMessages/>
```

Next we need to check the count of the results obtained when ApplyFilter is called, the change is below.

```
        ssc = new ApexPages.StandardSetController(Database.Query(query));

        if(ssc.GetRecords().Size() == 0)
        {
            ApexPages.AddMessage(new ApexPages.Message(ApexPages.
    Severity.Info, 'No matching Accounts found.'));
        }

        return null;
    }
```

Revisit the page to test this functionality, and you should see a nicely formatted yellow information message when choosing a filter with no matching results.

# Chapter 5
# Building Wizards With Visualforce

One of the major advantages custom built Visualforce pages can offer over the standard user interface is they can be tailored to facilitate a specific process. Users are often familiar with the concept of wizards, step-by-step screens that guide them through a process to achieve the desired goal, while helping ensure that nothing is missed or erroneously entered along the way. We're going to take a look at how we can create a group of Visualforce pages that works in a similar way to a wizard, but rather than just working through a process to create a single outcome, the result will be a hierarchy of related objects.

When creating objects in Salesforce, the user interface is very much segregated in that you create one object, then the next, and specify the relationship between the two. The page we're going to write will make use of a custom Apex controller to make an easy-to-use data entry method for a basic project management system, creating several related objects in one go. We'll start by looking at how we navigate between pages using a custom controller, then at how information is moved between the controller and the page in both directions, and finally putting it all together to create the finished product.

Before we can get going with any code, however, we're going to need to create some custom objects in the development org that will comprise a project as a whole. The hierarchy to create is displayed below and loosely borrows from the Agile SCRUM methodology in that a project is built up from multiple sprints, and each sprint contains stories. If you're not familiar with SCRUM, then for our purposes it does no harm to consider sprints as milestones, and stories simply as tasks. There is a master-detail relationship between projects and sprints (since sprints must belong to a project), and the same again between sprints and stories.

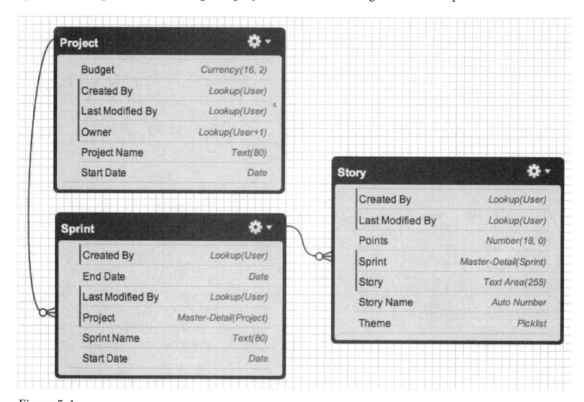

*Figure 5-1:*

Once you've built up the same data model, it's time to start creating our pages.

## Controller Extensions

There are two main ways of creating Apex-based controllers for Visualforce pages, the first being controller extensions and the other, custom controllers. As you might have guessed from the name, a controller extension extends a standard controller, and provides functionality for what is already provided by the system. You'll recall that standard controllers offer the basic actions that are common throughout Salesforce, creating new records, editing them, cancelling edits or saving changes, etc. They automatically handle the loading of existing records based on an ID parameter passed in the URL.

Custom controllers come with none of this pre-built functionality, and it's up to you as the developer to write all of it. Since our hierarchy of objects has project at the top, we're going to take advantage of the `Project__c` standard controller to save some work, despite the fact that we'll still have to provide such functionality for the other objects we're dealing with.

# Navigating Between Pages Using a Controller

The first step is to create the three pages that will work together with a single controller extension in order to provide interfaces for each of the objects. These will all take on the same form, and include some familiar Visualforce elements. All three pages will use the same `Project__c` `standard` controller, and will be named ProjectCreate1, ProjectCreate2, and ProjectCreate3. Throughout this chapter, I'll refer to the pages by their number for the sake of brevity. The source for the first page is below The page block titles for pages two and three should be 'Sprint Details' and 'Story Details,' respectively.

```
<apex:page standardController="Project__c" title="Project Creation">
    <apex:form>
        <apex:pageBlock title="Project Details">
        </apex:pageBlock>
    </apex:form>
</apex:page>
```

Since the first page will be gathering input related to the `Project__c` record that will be created, we can go straight ahead and add some input fields since we have the luxury of working with the standard controller. The following code snippet goes between the page block tags of the first page to provide input fields for the name field and the two custom fields defined.

```
<apex:inputField value="{!Project__c.Name}"/>
<apex:inputField value="{!Project__c.Start_Date__c}"/>
<apex:inputField value="{!Project__c.Budget__c}"/>
```

Now that the pages are in place, we can create the skeleton for the controller extension. Create a new Apex class and give it the name `ProjectCreateExtension`, so that it's clearly related to the pages and also makes it immediately obvious that it's a controller extension, without needing to view the source.

In order to access the standard controller inside our extension, we need to define a constructor for the class, which is a method that returns no values but is responsible for any setup that must be done when an instance of the class is created. Controller extension constructors must take one argument that's a reference to the standard controller created by the system when we view a page. This means that the functionality offered by the controller will be available to us inside the constructor, but nowhere else, so we'll also add a private variable (meaning a variable only accessible inside the class) that will store the reference provided.

```
public class ProjectCreateExtension
{
    private ApexPages.StandardController sc;

    public ProjectCreateExtension(ApexPages.StandardController
standardController)
    {
        // store a reference to the standard controller
        sc = standardController;
    }
}
```

In the same way that standard controllers offer actions that we can use in Visualforce pages (like Save), our controller extension will provide custom actions. These are public class methods that can be triggered from Visualforce tags, such as `<apex:commandButton>`, in order to do some processing. Furthermore, these actions can return references to other Visualforce pages, and this is how we'll implement navigation. These references take the form of the `PageReference` class, but we don't need to get bogged down in details since there's a simple shortcut to get a reference to a page, and that is `Page.<page name>`.

The following method defines the action that will navigate to Page 1, so add that to the class, plus two more methods for Pages 2 and 3.

```
public PageReference ToPage1()
{
    return Page.ProjectCreate1;
}
```

Once the methods are in place and the code has been saved without error, we can return to the first page and add a button that triggers the action to navigate to Page 2. As usual with Visualforce pages that mimic the standard look and feel of the system, the button will be nested inside `<apex:pageBlockButtons>` tags that go immediately inside of the `<apex:pageBlock>` itself:

```
<apex:pageBlock title="Project Creation">
    <apex:pageBlockButtons location="bottom">
        <apex:commandButton action="{!ToPage2}" value="Continue"/>
    </apex:pageBlockButtons>
```

If we try to save the page at this point we'll be rewarded with an error to the effect that "ToPage2" is an unknown method, and that's because all the page knows about at the moment is the standard controller we previously specified. We inform a page of our extension by using the "extensions" parameter in the `<apex:page>` tag:

```
<apex:page standardController="Project__c"
extensions="ProjectCreateExtension" title="New Project">
```

Once that's been added, the page should save with no errors, and once it has, it's time to give it a quick test. To access it quickly, you can either manually navigate to the URL for the page (<instance>.salesforce.com/apex/CreatePage1. For example, cs1.salesforce.com/apex/CreatePage1), or click the "Preview" button in the top right corner of the window if you're using the Developer Console. To make it easier in the long run, we'll create a custom tab for the `Project__c` object. Inside the setup screens, navigate to **Build > Create > Tabs**. Click the **New** button for Custom Object Tabs, choose the **Project** object from the picklist, and pick a style for the tab. Click **Next, Next** again, and then **Save**. You can add the new tab to your tab bar by clicking the "+" sign in the bar and then the customize button.

Since the page will be used to create new `Project__c` records and uses the `Project__c` standard controller, we are also able to override the "New" button for projects. Navigate to the configuration for the `Project__c` object under **Build > Create > Objects** and scroll down to the section labeled **Buttons, Links and Actions**. Click the **Edit** link on the "New" row and then on the next page choose Visualforce Page from the radio buttons. The picklist on the screen will update to show all Visualforce pages using the `Project__c` standard controller, so choose **ProjectCreate1** and save the change. Now the page is easily accessible by navigating to the new **Projects** tab and clicking the standard **New** button.

When you navigate to the page, you should see it as shown below, and since none of our fields are marked as required in the custom object setup, clicking the **Continue** button should take you to the next page with the page block labelled "Sprints." So far, so good!

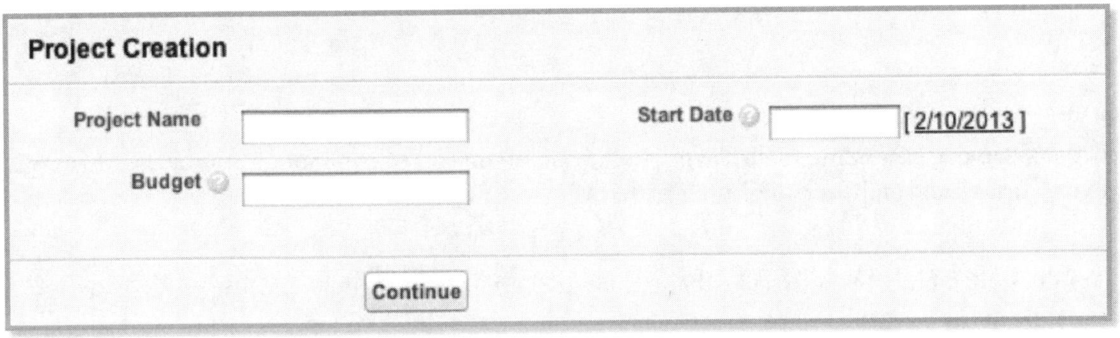

*Figure 5-2:*

Now that Page 1 is looking good, we can focus on the second page, so modify this page to add a button labelled "Project Details" that will return the user to Page 1. We're not going to add navigation to the final page yet as that will be a little more complicated; that page will be used for adding stories to sprints, and so will need to know which sprint is being worked on. Before we can focus on that, we need to provide the user with a way to create milestones.

## Moving Data Between Pages and Controller

When adding the navigation, we saw how pages can trigger actions in our custom controller in order to take some effect, but so far no data has been moved between them. Private variables in the controller are only visible to the controller itself. Nothing outside of it can access them, whereas public variables are visible to other classes and (the interesting part) Visualforce pages. Although other classes can reference public variables directly, pages must access them through special methods called getters and setters, which as their names imply, get variable values and set them,

Written out proper, all getters are named get<variable>, take no parameters, and return the value of the variable. For example, if we had a String variable declared in the controller like so:

```
private String hello = 'Hello, World!'
```

The corresponding getter would be:

```
public String getHello()
{
    return hello;
}
```

Note that although the string variable itself is private, because the getter method is public, the value of the variable is accessible in the page. If you want to give this a try and display this variable in your page, you can't use <apex:outputField> as it's not a field on an object, but you can use a more specific tag called <apex:outputText>, which works in the exact same way:

```
<apex:outputText value="{!hello}"/>
```

The getter for our variable does not return a value and so its return type is defined as void (nothing, nadda, zip), but it does take a parameter, and that's the new string value to assign to the variable.

```
public void setHello(String value)
{
    hello = value;
}
```

In a fashion corresponding to displaying the variable, you can collect input from the user to assign to the variable through an <apex:inputText> tag:

```
<apex:inputText value="{!hello}"/>
```

At this stage, it probably seems like there's a lot of overhead involved in allowing pages to access variables in the controller, so you'll be relieved to know that the developers of the platform provided a neat shortcut to take the pain out of dealing with basic functionality. To declare a string variable as being readable and writable from pages, you can use the syntax below to replace both of the two explicit methods above.

```
Public String {get; set;}
```

To ensure the page can only read or only write, you can declare either the getter or the setter to be private, making them hidden from the page.

```
// read only string
public String hello {get; private set;}
```

The downside with using the shorter syntax is that you can't assign a value to the variable when you declare it, so instead, you need to do so elsewhere, and the constructor can be a good place to do this in simple classes:

```
public ProjectCreateExtension(ApexPages.StandardController
standardController)
{
    sc = standardController;
    hello = 'Hello, World!';
}
```

## Adding Sprints To the Project

The aim for our page is to help the user build up a hierarchy of data without the overhead of having to create all the necessary relationships manually. The Sprint__c object is a child to the Project__c object, by way of a master-detail relationship, so each sprint record will need to contain the ID of the project it's to be attached to when it's created. Therefore, before we can go ahead and create any sprint records with the second page, we need to ensure that the project has been saved to the database, and assigned an ID.

Rather than implement a separate save button to do the job, we can save the project record automatically when the user navigates from the Page 1 to Page 2. Since we'd only want this save to occur when navigating from Page 1 to Page 2, and not when navigating from Page 3, we'll modify the ToPage2 action method to check which page we're navigating from.

The system method `ApexPages.CurrentPage()` returns a page reference for the current page. Calling `GetURL()` on that reference will let us know the URL of the current page. We can leverage this to ensure that we'll only save the project record when the current page is Page 1, though it's likely to contain a lot of information we don't care about. We ignore that information by using the String method `StartsWith()` to just check whether the beginning of the URL is a match, and also `ToLowerCase()` to convert the string to lower case, meaning we need not worry about case mismatches:

```
public PageReference ToPage2()
{
    if(ApexPages.CurrentPage().GetURL().ToLowerCase()StartsWith('/
apex/projectcreate1'))
    {
        // Save code will go here
    }
    return Page.ProjectCreate2;
}
```

At the beginning of this chapter, there was a brief discussion about the functionality provided by standard controllers. Recall that they can be used to save records. Also, we saved a reference to the standard controller inside of our extension, which means it's now available for us to use whenever we need to do so. When adding a command button to a page to save a record using the standard controller, the action used is called 'save,' and this corresponds directly to a save method provided by the Apex class StandardController. Thus, the final change we need to make to the action method ToPage2 is to call that method:

```
public PageReference ToPage2()
{
    if(ApexPages.CurrentPage().GetURL().StartsWith('/apex/
CreateProject1'))
    {
        sc.Save();
    }
    return Page.ProjectCreate2;
}
```

Now that saving the project has been taken care of, we're ready to go about the task of creating the interface that will allow the user to add sprints to our project. The form this page will take will comprise a form for collecting sprint information at the top, and a list of those already added below. The form itself is nothing new and should need no explanation; the one difference between this and the project page is that we're not using the standard `Sprint__c` controller, so we need to create a public `Sprint__c` variable in the controller to write information to. The form input fields use the name of this variable rather than `Sprint__c`.

Creating the variable in the controller is simple and uses the getter syntax we saw earlier. We'll place it under our private variable used to hold the standard controller reference:

```
private ApexPages.StandardController sc;
public Sprint__c sprint {get; set;}
```

Don't forget, this variable needs to be initialized to hold a new `Sprint__c` object, so we'll take care of that inside the constructor:

```
// create a new sprint instance to collect user input
sprint = new Sprint__c();
```

Now build up Page 2 in the same manner as Page 1, but use the sprint variable name to indicate to the page that that's where information is to be stored (note, if you didn't add the `extensions="ProjectCreateExtension"` attribute to Page 2 earlier, you'll need to do so now).

```
<apex:pageBlock title="Sprint Details">
    <apex:inputField value="{!sprint.Name }"/>
    <apex:inputField value="{!sprint.Start_Date__c}"/>
</apex:pageBlock>
```

Saving the information for the sprint record is a little different from doing so for the project. We don't have the `Sprint__c` standard controller to work with, so we must define our own save action method, which can be called from the page. To store the user's input in the database, we use what's known as a DML (Data Manipulation Language) operation, Insert. Insert is one of four such operations, the other three being update, upsert (which combines updating existing records and inserting new ones), and delete.

Because this object is a child on a master-detail relationship, we must ensure that the lookup to the parent is set before trying to save it or we'll receive an error from the system. When we saved the project record, it was updated with its new ID, and we can retrieve that from the standard controller using the method `GetRecord()` to get a reference of the record itself. Because the StandardController class can work with any object type, the `GetRecord()` method returns a generic SObject. There's no need to worry about the details, but you should know that when using this method, you need to tell the system what type of object the result should be interpreted as. This is done by prefixing the call to the method with the type we want in brackets. This is known as type casting.

```
Project__c project = (Project__c)sc.GetRecord();
sprint.Project__c = project.Id;
update sprint;
```

We want the user to be able to create multiple sprint records for a single project, so after saving the record, we'll keep a copy of it in a list in the controller extension so that we can keep track of all the records entered.

The list is stored in a controller member variable. The declaration looks like the following and should be placed with the other variables at the top of the class.

```
public List<Sprint__c> sprints {get; set;}
```

The List class is known as a collection object, and is capable of representing lists of any type of object, which is specified in the angle brackets after the List class name. Once more we must create an instance of this list and assign it to the variable inside the constructor.

```
// create a new list to store the sprints added by the user
sprints = new List<Sprint__c>();
```

When we insert the record, the information is saved and our variable updated with the unique ID assigned to it. We'll then use the Add method on the List class to add the new record to our list, and finally create a new Sprint__c instance so the user is presented with a clean form for adding the next record. The method must return a null PageReference to make the page refresh when the action is called; if we don't do this, the user will not see empty fields ready for the next record. The full body of our custom save method is below.

```
public PageReference SaveSprint()
{
    Project__c project = (Project__c)sc.GetRecord();
    sprint.Project__c = project.Id;
    insert sprint;

    sprints.Add(sprint);
    sprint = new Sprint__c();

    return null;
}
```

Once you've added this method to the extension, you'll need to add a command button to Page 2, wrapped in <apex:pageBlockButtons> tags, in the same way as for Page 1, though the action attribute should reference the new save method using {!SaveSprint}.

At this stage, if you test the page by starting on Page 1 and press continue, you might find the lack of feedback when saving sprints somewhat disconcerting, and end users most definitely would. Since a user is going to want to know what they've already added to a project, we can display the list of sprints being built up in the extension in another page block below the form, and <apex:pageBlockData> is the perfect tool for such a job. More information on this tag can be found in Chapter 4, though essentially, it loops over a list of records, outputting a table row for each, where the columns are specified using <apex:column> tags.

The following Visualforce snippet is all that's needed to display the list of already entered sprints and shouldn't pose any difficulty; this new page block goes below the one containing the input form.

```
<apex:pageBlock title="Sprints">
    <apex:pageBlockTable value="{!sprints}" var="s">
        <apex:column value="{!s.Name}"/>
        <apex:column value="{!s.Start_Date__c}"/>
    </apex:pageBlockTable>
</apex:pageBlock>
```

## Adding Milestones

Everything is coming together nicely; we now have the ability for the user to create a project and easily attach multiple sprints to it as child records, so the next logical step is to work on the third page, which will allow stories to be added to sprints. The work here will largely be a mirror image of what we have done for the sprints already, especially for the page itself, but there are some differences that need to be considered. For the sprints, there was only one project that they could be attached to. Now that we're adding stories to sprints, we must allow the user to choose a particular sprint to add stories to from the list on Page 2.

We already have an action method in place to navigate from Page 2 to Page 3, but what's missing is some indication of which sprint record Page 3 will be adding stories to. The easiest way to let a user choose a sprint to work with is for them to click it, so with that mind, we can turn the sprint name in the list into a link using <apex:commandLink>. When calling actions from an <apex:commandLink> or similar, we can use <apex:param> to specify particular parameters that should be assigned to member variables in the controller.

First, create the variable to assign to. All this needs to be is a public String:

```
public String selectedSprint {get; set;}
```

Next, we modify the table to add a third column with a link to add stories to the sprint in that row. Instead of specifying a value in the <apex:column> tag, we create a pair of tags, inside which we place a pair of <apex:commandLink> tags, and inside those goes the <apex:param> tag. This <apex:param> tag in turn specifies the value we want to pass to the controller (sprint ID) and the variable to assign it to:

```
<apex:column headerValue="Action">
    <apex:commandLink action="{!ToPage3}" value="Add Stories">
        <apex:param value="{!s.Id}" name="selected"
assignTo="{!selectedSprint}"/>
    </apex:commandLink>
</apex:column>
```

Page 3 itself will function much like Page 2: add a list of stories as a member variable to the controller, a story variable to capture input, and write a custom save action method to insert the story into the database and add it to the list. This time, the value for the master-detail lookup field will come from the selectedSprint member variable, as the user will expect the stories to be added to the sprint they clicked. The save method will look like this:

```
public PageReference SaveStory()
{
    story.Sprint__c = selectedSprint;
    insert story;

    stories.Add(story);
    story = new Story__c();

    return null;
}
```

The mark-up for the page is almost identical to the mark-up for Page 2, and should need no explanation:

```
<apex:pageBlock title="Story Details">
    <apex:pageBlockButtons>
        <apex:commandButton action="{!SaveStory}" value="Save"/>
```

```
        </apex:pageBlockButtons>
        <apex:pageBlockSection>
            <apex:inputField value="{!story.Theme__c}"/>
            <apex:inputField value="{!story.Points__c}"/>
            <apex:inputField value="{!story.Story__c}"/>
        </apex:pageBlockSection>
    </apex:pageBlock>
    <apex:pageBlock title="Stories">
        <apex:pageBlockTable value="{!stories}" var="s">
            <apex:column value="{!s.Theme__c}"/>
            <apex:column value="{!s.Points__c}"/>
            <apex:column value="{!s.Story__c}"/>
        </apex:pageBlockTable>
    </apex:pageBlock>
```

One extra thing to add to this page is a button to allow the user to return to Page 2 so they can add stories to other sprints. We already have the action method for doing this, ToPage2, but in our data model we made the story field on the story object required, as a record without that data is useless. The side effect of this is that if the user attempts to navigate back to Page 2 with that field empty, they'll receive an error from the system saying that it's required. Clearly, we don't want them to have to write a value in the field just to navigate away from it, so we must use the attribute 'immediate' on the command button. It calls the action method on the controller without performing any data validation or sending any data to it.

```
<apex:commandButton action="{!ToPage2}" value="Sprints"
immediate="true"/>
```

With that milestone, our project is nearing completion, but if you take the time to test adding stories to multiple sprints, you'll notice a rather glaring bug: when you click "Add Stories" on a second sprint, the list of existing milestones still shows the ones from the previous story. Clearly, this is undesirable, will only lead to confusion for the end user, and so must be avoided.

What we need to do is ensure that the list of stories is relevant to the selected sprint, and a good time to do that is when the selected sprint changes, i.e., in the ToPage3 action method. One option is to manage the lists for all sprints inside the controller, using a map to access a different list of stories for each sprint ID. Another option, and the one we will use, is to ask the database for the list of milestones related to the newly chosen sprint.

In the ToPage3 action method, we update the stories list variable, assigning it to the result of a simple SOQL query. If you're familiar with SOQL, feel free to skip the rest of this paragraph, if not, read on. The basic form of a SOQL query is

```
SELECT fields FROM object WHERE condition
```

where `fields` is a comma-separated list of field API names on the object being queried, `object` is the object API name of that object, and `WHERE condition` is an optional part allowing you to filter the data retrieved. Our table displays the story theme, points value, and story from the story object, so the first part of the query is `SELECT Theme__c, Points__c, Story__c FROM Story__c`. If we left the query at that, it would return all of the story records in the database, which is definitely not what we're aiming to achieve. As you might have guessed, since we want the stories for a particular sprint, we need to use a conditional clause that uses the `Sprint__c` lookup field on the story object; we want all the stories for the sprint clicked, and the ID of that sprint is in the selectedSprint member variable. We can merge values of variables into SOQL queries by prefixing them with a colon, so the whole query becomes:

SELECT Theme__c, Points__c, Story__c FROM Story__c WHERE Sprint__c = :selectedSprint."

The query is executed in code by putting it in square brackets ("[ ]"), and the result is a list of matching records in a list.

```
public PageReference ToPage3()
{
    stories = [SELECT Id, Theme__c, Points__c, Story__c FROM Story__c
where Sprint__c = : selectedSprint];
    return Page.ProjectCreate3;
}
```

Now when navigating back to the sprints page and choosing a new sprint to add stories to, the list is refreshed and always shows the correct information.

## Tidying Up

Our pages are now fully functional in terms of achieving what we set out to do, though there are a few minor changes we should consider to make life a little easier for end users.

One major sticking point at the moment is that there's no way to navigate away from our three pages back to the standard user interface, and an easy solution to this is to add another command button to the second page (since users will spend most of their time there) that links back to the standard detail page for the project record. Once again, having the standard controller makes life easier, we can simply trigger the standard save action, the default behavior of which is to update the record in the database and return the user to the page we desire.

Another sensible idea is to let the user use the custom interface for editing old projects as well as for adding new ones. Hooking it up to the project objects "Edit" button is easy enough as the process is the same as we used before when overriding the "New" button. Once that's done, a new issue becomes apparent, and that is that any existing sprints will not show up on Page 2 because we're not querying the database. When working with new projects, it isn't an issue because we are creating the new sprint records in our controller and maintaining a list there. But now we need to ensure that list is populated with those already in the system too.

As with the milestones, this issue can be resolved by adding a SOQL query into the navigation action method used to navigate to Page 2, though we'll only need to do so when navigating from Page 1. We already have code to handle that (which we used to save the project record), so inside that existing if statement, we can now populate the list of sprints with information from the database. We're going to need the project's ID to find the applicable sprints, so we'll move the code that grabs the project record from the `SaveSprint()` method and move it into the if block.

So that the sprints can still obtain the project ID, we'll make the project variable used a member variable belonging to the class:

```
private Project__c project = null;
```

The SaveSprint() method should now start like this:

```
public PageReference SaveSprint()
{
    sprint.Project__c = project.Id;
    insert sprint;
```

And then the if statement inside ToPage2() is expanded like so:

```
public PageReference ToPage2()
{
    if(ApexPages.CurrentPage().GetURL().ToLowerCase().StartsWith('/
apex/projectcreate1'))
    {
        sc.Save();
        project = (Project__c)sc.GetRecord();
        sprints = [select Id, Name, Start_Date__c from Sprint__c
where Project__c = : project.Id];
    }
    return Page.ProjectCreate2;
}
```

Test the new functionality by clicking the **Edit** button while viewing a project record in the standard UI and everything should behave as expected.

## Test Coverage

Although our controller isn't particularly complicated, it's going to require test coverage if it's to be deployed into a production org. Testing Visualforce pages involves writing code that will act like an end user, using a special method called System.Assert() to ensure certain conditions are met along the way. Should one of the assertions fail, the test will fail and we'll know something isn't functioning as it should.

Test code should go into a new class using the @IsTest annotation. The initial skeleton looks like this:

```
@IsTest
public class ProjectCreateTests
{
    @IsTest
    public static void TestControllerExtension()
    {

    }
```

```
    }
```

Inside the `TestControllerExtension()` method, we write code that emulates a user's actions, and we have to start by specifying which page we're working with. Then we create an instance of the controller extension class, and since that relies on a standard controller, we have to create one of those to pass to it. In turn, creating a standard controller requires a record, so we'll create an empty `Project__c` record that will mimic the process of a user creating a new project.

```
Project__c project = new Project__c();
ApexPages.StandardController sc = new ApexPages.
StandardController(project);
ProjectCreateExtension pce = new ProjectCreateExtension(sc);
```

Next, the user will enter some information about the project and click the **Save** button. We can simulate this by manually assigning some values to the project record and then calling the `ToPage2()` action. By default, test methods cannot see data in the system, so we'll also add our first assertion: if we query the database for all `Project__c` records, there should only be one of them, the one saved when navigating to Page 2.

```
project.Name = 'Test Project';
project.Budget__c = 1000;
project.Start_Date__c = System.Today();

pce.ToPage2();
System.Assert([select Id from Project__c].Size() == 1);
```

If you run the tests at this point in the Developer Console by selecting **Test > New Run** and then choosing the test class in the popup, a run log will appear under the **Tests** tab at the bottom of the screen. Double-click that entry and expand it all the way to reveal the test class name, and then double-click that to update the results pane on the right-hand side. ProjectCreateExtension should be listed in there and showing as around 50 percent covered—double-clicking that will bring up the class with covered lines in highlighted blue and untested lines highlighted in red. Completing the test class is left as an exercise for the reader. The steps above will give you all the tools needed to finish the job and reach 100% code coverage.

# Chapter 6
# Building Charts With Visualforce

hart a course to Salesforce data visualization! VisualForce Charts give Salesforce users a way to visualize data at-a-glance from directly within a number of Salesforce contexts. Using familiar chart types such as pie charts, bar charts, line charts and more, you can extend the value of Salesforce by giving business users access to rich, real-time analytics beyond what you get with out-of-the-box reports and dashboards.

In this chapter we'll cover what our options are for creating custom charts with VisualForce. By the end of the chapter you'll have a clear understanding of the chart types available in VisualForce, where you can use VisualForce charts in Salesforce, and how to customize each chart type to meet business requirements.

## APPROACH

First we'll cover technical limitations and other constraints you'll need to take into consideration when designing and implementing VisualForce charts. Then we'll cover the various options for displaying your chart within Salesforce, as you'll have a number of contexts available for embedding VisualForce charts. Next we'll discuss the high-level architecture of VisualForce charts to understand how they work, how they need to be built, and then we'll get into the details you need to know to build great charts. Finally, we'll reinforce these concepts with examples and code samples.

# CONSIDERATIONS

Before we dive into designing and building VisualForce charts, there are a number of requirements and limitations that we need to take into consideration.

VisualForce renders charts in browsers at runtime using JavaScript. This is important to understand, and it limits how and where you can use VisualForce charts. For example, browsers must support Scalable Vector Graphics (SVG) in order to render VisualForce charts. VisualForce Charts will also not display in VisualForce pages rendered as PDF. If you plan to include VisualForce charts in email messages or email templates, you'll need to make sure that the recipients' email clients support JavaScript, otherwise the charts will not render.

Because VisualForce charts use JavaScript for rendering, it bubbles up errors and messages to the JavaScript console and not to VisualForce. This means that you won't be able to troubleshoot rendering errors using tools such as Salesforce Debug Logs or the Developer Console. Instead, you'll need to use a debugging tool such as the built-in JavaScript debuggers in modern browsers, such as Firefox or Chrome, or with a popular plugin such as Firebug for the Firefox browser.

# WHERE TO USE CHARTS

There are three primary places within Salesforce where VisualForce charts can be used:

1. Stand-alone VisualForce pages.

2. VisualForce pages embedded in the Detail page of a standard Page Layout.

3. In dashboards as custom VisualForce Dashboard Components.

Because we'll be talking about VisualForce Dashboard Components in detail in the next chapter, we'll focus on creating charts for standalone and embedded pages.

## Standalone VisualForce Pages

This will be the most straightforward context in which to display a VisualForce chart. Because you'll have full control of the page design, you can configure your charts to appear in any manner you wish. Your only constraints will be usability and aesthetics.

## Embedded VisualForce Pages

You can embed VisualForce pages in Page Layouts for the detail page of any standard or custom object, which allows you to create charts to visualize quantitative data contextually relevant to the record you're viewing. You'll need to use the Standard Controller for the object whose detail page you'll be embedding the chart into. Your page can use Controller Extensions, but not a custom Controller.

Unlike using charts in a standalone VisualForce page, your real estate on a Page Layout is constrained and you'll need to design your chart accordingly.

- Decide whether you're embedding the chart in a 1-Column or 2-Column section layout.

- Specify the width of the embedded page as either a % of the column, or a number of pixels. The default is 100% of the column width.

- Specify the height of the embedded page in pixels. The default is 200px.
- Choose whether to use scrollbars if the page size exceeds the height constraint.
- Choose whether a label should appear with the name of the embedded page.

# BUILDING VISUALFORCE CHARTS

We have some work to do before we can get a chart in place. We have to think about why we're building the chart (i.e. what business purpose will it serve), what we want it to look like when we turn it over to our business users, and where we'll be getting the data from to generate our chart.

## Getting Chart Data

A chart isn't a chart without its underlying data. You have a number of options for defining or retrieving data that will populate the values and labels in a chart series. You can use:

- A Standard Controller
- A Standard Controller with Extensions
- A Custom Controller
- No Controller

**Standard Controller:** As explained in detail in Chapter 3, a Standard Controller provides you with access to the Salesforce record in context. You also get access to up to five levels of ancestor (i.e. child, parent, grandparent, etc.) data, and one level of child data for the record in context. If you want to embed a VisualForce Page containing a Chart in a page layout, you'll need to use a Standard Controller or Standard Controller with Extension, as the detail page is generated for the record in context and leverages the Standard Controller for the object in context.

**Standard Controller with Extensions**: Controller extensions allow you to apply additional logic and retrieve data not inherently available in the Standard Controller.

**Custom Controller:** A custom Controller gives you full control of the data that is available to a VisualForce Page and any Charts contained on the page, but you won't inherently have access to data or actions provided by a Standard Controller. You must use a Custom Controller if your Chart will be used as a custom VisualForce Dashboard Component.

**No Controller:** You can provide chart data from sources other than a controller, for example custom JavaScript functions or arrays that do not interact with a controller.

## Processing Chart Data

Regardless of where your data comes from, something to keep in mind is that VisualForce Charts look for data to be provided in JSON `Name : Value` format. While you aren't necessarily on the hook for serializing the data yourself, knowing that JSON is the standardized format that underlies Chart data will help you with your overall charting strategy and architecture, especially if you plan to utilize visualizations other than VisualForce Charts that also consume data as JSON objects.

You have three options for providing source data for a VisualForce Chart to bind to:

- Controller method
- JavaScript Function
- JavaScript Array

## Controller Method

If you want to write a method in a Custom Controller or Controller Extension to provide Chart data, you need to make sure your method returns data as a List of either sObjects, AggregateResult objects, or Apex wrapper objects. If you're using a Standard Controller, you can access an sObjects List by referencing the children of the record in context.

When you use a Controller method, you don't need to worry about serializing to JSON as this will be handled for you server-side.

## JavaScript Function

If you don't have a Controller method for the Chart to use for its data, or if you want to apply additional client-side logic or processing, you can specify the name of a JavaScript function that will provide the Chart with its data.

This JavaScript function must either be present on the VisualForce page or referenced by the page, it must be constructed to accept a callback function as a parameter, and invoke that callback with the result object generated by the function.

## JavaScript Array

You can define a JavaScript array that contains JSON objects the Chart will use for its data. This is a good option if you'll be using data that comes from a source other than Salesforce, or if you'll be aggregating data from multiple sources client-side.

Using JavaScript arrays also gives you an interesting option for abstracting data into a reusable data model that can be consumed by other functions and components, such as custom JavaScript frameworks and components. For example, you can define an array that can be consumed by both a VisualForce Chart and a Google Chart on the same page, or populate an ExtJS store.

## Basic Chart Elements

Regardless of the specific type of chart you wish to create, there are some universal elements you need to think about when creating VisualForce charts.

### CONTAINER

Every VisualForce Chart must be created in a container. Chart containers are represented by the `<apex:chart>` standard component, which defines the basic attributes of a Chart, including where the data will be coming from and the size of the container.

## Colors

You'll see several references to colors within VisualForce Chart components. While the application of colors is specific to the context of the individual component, color attributes are universally defined in components using comma-separated HTML color values in hexadecimal notation. For example, if you want to define a sequence of color values for black, red, yellow, blue, and white, represent them as follows:

```
attributeName="#000000, #FF0000, #FFFF00, #0000FF, #FFFFFF"
```

## Axis

Most charts display data using axes, which represent data in multiple dimensions. The horizontal axis is referred to as the X-axis, and the vertical axis is the Y-axis.

The `<apex:axis>` component is a child of the `<apex:chart>` container and allows you to define attributes specific to the visual options for axis, including labels and scale.

## Legend

By default, VisualForce charts include a legend, represented as a box that displays a list of labels with their corresponding visual representation to serve as a key for the user viewing the chart.

The `<apex:legend>` component allows you to define attributes specific to the Legend, and must be a child of the `<apex:chart>` container.

Series

The type of chart rendered is defined by its Series. The Series is a child element of the `<apex:chart>` container, and is defined by specific VisualForce components and their associated attributes:

- Bar Chart: `<apex:barSeries>`

- Line Chart: `<apex:lineSeries>`

- Area Chart: `<apex:areaSeries>`

- Scatter Chart: `<apex:scatterSeries>`

- Pie Chart: `<apex:pieSeries>`

- Gauge Chart: `<apex:gaugeSeries>`

- Radar Chart: `<apex:radarSeries>`

# Creating the Chart Container

This is where we define the general look-and-feel of our VisualForce Chart. The `<apex:chart>` component has three required Attributes: `height`, `width`, and `data`. The full list of `<apex:chart>` attributes is as follows:

| <apex:chart> Attribute | Description |
| --- | --- |
| animate [Boolean \| Optional] | Do you want your chart to render with a simple animation? You cannot specify any attributes for the animation itself, only whether it animates on render. The default value is True. |
| background [String \| Optional] | Controls the background color of the chart using HTML hexadecimal color values. The default value is #FFFFFF (a plain white background). |
| colorSet [String \| Optional] | Specifies the colors assigned to each series used by charts in this container and overrides their default values, using a comma-separated set of HTML hexadecimal color values. If an individual data series within this container also includes a colorSet attribute, it overrides the values specified here. |
| data [Object \| REQUIRED] | Specifies the data used by the underlying chart. See 'Getting Chart Data' above for options. |
| floating [Boolean \| Optional] | Specifies whether to use CSS absolute positioning to "float" the chart outside the normal bounds of the HTML document. |
| height [String \| REQUIRED] | Defines the height of the container, specified as either an integer for a number of pixels, or as a percentage of the height of the HTML element that contains this chart. |
| hidden [Boolean \| Optional] | Specifies whether the chart is hidden when the page loads. |
| id [String \| Optional] | Specifies a unique identifier that allows this chart to be referenced by other VisualForce components on the same page. |
| legend [Boolean \| Optional] | Specifies whether the default chart legend should be displayed. Using <apex:legend> allows you to specify additional Legend attributes. The default value is True. |
| name [String \| Optional] | Generates a name for the JavaScript object that gets created at runtime. This name can be used by other JavaScript functions and inherits any namespace defined by the parent VisualForce Page or Component, and must be unique across all VisualForce Chart components. |
| rendered [Boolean \| Optional] | Specifies whether the Chart is rendered on the page. The default value is True. |
| renderTo [String \| Optional] | Specifies whether or not to render the Chart to a specific DOM element present on the page. |
| resizable [Boolean \| Optional] | Specifies whether or not the Chart can be resized. |
| theme [String \| Optional] | Specifies the name of the theme that defines sets of colors to be applied to your Chart series. Do not specify a theme if you're defining Chart colors using the colorSet attribute. |
| width [String \| REQUIRED] | Defines the width of the container, specified as either an integer for a number of pixels, or as a percentage of the height of the HTML element that contains this chart. |

# Bar Charts

A bar chart represents data as rectangular-shaped bars that can be plotted horizontally or vertically. A bar chart is a good choice for representing values for comparison, with data being described as the intersection of X and Y coordinates. Bar charts will have one axis that represents the subject being compared and an axis that represents specific data values.

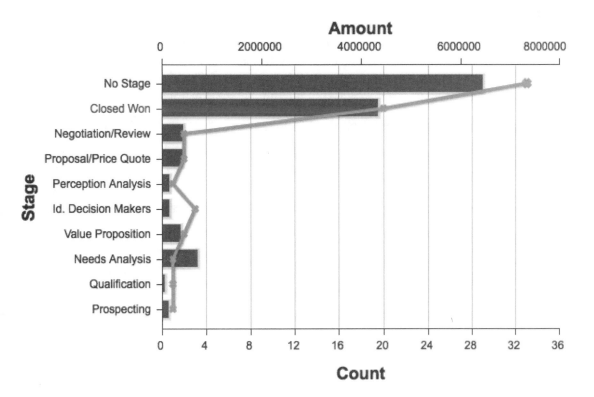

For more complex comparisons, bar charts can be stacked or grouped to provide additional context. Stacked bar charts show how multiple subcategories can be combined to create a single aggregated bar, with each subelement assigned its own color or pattern within the bar. Grouped bar charts show two or more bars within each category, with each bar being assigned its own color or pattern.

Bar Charts are created by including the <apex:barSeries> component in your chart.

| <apex:barSeries> Attribute | Description |
|---|---|
| axis [String \| REQUIRED] | Specifies the axis that the barSeries will bind to, as defined in an <apex:axis> component. Values include: top, bottom, left, right. |
| colorSet [String \| Optional] | Specifies the bar fill colors using a comma-separated set of HTML hexadecimal color values. |
| colorsProgressWithinSeries [Boolean \| Optional] | Use True to cycle through your colorSet and apply a different color to each bar or bar segment in this barSeries, with colors restarting from the beginning after using all colors in the colorSet. Use false if you want to have all bars in a barSeries use the same color from a colorSet, and then cycle through the remaining colors in the colorSet for each additional barSeries defined in this Chart. |
| groupGutter [Integer \| Optional] | Specifies the percentage of the bar width to apply to the spacing between groups of bars. |
| gutter [Integer \| Optional] | Specifies the percentage of the bar width to apply to the spacing between the individual bars. |
| highlight [Boolean \| Optional] | Specifies whether or not a bar is highlighted when you hover the mouse over it. The default value is True. |
| highlightColor [String \| Optional] | If you have specified a value for 'highlight,' use this attribute to specify the HTML hexadecimal color value of the highlighted bar. |
| highlightLineWidth [Integer \| Optional] | Defines the width of the line that borders the highlighted Bar, specified as an integer for the number of pixels. |
| highlightOpacity [String \| Optional] | Defines the amount of opacity applied to the color of the highlighted Bar. This is specified as a decimal value from 0.0 - 1.0, with lower values making the color more transparent. |
| highlightStroke [String \| Optional] | Specifies the color of the line that borders the highlighted Bar using HTML hexadecimal values. |
| id [String \| Optional] | Specifies a unique identifier that allows this barSeries to be referenced by other VisualForce components on the same page. |
| orientation [String \| REQUIRED] | Specifies whether you want the Bars in your Chart to be 'vertical' or 'horizontal.' The default value is 'vertical.' |
| rendered [Boolean \| Optional] | Specifies whether or not the Series is rendered on the page. The default value is True. |

| <apex:barSeries> Attribute | Description |
|---|---|
| rendererFn [String \| Optional] | If you want to use a custom JavaScript function to apply additional formatting or process data, specify the name of the function as a String. |
| showInLegend [Boolean \| Optional] | Specifies whether or not the Series should be included in the Legend for the Chart. The default value is True. |
| stacked [Boolean \| Optional] | If True, the Bars in this barSeries are stacked. If False, the Bars are grouped. |
| tips [Boolean \| Optional] | Specifies whether or not a tool tip in the format of "xField: yField" displays when the mouse hovers over a Bar. The default value is True. |
| title [String \| Optional] | Specifies the title of the Series to be used in the Legend. If you are using multiple Series in a stacked Chart, specify each name separated by a comma in "Title1, Title2, Title3" format. |
| xField [String \| REQUIRED] | Specifies a required attribute that determines the field in the Chart data object containing the values for each data point on the X-axis. |
| xPadding [Integer \| Optional] | Specifies the amount of padding that should appear between Bars and the left and right axes. |
| yField [String \| REQUIRED] | Specifies a required attribute that determines the field in the Chart data object containing the values for each data point on the Y-axis. |
| yPadding [Integer \| Optional] | Specifies the amount of padding that should appear between Bars and the top and bottom axes. |

## LINE CHARTS

Typically used to visualize data trends over a period of time, line charts represent data as a series of points connected by line segments.

Like Bar Charts, Line Charts are two-dimensional, with a horizontal X-axis and a vertical Y-axis. To aid in visualization, line charts can have parallel lines drawn that extend from either axis; you can create a grid by extending lines from both the X-axis and Y-axis.

Line Charts can include multiple series, allowing you to compare multiple data points. Line Charts can also be combined with Bar Charts to create a visual overlay that displays multiple related data series.

| <apex:lineSeries> Attribute | Description |
|---|---|
| axis [String \| REQUIRED] | Specifies the axis the lineSeries will bind to, as defined in an <apex:axis> component. Values include: top, bottom, left, right. |
| fill [Boolean \| Optional] | Specifies whether you want to fill the area between the line and the axis with a color. You can also optionally specify the color of the fill using the fillColor attribute, otherwise the fill color defaults to the same color as the line. The default value is false. |
| fillColor [String \| Optional] | If you have chosen to use a fill, you can specify its HTML hexadecimal color value. |
| highlight [Boolean \| Optional] | Specifies whether or not points on the lineSeries are highlighted when you hover the mouse over them. The default value is True. |
| highlightStrokeWidth [String \| Optional] | Defines the width of the line that appears over the highlighted line in the lineSeries, specified as String. |
| id [String \| Optional] | Specifies a unique identifier that allows this lineSeries to be referenced by other VisualForce components on the same page. |
| markerFill [String \| Optional] | Specifies the HTML hexadecimal color value used for the data point markers in this lineSeries. If this attribute is not defined, the color defaults to the same color of the line. |
| markerSize [Integer \| Optional] | Specifies the size of the data point markers in this lineSeries. If this attribute is not defined, the size defaults to 3. |
| markerType [String \| Optional] | You can specify whether the data point marker will be a "circle" or a "cross." If you don't define this attribute, the data point marker shape defaults to the next shape in the sequence. |
| opacity [String \| Optional] | Defines the amount of opacity applied to the filled area that appears beneath the line. Specified as a decimal value from 0.0 - 1.0, with lower values making the color more transparent. |
| rendered [Boolean \| Optional] | Specifies whether or not this lineSeries is rendered on the page. The default value is True. |
| rendererFn [String \| Optional] | If you want to use a custom JavaScript function to apply additional formatting or process data, specify the name of the function as a String. |
| showInLegend [Boolean \| Optional] | Specifies whether or not the lineSeries should be included in the Legend for the Chart. The default value is True. |

| <apex:lineSeries> Attribute | Description |
|---|---|
| smooth [Integer \| Optional] | Specifies the amount of smoothing applied to the line. A lower number indicates more smoothing is applied. Use a value of 0 to disable smoothing and simply show a straight line between data points. |
| strokeColor [String \| Optional] | Specifies the HTML hexadecimal color value used for the line in this lineSeries. |
| strokeWidth [String \| Optional] | Defines the width of the line, specified as an integer. |
| tips [Boolean \| Optional] | Specifies whether or not a tool tip in the format of "xField: yField" displays when the mouse hovers over a data point. The default value is True. |
| title [String \| Optional] | Specifies the title of the lineSeries used in the legend. |
| xField [String \| REQUIRED] | Specifies a required attribute that determines the field in the Chart data object containing the values for each data point on the X-axis. |
| yField [String \| REQUIRED] | Specifies a required attribute that determines the field in the Chart data object containing the values for each data point on the Y-axis. |

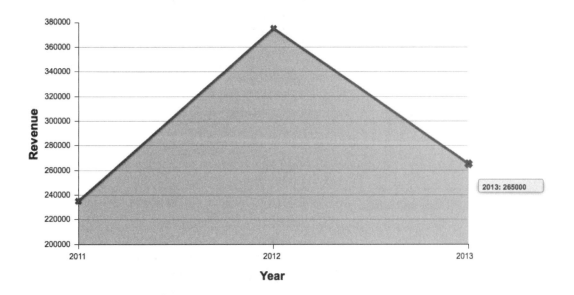

## AREA CHARTS

Area Charts are fundamentally similar to Line Charts, with the exception being that the area between the axis and the line are filled with colors or patterns. Area charts are great for visualizing trends of related categories over time, usually representing aggregated totals or percentages.

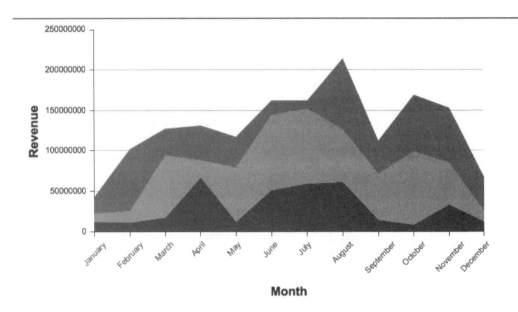

## Creating a VisualForce Area Chart

Specify a data series to be rendered as shaded areas in a Visualforce chart. It's similar to a line series with the fill attribute set to true, except that multiple Y values for each X will "stack" as levels upon each other.

At a minimum, you must specify the fields in the data collection to use X and Y values for each point along the line that defines the amount of area each point represents, as well as the X and Y axes to scale against. Add multiple Y values to add levels to the chart. Each level takes a new color.

| <apex:areaSeries> Attributes | Description |
|---|---|
| axis [String \| REQUIRED] | Specifies the axis that the areaSeries will bind to, as defined in an <apex:axis> component. Values include: top, bottom, left, right. |
| colorSet [String \| Optional] | Specifies the bar fill colors using a comma-separated set of HTML hexadecimal color values. |
| highlight [Boolean \| Optional] | Specifies whether or not an area is highlighted when you hover the mouse over it. The default value is True. |
| highlightLineWidth [Integer \| Optional] | Defines the width of the line that surrounds the highlighted area, specified as an integer for the number of pixels. |
| highlightOpacity [String \| Optional] | Defines the amount of opacity applied to the color of the highlighted area. Specified as a decimal value from 0.0 - 1.0, with lower values making the color more transparent. |

| <apex:areaSeries> Attributes | Description |
| --- | --- |
| highlightStrokeColor [String \| Optional] | If you have specified a value for 'highlight,' use this attribute to specify the HTML hexadecimal color value of the highlighted area. |
| id [String \| Optional] | Specifies a unique identifier that allows this areaSeries to be referenced by other VisualForce components on the same page. |
| opacity [String \| Optional] | Defines the amount of opacity applied to the filled area. Specified as a decimal value from 0.0 - 1.0, with lower values making the color more transparent. |
| rendered [Boolean \| Optional] | Specifies whether or not this areaSeries is rendered on the page. The default value is True. |
| rendererFn [String \| Optional] | If you want to use a custom JavaScript function to apply additional formatting or process data, specify the name of the function as a String. |
| showInLegend [Boolean \| Optional] | Specifies whether or not this areaSeries should be included in the legend for the chart. The default value is True. |
| tips [Boolean \| Optional] | Specifies whether or not a tool tip in the format of "xField: yField" displays when the mouse hovers over a data point. The default value is True. |
| title [String \| Optional] | Specifies the title of the areaSeries to be used in the legend. If you're using multiple series in a stacked chart, specify each name separated by a comma in "Title1, Title2, Title3" format. |
| xField [String \| REQUIRED] | Specifies a required attribute that determines the field in the Chart data object containing the values for each data point on the X-axis. |
| yField [String \| REQUIRED] | Specifies a required attribute that determines the field in the Chart data object containing the values for each data point on the Y-axis. |

## SCATTER CHARTS

Scatter Charts and Line Charts might look similar at first blush, but there are fundamental differences between the two. A Line Chart represents data as evenly distributed values along the X-axis, while a Scatter Chart uses two axes to display data values: one along the Y-axis and one along the X-axis. Unlike a Line Chart, values in a Scatter Chart are represented individually and are not connected.

Line Charts tend to be used to show data sequentially, whereas Scatter charts are used to visualize larger, grouped data sets to find correlations or patterns in the data. Scatter charts allow you to compare data without constraining to a sequence or time period.

| `<apex:scatterSeries>` Attributes | Description |
|---|---|
| `axis [String \| REQUIRED]` | Specifies the axis that the scatterSeries will bind to, as defined in an `<apex:axis>` component. Values include: top, bottom, left, right. |
| `highlight [Boolean \| Optional]` | Specifies whether or not a data point is highlighted when you hover the mouse over it. The default value is True. |
| `id [String \| Optional]` | Specifies a unique identifier that allows this scatterSeries to be referenced by other VisualForce components on the same page. |
| `markerFill [String \| Optional]` | Specifies the HTML hexadecimal color value used for the data point markers in this scatterSeries. |
| `markerSize [Integer \| Optional]` | Specifies the size of the data point markers in this scatterSeries. |
| `markerType [String \| Optional]` | You can specify whether the data point marker will be a "circle" or a "cross." If you do not define this attribute, the data point marker shape defaults to the next shape in the sequence. |
| `rendered [Boolean \| Optional]` | Specifies whether or not this scatterSeries is rendered on the page. The default value is True. |
| `rendererFn [String \| Optional]` | If you want to use a custom JavaScript function to apply additional formatting or process data, specify the name of the function as a String. |
| `showInLegend [Boolean \| Optional]` | Specifies whether or not this scatterSeries should be included in the legend for the chart. The default value is True. |
| `tips [Boolean \| Optional]` | Specifies whether or not a tool tip in the format of "xField: yField" displays when the mouse hovers over a data point. The default value is True. |
| `title [String \| Optional]` | Specifies the title of the scatterSeries to be used in the legend. |
| `xField [String \| REQUIRED]` | Specifies a required attribute that determines the field in the Chart data object containing the values for each data point on the X-axis. |
| `yField [String \| REQUIRED]` | Specifies a required attribute that determines the field in the Chart data object containing the values for each data point on the Y-axis. |

## PIE CHARTS

Pie charts are probably the most commonly used chart type in business. Pie charts represent a data set in the shape of a full circle. Think of a fresh-baked apple pie with individual data values represented as slices of the pie, referred to as "wedges," sized proportionately relative to the value compared to the whole.

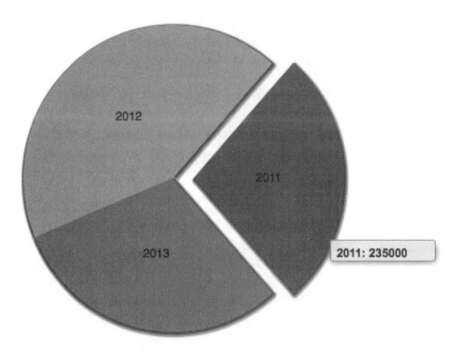

Pie charts are great for representing a simple data set that compares a limited number of categories or values. Pie charts are not good for representing values over time, and they tend to become unruly when too many categories are represented on a single chart.

| <apex:pieSeries> Attributes | Description |
|---|---|
| colorSet [String \| Optional] | Specifies the fill colors of each wedge in sequence using a comma-separated set of HTML hexadecimal color values. |
| dataField [String \| REQUIRED] | Specify the name of the field that appears in each data record that will contain the data values for pie wedges. |
| donut [Integer \| Optional] | If you want to have a "donut" hole appear in the center of your pie chart, specify an integer value from 0-100. This number represents the percentage of the pie radius, so a value of 0 means no hole appears, and a value of 100 means the hole consumes the entire pie. |

| <apex:pieSeries> Attributes | Description |
|---|---|
| highlight [Boolean \| Optional] | Specifies whether or not each pie wedge is highlighted when you hover the mouse over it. The default value is True. |
| id [String \| Optional] | Specifies a unique identifier that allows this chart to be referenced by other VisualForce components on the same page. |
| labelField [String \| Optional] | Specify the name of the field that appears in each data record that contains the label for each pie wedge. If you don't specify a value for this attribute, each pie wedge receives a generic label of "name." |
| rendered [Boolean \| Optional] | Specifies whether this pieSeries is rendered on the page. The default value is True. |
| rendererFn [String \| Optional] | If you want to use a custom JavaScript function to apply additional formatting or process data, specify the name of the function as a String. |
| showInLegend [Boolean \| Optional] | Specifies whether or not this pieSeries should be included in the legend for the chart. The default value is True. |
| tips [Boolean \| Optional] | Specifies whether or not a tool tip in the format of "labelField: dataField" displays when the mouse hovers over a pie wedge. The default value is True. |

## Gauge Charts

Gauge charts make for good dashboard components, as they are shaped like an instrument you typically find on your car's dashboard to measure things like speed, RPM, etc. A Gauge Charts look like a donut cut in half.

Use Gauge Charts to measure progress against a stated goal. Shade different regions of the chart to show markers/progress against the goal. For example, if you are a salesperson with a quota, you can track your closed revenue against your quota goal with a gauge chart.

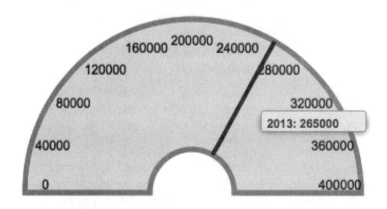

| <apex:gaugeSeries> Attributes | Description |
|---|---|
| colorSet [String \| Optional] | Specifies the gauge fill colors using a comma-separated set of HTML hexadecimal color values. |
| dataField [String \| REQUIRED] | Specify the name of the field that appears in each data record that will contain the data value for the gauge level. Note that only data from the first record is used. |
| donut [Integer \| Optional] | Specify the size of the hole that appears in the center of your Gauge Chart as an integer value from 0-100. This number represents the percentage of the radius of the gauge, so a value of 0 means no hole appears, and a value of 100 means the hole consumes the entire gauge. |
| highlight [Boolean \| Optional] | Specifies whether or not each gauge level is highlighted when you hover the mouse over it. The default value is True. |
| id [String \| Optional] | Specifies a unique identifier that allows this gaugeSeries to be referenced by other VisualForce components on the same page. |
| labelField [String \| Optional] | Specify the name of the field that appears in each data record containing the label for the gauge level. If you don't specify a value for this attribute, a generic label of "name" is assigned. Similar to the dataField attribute, only the label from the first record is used. |
| needle [Boolean \| Optional] | Set this value to True if you want a needle to appear on the gauge chart. The default value is False. |
| rendered [Boolean \| Optional] | Specifies whether or not this gaugeSeries is rendered on the page. The default value is True. |
| rendererFn [String \| Optional] | If you want to use a custom JavaScript function to apply additional formatting or process data, specify the name of the function as a String. |
| tips [Boolean \| Optional] | Specifies whether or not a tool tip in the format of "labelField: dataField" displays when the mouse hovers over a gauge level. The default value is True. |

## RADAR CHARTS

Radar Charts might look complex on the surface, but at the heart they are basically Line Charts wrapped into a circular axis. You might have heard radar charts referred to as "spider" charts because of the resemblance to a spider web.

Radar Charts plot values for each category along an axis that starts in the center of the chart and extends to the outer edge of the outermost ring of the chart. They are commonly used to show similarities across different categories in a data set and to help identify outliers.

| <apex:radarSeries> Attributes | Description |
| --- | --- |
| fill [String \| Optional] | If you want to fill the area inside of a line, use an HTML hexadecimal value for your desired color. If you don't specify a color, the next color in the sequence for the inherited colorSet or theme is used. If you specify "none" for the value, no fill is applied. In this case, you'll need to specify values for marker and stroke attributes, as you'll only see lines and markers, and they are not visible by default. |
| highlight [Boolean \| Optional] | Specifies whether or not a data point is highlighted when you hover the mouse over it. The default value is True. |
| id [String \| Optional] | Specifies a unique identifier that allows this radarSeries to be referenced by other VisualForce components on the same page. |
| markerFill [String \| Optional] | Specifies the HTML hexadecimal color value used for the data point markers in this. |
| markerSize [Integer \| Optional] | Specifies the size of the data point markers in this radarSeries. |
| markerType [String \| Optional] | You can specify whether the data point marker will be a "circle" or a "cross." If you don't define this attribute, the data point marker shape defaults to the next shape in the sequence. |
| opacity [String \| Optional] | Defines the amount of opacity applied to the filled area. Specified as a decimal value from 0.0 - 1.0, with lower values making the color more transparent. |
| rendered [Boolean \| Optional] | Specifies whether or not this radarSeries is rendered on the page. The default value is True. |
| showInLegend [Boolean \| Optional] | Specifies whether or not this radarSeries should be included in the legend for the chart. The default value is True. |
| strokeColor [String \| Optional] | Specifies the HTML hexadecimal color value used for the line in this series. |

| <apex:radarSeries> Attributes | Description |
|---|---|
| strokeWidth [String \| Optional] | Defines the width of the line, specified as an integer. |
| tips [Boolean \| Optional] | Specifies whether or not a tool tip in the format of "xField: yField" displays when the mouse hovers over a data point. The default value is True. |
| title [String \| Optional] | Specifies the title of the radarSeries used in the legend. |
| xField [String \| REQUIRED] | Specifies a required attribute that determines the field in the Chart data object containing the values for each data point on the X-axis.  In a radarSeries, the X-axis circles the perimeter. |
| yField [String \| REQUIRED] | Specifies a required attribute that determines the field in the Chart data object containing the values for each data point on the y-axis. In a radarSeries, the Y-axis runs from the center of the chart to the outermost edge. |

## Summary

In this chapter we learned about the different options for creating custom charts in VisualForce, including the chart types available and how to configure each type to meet the requirements of your business users. You should have a better understanding of how to get data for your chart and process it for rendering, as well as where VisualForce Charts can be used in Salesforce.

Now get charting!

# Chapter 7
# Building Dashboards with Visualforce

You'll be hard pressed to find an experienced Salesforce user that hasn't learned to love the dashboard. Dashboards provide an at-a-glance visualization of business metrics and key performance indicators for every Salesforce user across every role in an organization, but sometimes the dashboard components available out-of-the box just don't meet business requirements.

In this chapter we'll cover how you can incorporate custom Visualforce components into dashboards to provide a wealth of data to business users that they cannot capture using standard dashboard components.

We'll discuss what you need to take into consideration when designing and implementing custom Visualforce dashboard components, as well as introduce common design patterns and ideas. From there we'll walk through the process of building a dashboard component in Visualforce and adding it to a Salesforce Dashboard.

## Considerations

Adding a Visualforce page to a Salesforce Dashboard is not a difficult undertaking, but there are some key technical requirements and limitations that you'll need to understand.

Because screen real estate is constrained on a dashboard, you'll need to design your custom Visualforce dashboard components to fit within the containers in which they are rendered. If your component is much larger than your container, it might not function properly, and might affect the aesthetics of your dashboard. You are also subject to the Salesforce limit of 20 components per dashboard.

For a Visualforce page to be usable as a dashboard component, it must use either a custom controller, no controller at all, or reference another page that binds to the StandardSetControler class. Visualforce pages that use a standard controller cannot be used as dashboard components, and will not appear as Data Source options.

If you plan on using a Visualforce page as a custom dashboard component, be sure to enable access to the page in every user profile that will be accessing the dashboard. If a profile has not been given access to a page, the logged-in user will receive an error stating, "Content cannot be displayed: You do not have sufficient privileges to access the page: (Name of Visualforce page)."

Custom Visualforce dashboard components are rendered as IFrames, which might cause issues in some browsers. You'll need to test your components accordingly.

## Use Cases for Visualforce Dasboard Components

While the primary use case for building custom dashboard components is to display data visualizations that are not possible to create using standard dashboard components, a key feature of Salesforce dashboards is that you can incorporate custom Visualforce components alongside standard dashboard components. This means you don't have to decide between using one or the other, and it allows you to extend the value of existing dashboards by providing additional context and functionality.

## Charts

Since the predominant standard component types used in dashboards are charts representing underlying reports as data sources, it's only fitting that charts are also a common design choice for custom Visualforce dashboard components.

In the previous chapter we learned how to create Bar Charts, Line Charts, Area Charts, Scatter Charts, Pie Charts, Gauge Charts, and Radar Charts. As long as the Visualforce pages containing your Visualforce charts adhere to controller restrictions, you can use them as custom Visualforce dashboard components.

Because standard Salesforce dashboard components offer a wide selection of chart types to choose from, you'll want to create custom dashboard components for charts only if it's not possible to use a standard component due to data limitations, or if the chart types or styling that your business users require can only be created using a custom chart component.

Visualforce Charts are not your only option for creating and displaying charts. Google Charts provides many data visualization options to choose from for creating charts for custom dashboard components, as do a number of JavaScript frameworks and third-party charting packages. One thing to keep in mind if you decide to leverage a third party for generating charts is that if the tool uses Adobe Flex to render the visualizations, many tablets and mobile devices will not be able to display them due to limited support for Adobe Flash on these devices.

## Real-Time Updating Charts

A significant limitation of Salesforce dashboards is that they do not refresh in real time. Dashboards are either refreshed manually by clicking a button, or on a daily, weekly, or monthly schedule. For a Salesforce dashboard to display data that's refreshed more frequently, you'll need to create a custom Visualforce dashboard component.

An emerging design pattern is to use a JavaScript library that supports rich, animated content that leverages AJAX for frequent data refreshes. The ExtJS framework from Sencha is a great example of a JavaScript framework that contains a wide array of beautiful charts and other visualizations that support animation with either scheduled or real-time data refreshing. See Chapter 10 for more information on using JavaScript with Visualforce.

## Rotating Content

If your organization's content refreshes often, such as announcements or press releases, you can create a Visualforce page to display the content in a form factor tailored for a Salesforce dashboard. The content can be refreshed at any time, because it's not subject to the refresh frequency limitations of standard Dashboard components.

## Tailored Content

Even though custom Visualforce dashboard components are limited to Visualforce pages that adhere to controller limitations for custom components, you still get access to a wealth of contextual information with Visualforce global variables and Apex methods.

With this contextual information, you can tailor the content displayed in a custom Visualforce dashboard component to the logged-in user based on criteria such as their assigned Role or Profile, membership in a Chatter Group or Public Group, or even the time of day.

## Interactive Content

Dashboards do not need to be read only. If your business users require a component that allows for any level of real-time interaction, you'll need to use a custom Visualforce dashboard component.

For example, if your company wants to conduct employee surveys from within Salesforce, you can design the survey as a Visualforce page and embed it as a custom dashboard component in a dashboard that every employee sees on their Home tab when they log in to Salesforce.

## Tables, Lists, and Grids

Sometimes your business users don't need eye-popping visualizations to get the intelligence they need from Salesforce and other data. Sometimes a simple table, list, or grid will do the trick. While Salesforce offers the Metric and Table standard components, you can build Visualforce pages with either standard Visualforce components or custom JavaScript visualizations to show data in a table, list, or grid format.

## Data Mashups

If your organization is like most organizations, you likely have systems in place other than Salesforce that contain company data. While standard dashboard components are dependent on underlying reports for their source data, and those reports are limited to data that resides in Salesforce, custom Visualforce dashboard components are not subject to the same limitation.

Sometimes your business users want to see data that's aggregated from multiple source systems or services. If spending hours pulling the data together in Excel spreadsheets or making an investment in a business intelligence (BI) tool are not attractive options, a custom Visualforce dashboard component might be the ideal solution.

## Embedded Web Content

If content from another website adds context to a Salesforce dashboard, you can create a simple Visualforce page with an `<apex:iframe>` component that displays the website in a frame that can be sized to fit within the available real estate of a dashboard component.

As mentioned earlier, some browsers might have issues with IFrames, so test this solution thoroughly before rolling it out to your business users.

## JavaScript Widgets

Search the web and you can find templates and toolkits for consuming data from a virtually unlimited number of services using JavaScript and AJAX. Many services also provide pre-built widgets for interacting with the service.

Bound only by your imagination, you can use JavaScript widgets in Visualforce pages used as dashboard components to add contextually relevant data to your Salesforce dashboards. Some examples include:

| | |
|---|---|
| Twitter | Use the Twitter Widget to embed your company Twitter feed right in a Salesforce dashboard. |
| Facebook | Use a Facebook Plugin to view activity on your company Facebook page. |
| News Feed | Aggregate relevant news about your organization, customer, or industry in a single view that can be displayed on the Home tab when Salesforce users log in. |
| Currency Converter | Give your business users access to financial tools, such as a currency converter in a dashboard. |
| Weather | Embed a weather widget in a dashboard used on the Home tab and you can display today's weather based on the logged-in user's zip code or city and state. |
| Stock Ticker | Have your company's stock or major indexes tracked in a dashboard component. |

# Building Visualforce Dashboard Components

The process for building a Visualforce dashboard component is straightforward – you need a Visualforce page that adheres to the controller restrictions for Visualforce dashboard components, and you need a Salesforce dashboard.

# Adding Visualforce Pages to Dashboards

When you have identified the Salesforce dashboard you want to use or have created a new one, you'll need to edit the dashboard to include your custom component.

There are two ways to add a Visualforce page as a dashboard component. The first way is to drag the "Visualforce Page" component type from the 'Components' tab to the column in which you want it to display. Once the component has been dropped into the appropriate place on your dashboard, you can provide values for the Header and Footer. You'll then need to click the 'Data Sources' tab and expand the list of available Visualforce Pages, then drag and drop the desired page on top of the component. If the Visualforce page you're looking for doesn't appear, you need to check whether your page meets the controller requirements for a custom Visualforce dashboard component.

The second way to add a Visualforce page to a dashboard is to simply skip the step of first dragging and dropping the Visualforce Page container, and proceed to dragging and dropping the Visualforce Page Data Source directly in the dashboard. By doing this, the component container will be automatically created for you.

Either method achieves the same outcome, it's just a matter of preference.

# Visualforce Page Component Configuration

There are a number of options for customizing the look and feel of the Visualforce Page component once you drag and drop it on the dashboard, and add the Visualforce Page data source.

| Edit Header | Enter the text you want to display in the header of this component. |
| --- | --- |
| Edit Footer | Enter the text you want to display in the footer of this component. |
| Clear Source | If you want to remove the Visualforce Page data source, click the 'X' that appears on the right side of the selected component. |
| Height | If you click the wrench icon for 'Edit Attributes' on the component, you'll be given the option to set the height of the container in pixels. You can either leave this value blank and accept the default height for the container, or specify a value from 1-1000 pixels. |

# Component Container Size Limitations

Salesforce dashboards can contain up to three columns, and each column can be set to one of three widths: Narrow, Medium, or Wide. Unlike the Height setting for the component, which is customizable, the width of the component is determined by the width of the column in which it appears.

It's important to know which width your custom dashboard component will be constrained to, as it might impact how your Visualforce page appears when rendered in a dashboard.

When a Visualforce page is included as a custom dashboard component, it's rendered in a containing IFrame. Within the IFrame, the document body is rendered with a 10-pixel margin on the left and right sides, reducing the usable real estate by 20 pixels.

| Narrow | When a Visualforce page is rendered in a Narrow column, the containing IFrame will have a width of 240px, with the document body constrained to 220px. |
|--------|------|
| Medium | When a Visualforce page is rendered in a Medium column, the containing IFrame will have a width of 280px, with the document body constrained to 260px. |
| Wide | When a Visualforce page is rendered in a Wide column, the containing IFrame will have a width of 400px, with the document body constrained to 380px. |

## Dashboards in Practice

## Creating a Sales Leaderboard Dashboard Component

We have learned about incorporating Visualforce pages into dashboards as custom components, but what does this look like in practice?

As mentioned previously, sometimes a simple table can go a long way in providing relevant, real-time data to your business users when they are viewing their Home tab in Salesforce or viewing one of their dashboards.

For this example, we are going to create a Sales Leaderboard that shows the top five salespeople by Closed Won opportunities in the current year. The Leaderboard will display the name of the salesperson, the number of Closed Won opportunities, and the amount of revenue closed so far this year – and to give it a little bit of a "wow" factor, we're also going to include the Chatter profile picture for each of the top salespeople.

## Creating the Controller

Do you remember what the major limitation is for Visualforce pages that you want to embed as custom dashboard components? That's right, our page must either use a custom controller, or no controller at all.

In this example, we're going to use a custom controller to generate all of the data that we'll need to render our Sales Leaderboard. Since we want to see summaries of all Opportunity data, we're not going to declare the class 'With Sharing,' and to keep things simple, we'll skip a constructor.

```
public class sampleController {

}
```

## Rolling Up Opportunity Data

Since we want to look at all Opportunities that have been marked as Won for this year, the most straightforward way will be to leverage the powerful SOQL aggregate functions.

For this example, we'll be performing a COUNT on the Opportunity Name field (since every record has a name, this will give us an accurate count), and a SUM on the Amount field to give us the sum of all Opportunities that meet the criteria that we define in our Where clause – which in this example will be 'CloseDate = THIS_YEAR' and 'IsWon = TRUE.' We'll GROUP BY ROLLUP on the 'OwnerId' field so that we group the aggregations by each salesperson, and we'll ORDER BY the SUM(Amount) aggregation, in DESC order (because we want to display our top salespeople from the most revenue to the least).

We'll put our AggregateResult objects into a List that will be available to other methods in our controller.

```
public List<AggregateResult> aggregateOpps {

        get {

                if (aggregateOpps == null) {
                        aggregateOpps = new List<AggregateResult>();

                        for(AggregateResult o : [

                                SELECT OwnerId, SUM(Amount) amt,
        COUNT(Name) cnt

                                FROM Opportunity
                                WHERE CloseDate = THIS_YEAR AND IsWon =
        TRUE

                                GROUP BY ROLLUP(OwnerId)
                                ORDER BY SUM(Amount) DESC

                        ]){

                                if(o.get('OwnerId') != null &&
        o.get('amt') != null && o.get('cnt') != null) {

                                        aggregateOpps.add(o);

                                }

                        }

                }

                return aggregateOpps;

        }

        set;

}
```

## Retrieving User Data

We'll need to match up our AggregateResult objects with the corresponding User information to give the data the context it needs to display information about the salespeople that crack the Sales Leaderboard.

The first step is to create a Set that will contain the IDs of the User records we want to retrieve from Salesforce. To populate this Set, we'll simply iterate over our AggregateResult List, cast the object values for `OwnerId` to String values, and add them to our Set.

```
public Set<Id> ownerIds {

    get {

        if (ownerIds == null) {

            ownerIds = new Set<Id>();

            for (AggregateResult ar : aggregateOpps) {

                ownerIds.add(String.ValueOf(ar.
get('OwnerId')));

            }

        }

        return ownerIds;

    }

    set;

}
```

Next, we'll create a Map that will contain the User data we'll match up with the AggregateResult objects in our List. Since we have 'OwnerId' as a value we can use to combine Opportunity data with User data, we'll use the User ID for our Map keys, and we'll use the User sObject for our Map values. Since we want to display the name and small Chatter profile image for each salesperson in our Sales Leaderboard, we'll retrieve the 'Name' and 'SmallPhotoUrl' attributes from the User object.

**NOTE:** the 'SmallPhotoUrl' field will only be available if you have enabled Chatter in your Salesforce org.

```
public Map<Id, User> salesUsers {

    get {

        if(salesUsers == null) {

            salesUsers = new Map<Id, User>();
```

```
            for(User u : [SELECT SmallPhotoUrl, Name, Id From User
WHERE Id IN :ownerIds]) {

                    salesUsers.put(u.id, u);

            }

            }

            return salesUsers;

        }

        set;

    }
```

## Creating a Wrapper Class

Since we'll be "mashing up" data from two different sources – our List< AggregateResult> and our Map<Id, User> - a best practice is to create a Wrapper Class to combine the data.

In the Wrapper Class, we'll declare String variables for the name and picture URL for each salesperson, an Integer variable for the Opportunity count, and a Double variable for the sum of the Closed Won Opportunities. The constructor for our Wrapper Class will take values from both the List< AggregateResult> and our Map<Id, User> to return a new object that we'll cast to a List to be consumed by our Visualforce page.

```
        public class leaderData {

            public String leaderName { get; set; }
            public String leaderPic { get; set; }
            public Integer oppCount { get; set; }
            public Double oppAmount { get; set; }

            public leaderData(String leaderName, String leaderPic, Integer
oppCount, Double oppAmount) {

                this.leaderName = leaderName;
                this.leaderPic = leaderPic;
                this.oppCount = oppCount;
                this.oppAmount = oppAmount;

            }

        }
```

Finally, we'll create a Get method to grab the data we need from each object in the List< AggregateResult> and match it up with the corresponding User fields from the sObject value that corresponds to the ID key in our Map<Id, User>. We'll construct new objects and cast them to a new List that our Visualforce PageBlockTable will consume when rendering the Sales Leaderboard.

```
public List<leaderData> getLeaders() {

    List<leaderData> leaders = new List<leaderData>();

    if(aggregateOpps != null && salesUsers !=null) {

        for(AggregateResult ar : aggregateOpps) {

            leaders.add(new leaderData(salesUsers.get(String.
ValueOf(ar.get('OwnerId'))).Name, salesUsers.get(String.ValueOf(ar.
get('OwnerId'))).SmallPhotoUrl, Integer.ValueOf(ar.get('cnt')),
Double.ValueOf(ar.get('amt'))));

        }

    }

    return leaders;
}
```

## Creating the Visualforce Page

Now that the heavy lifting is complete, the Visualforce page itself is pretty simple. We need to tell our Page component that we'll be using a custom controller. We can also set the `tabStyle` attribute so that our table is rendered with the same look-and-feel as items that appear in the Opportunity tab.

To render the table, we'll first render an `<apex:pageBlock>` component to contain the table. Then we'll render an `<apex:pageBlockTable>` with the `Value` attribute set to the object List variable in our controller, a simple variable name in the `Var` attribute, and we'll limit the number of 'Rows' to five so that we display the top five salespeople.

Within the `<apex:pageBlockTable>` we'll define our four columns. In the first column, we'll use an `<apex:image>` component to render the small Chatter profile picture for the User in the `<apex:column>` component. In the second column, we'll render the name of the salesperson along with a column header by specifying 'Name' for the value of the `headerValue` attribute of our `<apex:column>` For the third column, we'll render the Opportunity count value with a 'headerValue' of 'Count.' In the last column, we'll need to do a little formatting of the output so that it displays using our preferred convention for displaying a currency value. This is achieved by including an `<apex:outputText>` component with additional formatting attributes.

```
<apex:page controller="sampleController" tabStyle="Opportunity">

    <apex:pageBlock >

        <apex:pageBlockTable value="{!leaders}" var="l" rows="5">
            <apex:column >
```

```
                <apex:image url="{!l.leaderPic}" />
            </apex:column>
            <apex:column value="{!l.leaderName}"
 headerValue="Name"/>
            <apex:column value="{!l.oppCount}" headerValue="Won"/>
            <apex:column headerValue="Revenue">
               <apex:outputText value="{0, number, 0,000}">
                       <apex:param value="{!l.oppAmount}" />
               </apex:outputText>
            </apex:column>
        </apex:pageBlockTable>
    </apex:pageBlock>
</apex:page>
```

You can now view your page to test it and make sure it looks and feels the way you want it to by going to the URL for the Visualforce page:

https://{Instance_name}.salesforce.com/apex/{Visualforce page name}

## Creating the Custom Visualforce Dashboard Component

This is where the magic happens. Navigate to and edit the Salesforce Dashboard where you want the new Sales Leaderboard to display.

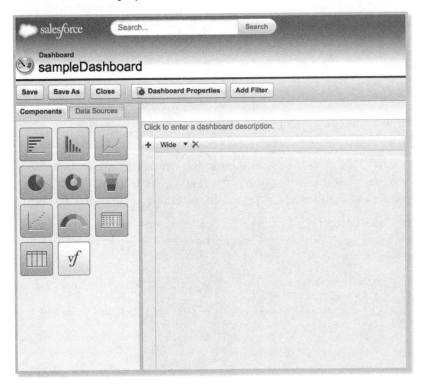

Drag the 'Visualforce Page' component from the 'Components' tab and drop it in the position on the column where you want it to display.

Edit the component's Header to give it a descriptive title, such as "Sales Leaderboard."

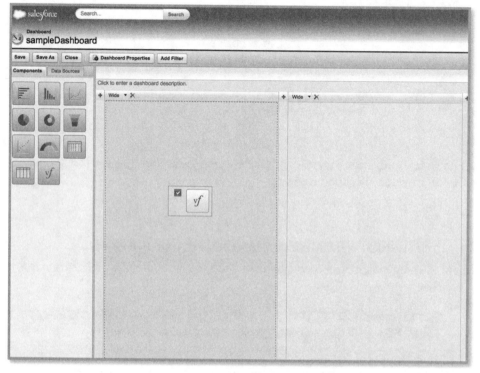

*Figure 7-2. Dropping the component into position and editing the Header of the component.*

Next, drag the Visualforce page from the 'Visualforce Pages' menu under the 'Data Sources' tab and drop it on the component. as shown in Figure 7-3.

Save the dashboard. How does the preview look? If it needs any tuning, click the wrench icon and set the component height if you need more real estate. To display the full Sales Leaderboard with five salespeople and their small Chatter profile pictures, a height of 420px is optimal.

If you want the Sales Leaderboard component to display on a dashboard that you have assigned to the Home tab, you'll need to make sure it's positioned at the top of one of the three columns in a dashboard. See Figure 7-4.

Close the dashboard editor. Your Sales Leaderboard component is now live and should look similar to Figure 7-5. Nice work!

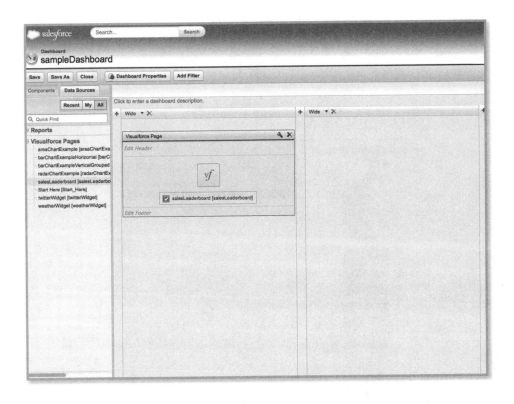

*Figure 7-3.* Dragging the Visualforce page and dropping it onto the component.

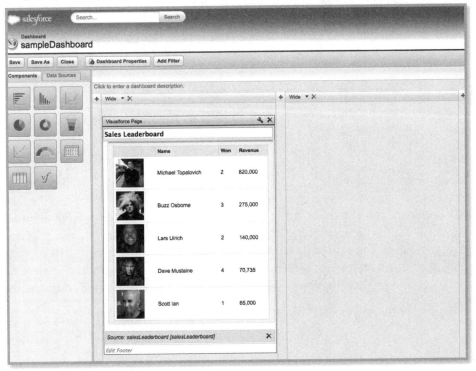

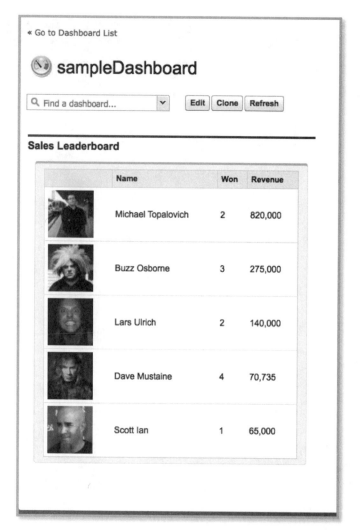

*Figure 7-5. The completed Sales Leaderboard*

## Summary

In this chapter we learned about how to incorporate Visualforce pages as custom dashboard components to give your business users access to information that goes far beyond the limitations of standard dashboard components. Common and emerging design patterns were discussed, and we learned about the limitations and configuration options available for custom Visualforce dashboard components. You should feel comfortable adding Visualforce pages to dashboards as components, as well as have enough information to troubleshoot any issues that might emerge during the design and implementation of your custom Visualforce dashboard components.

# Chapter 8
# Streaming Realtime Data into Visualforce

- About the Streaming API
- Setup and Configuration
- Creating a Push Topic
- Using RemoteActions
- About the Streaming API

The salesforce.com Streaming API provides a near real-time feed of notifications from events occurring within your organization's database. A client can subscribe to this feed of data from the server and can take action on the notifications received from the subscription channel. This chapter will provide an overview of the Streaming API and demonstrate how to setup and configure your Salesforce environment to subscribe to Push Topic channels in Visualforce pages. Additionally, we'll explore a variety of techniques to process the event notifications and handle the interactions with Visualforce controllers.

We'll work through three examples of how to implement the Streaming API in Visualforce pages. The first example will show how to subscribe to a channel, and handle the messages on the client side with JavaScript. This does not require a controller, but the data provided to the end user goes no farther than the extent of the channel notification. The next example will build upon the previous example, but query for additional information by invoking an @RemoteAction method from a controller to deliver additional reference fields. Finally, we'll use a Visualforce ActionFunction to deliver notification data to a custom controller, which will process and retain the data in the view state for a feed of updates to the end user. All of these examples will be using the Case object as the subject for the Push Topic.

# Streaming API Overview

The salesforce.com Streaming API operates on a topic publish/subscribe model. In this model, the server delivers messages within a specified channel (topic) to subscribers (clients). The subscriber performs an initial handshake with the server for authentication and designates the channel with which they want a subscription. Once the handshake is complete and a connection to a channel is established, the subscriber begins to receive a feed of notifications from the channel. The Streaming API is a forward moving, one-way feed of data. Subscribers receive notifications from the server upon relevant database events, but cannot respond to or request additional details from notifications received from the Streaming API. Furthermore, past notifications not received from a lost connection or other issues cannot be recovered or queried. Any additional actions or interactions based on the notifications must be performed via other means.

A channel, in terms of the Streaming API, is created by defining a Push Topic. A Push Topic is a record within Salesforce that defines a series of attributes about the channel. The most critical attribute of a Push Topic is the query. A Push Topic query follows the same syntax as any other SOQL query. This SOQL query defines which records qualify for notifications within the channel. For example:

```
SELECT Id, name, accountId, amount, stageName
FROM Opportunity
WHERE isClosed = false
```

In this example, only DML actions on records with the isClosed flag set to false will provide notifications to the channel. While the query attribute of a Push Topic is SOQL, you cannot use every feature of SOQL's syntax. Most notably, Push Topic queries do not support relationships. Adding "account.name" to the query defined above will result in a failure while attempting to create or update a Push Topic. For a full list of supported Push Topic queries, check the salesforce.com Streaming API documentation.

There are two more important attributes of a Push Topic. NotifyForFields is an enum that is defined as All, Referenced, Select, or Where. If "All" is selected, a notification will be sent regardless of which fields are updated on the record. However, the notification message will only contain the fields defined in the query. The default value is "Referenced;" it will only issue notifications if a field that is referenced in the SOQL query has changed. Similarly, the "Select" and "Where" options generate notifications only if a field value has been updated in the SELECT or WHERE clauses, respectively. NotifyForOperations is another enum that is defined as All, Create, or Update. The default selection is "All" and generates notifications for both Create and Update actions in the database for records that are found by the Push Topic query. The Create and Update options limit notifications to their respective DML events.

It is important to remember that notifications delivered within channels on the Streaming API occur only upon DML actions on records in the database. Passive changes on fields via formulas, lookups being cleared, etc., will not initiate a notification. However, time-based workflows can initiate a DML event, and can therefore create channel notifications where applicable. Time-based workflow can be helpful in initiating proactive notifications from the system. An example can be a time-based workflow that checks a box or sets a date field based on business rules. When the workflow fires, the record is updated with a field update from a workflow action. The DML event can initiate a Push Topic notification that is filtering based on the field being updated from the time-based workflow action. The final result is a declarative mechanism for delivering notifications to subscribers without hands-on interaction from a user or scheduled jobs.

# Environment Setup and Configuration

The Streaming API notification delivery is based on connectivity through long-polling, or Comet programming. This is achieved by transporting messages utilizing the Bayeux Protocol via an implementation of an AJAX-based framework called CometD. The technologies are very compelling, and can be explored further at:

```
http://cometd.org/documentation
http://cometd.org/documentation/bayeux
```

In order to negotiate access to the notification channels in Visualforce pages, we need to add a few static resources from CometD. The CometD compressed archive can be downloaded at:

```
http://download.cometd.org/cometd-2.2.0-distribution.tar.gz
```

Once you have a copy of this archive, you'll need to extract it to a directory that can be easily accessed. We'll be uploading some of the files from this extract to your organization's static resources. Once the archive is extracted, we'll need to take another step to extract the cometd.js file from the cometd-javascript-common-2.2.0.war web application archive. In a Mac environment, this can be achieved by opening a terminal in the extracted directory at:

```
[Your Path]/cometd-2.2.0/cometd-javascript/common/target
```

Once the terminal is open, execute the following command:

```
jar xvf cometd-javascript-common-2.2.0.war org/cometd.js
```

This will place the cometd.js file in the same directory listed above. Once this process is complete, navigate to your static resources in Salesforce by clicking:

```
[Your Name]>Setup>Develop>Static Resources
```

Create the following static resources from your extracted CometD archive.

| Static Resource Name | CometD Extract Path |
| --- | --- |
| cometd | cometd-2.2.0/cometd-javascript/common/target/org/cometd.js |
| jquery | cometd-2.2.0/cometd-javascript/jquery/src/main/webapp/jquery/jquery-1.5.1.js |
| json2 | cometd-2.2.0/cometd-javascript/jquery/src/main/webapp/jquery/json2.js |
| jquery_cometd | cometd-2.2.0/cometd-javascript/jquery/src/main/webapp/jquery/jquery.cometd.js |

Your environment is now set up to subscribe to channels and accept notifications from the Streaming API.

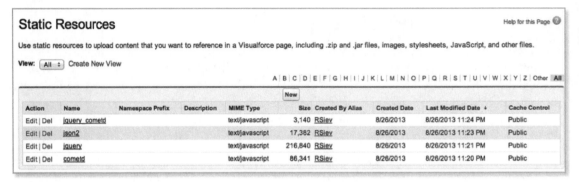

*Figure 8-1. Static Resources*

## Create a Push Topic

Push Topics can be created on almost all objects within Salesforce, including the CRM objects and custom objects. You can create a Push Topic by executing anonymous Apex via the developer console or through the IDE. To create a Push Topic from the developer console, click:

[Your Name] > **Developer Console**

Once the console loads, open an Execute Anonymous window by clicking:

Debug>Open Execute Anonymous Window

Execute the following code:

```
PushTopic pushTopic = new PushTopic();
pushTopic.ApiVersion = 28.0;
pushTopic.Name = 'CaseNotifications';
pushTopic.Description = 'Case Notifications';
pushTopic.NotifyForFields = 'Referenced';
pushTopic.NotifyForOperations = 'All';
pushTopic.Query = 'SELECT Id, caseNumber, accountId, contactId,
status, priority FROM Case';
insert pushTopic;
system.debug('Created new PushTopic: ' + pushTopic.Id);
```

Now that your Push Topic has been created, we need to test that it's working. There are a variety of ways to test, but the simplest way is to log into the Salesforce workbench at:

https://workbench.developerforce.com/login.php.

This is a tremendous tool for working with the Streaming API. It provides a reliable way to interact with the various channels by browsing and subscribing to Push Topics. It can also provide a sanity check if you ever lose your connection in a page and need to see if messages are being delivered in your channel. Once you have logged into the workbench, click: **Queries > Streaming Push Topics**

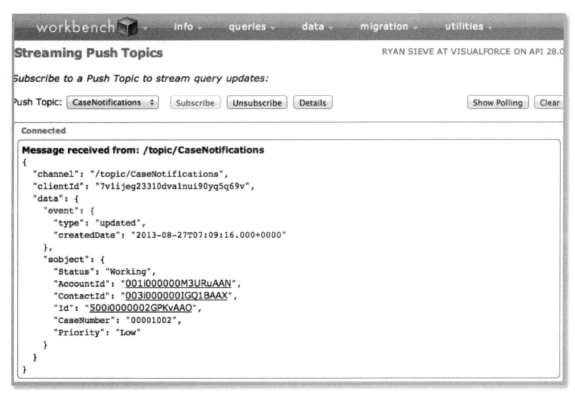

*Figure 8-2. Streaming Push Topics*

You can view all of your Push Topics by clicking the drop down list labeled "Push Topics." For our example, select the "CaseNotifications" channel and click the "Subscribe" button. You should see a dialog appear indicating that you have subscribed to "/topic/CaseNotifications."

In a separate browser tab or browser, find a Case record in your organization and change the value in the status or priority field. Return to the workbench, and you should see a new dialog appear indicating that a message was received from the channel. See Figure 8-4.

Now that you have verified your channel is delivering messages as expected, you're ready to start building pages to accept the feed of notifications from your channel.

## Visualforce Page with Client Side Processing

The first Visualforce page example will handle the subscription to the Push Topic channel and the processing of the notification completely on the client side. It will not require a custom controller, and provides a quick and easy starting point to working with the Streaming API in a Visualforce page. This example simply takes notifications received from the channel, and updates a PanelGrid with the message details. The intention of this page is to be modular, and to fit within a Dashboard Component. The end result is a near real-time dashboard component that shows the latest Case update details, and requires no Dashboard refresh, or screen refresh.

Message received from: /topic/CaseNotifications
{
  "channel": "/topic/CaseNotifications",
  "clientId": "7v1ijeg23310dva1nui90yq5q69v",
  "data": {
    "event": {
      "type": "updated",
      "createdDate": "2013-08-27T07:09:16.000+0000"
    },
    "sobject": {
      "Status": "Working",
      "AccountId": "001i000000M3URuAAN",
      "ContactId": "003i000000IGQ1BAAX",
      "Id": "500i0000002GPKvAAO",
      "CaseNumber": "00001002",
      "Priority": "Low"
    }
  }
}

*Figure 8-3.*

Let's begin by creating a new Visualforce page named, "SimpleCaseNotifications." Add the following attributes to the opening page tag:

| Attribute Name | Value |
| --- | --- |
| id | page |
| tabstyle | case |

Next, we need to add the static resources to the page with the following tags:

```
<apex:includeScript value="{!$Resource.cometd}"/>
        <apex:includeScript value="{!$Resource.jquery}"/>
        <apex:includeScript value="{!$Resource.json2}"/>
        <apex:includeScript value="{!$Resource.jquery_cometd}"/>
```

These IncludeScript tags load the JavaScript libraries from the static resources into the page, and will be used to manage the subscription to the channel and ongoing long-polling. We need to add one more block of JavaScript to the page, directly under the IncludeScript tags. This JavaScript is used to initiate the connection to the Streaming API, and subscribe to the "CaseNotifications" channel.

```
<script type="text/javascript">

        var j$ = jQuery.noConflict();
        j$(document).ready(function() {
```

```
        j$.cometd.init({
            url: window.location.protocol+'//'+window.location.
hostname+'/cometd/28.0/',
            requestHeaders: { Authorization: 'OAuth {!$Api.
Session_ID}'}
        });

        j$.cometd.subscribe('/topic/CaseNotifications',
function(message) {
            document.getElementById('{!$Component.page.
block.casenumber}').innerText = message.data.sobject.CaseNumber;
            document.getElementById('{!$Component.page.
block.casestatus}').innerText = message.data.sobject.Status;
            document.getElementById('{!$Component.page.
block.casepriority}').innerText = message.data.sobject.Priority;
            console.log(message);
        });
    });

</script>
```

Finally, add the body of the page as a simple page block and panel grid with text details. When the notifications are received in the channel, the JavaScript will update the elements in the DOM with the details. As additional notifications are received, these attributes will be overwritten to show the latest notification details.

```
<apex:sectionHeader title="Simple" subTitle="Case Notifications"/>
<apex:pageBlock id="block">
    <apex:panelGrid columns="2">
        <apex:outputLabel value="Case Number: " for="casenumber"
style="font-weight: bold;"/>
        <apex:outputText value="" id="casenumber"/>
        <apex:outputLabel value="Case Status: "
for="casestatus" style="font-weight: bold;"/>
        <apex:outputText value="" id="casestatus"/>
        <apex:outputLabel value="Case Priority: "
for="casepriority" style="font-weight: bold;"/>
        <apex:outputText value="" id="casepriority"/>
    </apex:panelGrid>
</apex:pageBlock>
```

Save your changes to the page. Your final markup should look like this:

```
<apex:page id="page" tabStyle="Case">

    <apex:includeScript value="{!$Resource.cometd}"/>
    <apex:includeScript value="{!$Resource.jquery}"/>
    <apex:includeScript value="{!$Resource.json2}"/>
    <apex:includeScript value="{!$Resource.jquery_cometd}"/>
```

```
<script type="text/javascript">

    var j$ = jQuery.noConflict();
    j$(document).ready(function() {

      j$.cometd.init({
            url: window.location.protocol+'//'+window.location.
hostname+'/cometd/28.0/',
            requestHeaders: { Authorization: 'OAuth {!$Api.
Session_ID}'}
          });

        j$.cometd.subscribe('/topic/CaseNotifications',
function(message) {
                    document.getElementById('{!$Component.page.
block.casenumber}').innerText = message.data.sobject.CaseNumber;
                    document.getElementById('{!$Component.page.
block.casestatus}').innerText = message.data.sobject.Status;
                    document.getElementById('{!$Component.page.
block.casepriority}').innerText = message.data.sobject.Priority;
                    console.log(message);
          });
      });

  </script>
  <apex:sectionHeader title="Simple" subTitle="Case Notifications"/>
  <apex:pageBlock id="block">
        <apex:panelGrid columns="2">
<apex:outputLabel value="Case Number: "
for="casenumber" style="font-weight: bold;"/>
              <apex:outputText value="" id="casenumber"/>
              <apex:outputLabel value="Case Status:  "
for="casestatus" style="font-weight: bold;"/>
              <apex:outputText value="" id="casestatus"/>
              <apex:outputLabel value="Case Priority:  "
for="casepriority" style="font-weight: bold;"/>
              <apex:outputText value="" id="casepriority"/>
        </apex:panelGrid>
  </apex:pageBlock>
</apex:page>
```

Navigate to your new page and verify that it loads without content in the PageBlock. Open another tab or browser and update the status or priority fields on a Case record, similar to how you tested using the workbench. You should see the page update with the notification details. You can also check for the same notification in the Workbench to explore additional details.

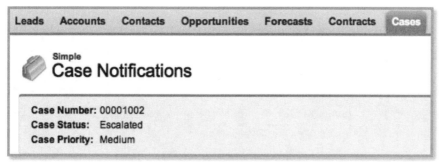

*Figure 8-4. The Case Notifications window.*

Notice the console.log(message) command in the supplemental JavaScript block. In Chrome, this logs the message received from the channel for review. Take some time and use the browser debugging tools of your choice, or the Salesforce Developer Workbench, to examine these messages. You'll notice the message content is delivered in JSON, and has more attributes than what is being added to the page. These can be valuable both in debugging, or displaying to the end user.

```
▼ Object 🔢
    channel: "/topic/CaseNotifications"
    clientId: "vpvkfo8tbgr1mjje95w9x4h160"
  ▼ data: Object
    ▼ event: Object
        createdDate: "2013-08-28T06:10:11.000+0000"
        type: "updated"
      ► __proto__: Object
    ▼ sobject: Object
        AccountId: "001i000000M3URuAAN"
        CaseNumber: "00001002"
        ContactId: "003i000000IGQ1BAAX"
        Id: "500i0000002GPKvAAO"
        Priority: "Low"
        Status: "Escalated"
      ► __proto__: Object
    ► __proto__: Object
  ► __proto__: Object
```

This simple page can also be dropped into a dashboard component to show a near real-time feed of updates to the user without requiring a screen refresh, or dashboard refresh.

This example is intentionally very simple. The goal is to demonstrate how a page can subscribe to a Push Topic channel, receive notifications, and take action to display the data to the user. This is achieved without the use of an Apex controller, and relies on client-side JavaScript to update elements in the DOM with the message details.

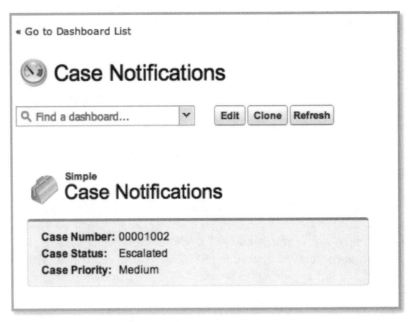

*Figure 8-5. Case Notifications.*

## Visualforce Page with RemoteAction

In the first example, the message contains all of the data needed to display to the end user. Oftentimes, requirements dictate that additional information from parent or child objects are displayed for user reference or interaction. While the channel notification holds vital pieces of information from the record being created or updated, it's reasonable to assume that additional supporting information might be needed at the time a notification is received.

RemoteAction methods can provide a simple and fast (both in development time and response time) way to query the database for additional data regarding the channel notification. A RemoteAction method can return an sObject record that has queried additional reference fields from the database that cannot be provided in the channel notification. This page will differ from the first example in that the notification serves as input parameters to the RemoteAction method. However, it resembles the first example by taking the RemoteAction response, and updating the DOM with the queried data.

This example page will show additional details regarding the name of the Account, Contact, and Owner related to the Case. These reference attributes are not delivered in the notification, nor will a push topic query support the delivery of the related fields. We are able to return these pieces of data to the user by invoking a RemoteAction method upon receipt of a channel notification. The RemoteAction will accept data delivered from the notification, and return the queried record with the additional reference data.

Begin by creating a new "with sharing" Apex class named "RemoteActionCaseNotificationsController." We'll only need a single method in this controller. Create a new method, using the @RemoteAction annotation, that returns a Case, as shown below.

```
public with sharing class RemoteActionCaseNotificationsController {

    @RemoteAction
    public static Case returnCase(string caseId){

            return [SELECT Id, caseNumber, status, priority,
    owner.name, account.name, contact.name
                    FROM Case
                    WHERE Id = :caseId];

    }

}
```

This query can be expanded to pull additional reference fields, as well as records in child relationships. Save your changes to this class.

Create a new Visualforce page named "RemoteActionCaseNotifications," with the same page tag attributes as the first example. Add the same <apex:includeScript> tags as well. The body of the page should resemble the first example; except we need to add additional <apex:outputLabel> and <apex:outputText> tags for the additional reference fields, as shown below.

```
<apex:sectionHeader title="Remote Action" subTitle="Case
Notifications"/>
<apex:pageBlock id="block">
    <apex:panelGrid columns="2">
            <apex:outputLabel value="Case Number: "
for="casenumber" style="font-weight: bold;"/>
            <apex:outputText value="" id="casenumber"/>
            <apex:outputLabel value="Case Status:     "
for="casestatus" style="font-weight: bold;"/>
            <apex:outputText value="" id="casestatus"/>
            <apex:outputLabel value="Case Priority:   "
for="casepriority" style="font-weight: bold;"/>
            <apex:outputText value="" id="casepriority"/>
            <apex:outputLabel value="Case Owner:      "
for="caseowner" style="font-weight: bold;"/>
            <apex:outputText value="" id="caseowner"/>
            <apex:outputLabel value="Account Name:    "
for="accountname" style="font-weight: bold;"/>
            <apex:outputText value="" id="accountname"/>
            <apex:outputLabel value="Contact Name:    "
for="contactname" style="font-weight: bold;"/>
            <apex:outputText value="" id="contactname"/>
    </apex:panelGrid>
</apex:pageBlock>
<apex:outputPanel layout="block" id="responseErrors"></
apex:outputPanel>
```

Following the first example, add a new JavaScript block, with the "ready," "init," and "subscribe" functions. However, leave the content of the subscribe method empty.

```
<script type="text/javascript">

var j$ = jQuery.noConflict();
j$(document).ready(function() {

        j$.cometd.init({
url: window.location.protocol+'//'+window.location.hostname+'/
cometd/28.0/',
            requestHeaders: { Authorization: 'OAuth {!$Api.
Session_ID}'}
            });

            j$.cometd.subscribe('/topic/CaseNotifications',
function(message) {

            });

    })
   </script>
```

Now create another Javascript function named "getRemoteCase," with a signature that will accept the ID of the record received in the channel notification. The contents of this method should invoke the RemoteAction method from the controller, and update the elements in the DOM for the user to review. Finally, add a call to the getRemoteCase method from within the subscribe method. Your final JavaScript code should look like:

```
<script type="text/javascript">

        var j$ = jQuery.noConflict();
        j$(document).ready(function() {

          j$.cometd.init({
            url: window.location.protocol+'//'+window.location.
hostname+'/cometd/28.0/',
            requestHeaders: { Authorization: 'OAuth {!$Api.
Session_ID}'}
            });

            j$.cometd.subscribe('/topic/CaseNotifications',
function(message) {
            getRemoteCase(message.data.sobject.Id);
          });

         function getRemoteCase(caseId) {
            Visualforce.remoting.Manager.invokeAction(
              '{!$RemoteAction.
RemoteActionCaseNotificationsController.returnCase}',
                caseId,
                function(result, event){
```

```
                    if (event.status) {
                            document.
getElementById('{!$Component.page.block.casenumber}').innerText =
result.CaseNumber;
                            document.
getElementById('{!$Component.page.block.casestatus}').innerText =
result.Status;
                            document.
getElementById('{!$Component.page.block.casepriority}').innerText =
result.Priority;
                            document.
getElementById('{!$Component.page.block.caseowner}').innerText =
result.Owner.Name;
                            document.
getElementById('{!$Component.page.block.accountname}').innerText =
result.Account.Name;
                            document.
getElementById('{!$Component.page.block.contactname}').innerText =
result.Contact.Name;
                    } else if (event.type === 'exception') {
                        document.
getElementById("responseErrors").innerHTML =
                            event.message + "<br/>\n<pre>" +
event.where + "</pre>";
                    } else {
                        document.
getElementById("responseErrors").innerHTML = event.message;
                    }
                },
                {escape: true}
            );
        }
    })
</script>
```

Recall the <apex:outputPanel> with the ID of "responseErrors." This panel will render a <div> on the page where error messages will appear if there is a problem with the query or RemoteAction method. The error message HTML delivers in the exception conditions of the JavaScript can be changed to fit your requirements.

You can test this page in the same fashion as the first example. Once the notification is received, the RemoteAction will fire and update the elements in the DOM with the queried reference data.

It's important to consider the performance of the page while adding the call to the server with the RemoteAction. There will be a slight delay between the channel notification and providing the information to the user once the additional reference fields are queried. In high-level performance benchmarks, this example typically returns data to the page from the RemoteAction within ~200-250 ms. This duration will likely extend if the query returns more fields, child relationships, or has other processing prior to returning the data. While the delay is nominal in this example, it should not be overlooked as you extend this functionality to support more complex interactions on the server and client side.

# Visualforce Page with ActionFunction

The previous example illustrates how a channel notification can be used to initiate interaction with the server to obtain additional data not available in the channel notification. This example also treats the notification as a signal to interact with the server for additional data, but will also be adding and managing elements in the view state, and rerender components in the form. This is achieved through the utilization of an <apex:actionFunction> tag. When the page loads, the ActionFunction tag generates a JavaScript function in the browser that handles an AJAX request from the user. We are taking advantage of this by generating an ActionFunction that allows the calling action to pass a parameter, and deliver it to the controller for further action.

This example will deliver the ID from the Case in the channel notification to the controller, which queries and retains Case details in the view state even after additional notifications have been received. The ActionFunction will also be utilized to rerender elements on the page to reflect updated data in the view state from the controller upon receipt of the data from the channel notification. The rerender will also be used to refresh Visualforce charts that reflect summary data on open Cases in the database.

Similar to the RemoteAction controller example, begin by creating a new "with sharing" Apex class named "ActionFunctionCaseNotificationController." Before we build any methods to process the channel notifications, we need to define a class wrapper to store the data queried on the incoming notifications. The class wrapper is simple, only containing a Case sObject and DateTime as member variables. It will also need a Comparable interface to store the incoming Cases in a descending sequence based on the DateTime it was received. As channel notifications are received, additional data will be queried from the system, stored in instances of this class wrapper, and tagged with a time stamp. For more information on the Comparable interface, please check the Apex documentation. Add the following class to your controller.

```
public class CaseWrapper implements Comparable{
        public Case c {get;set;}
        public DateTime ts {get;set;}

        //Return a descending timestamp sort,
//with the latest timestamp first after sort
        public integer compareTo(Object compareTo){
                CaseWrapper wrapperCompareTo = (CaseWrapper)compareTo;
                if(ts == wrapperCompareTo.ts){
                        return 0;
                }else if(ts > wrapperCompareTo.ts){
                        return -1;
                }else{
                        return 1;
                }
        }
    }
```

We need to add a couple of public variables in the controller to support the incremental Case data being stored in a collection. Add the following variables to your controller.

```
public string caseId {get;set;}
public Map<Id, CaseWrapper> mCaseWrappers {get;set;}
{ mCaseWrappers = new Map<Id, CaseWrapper>();}
```

The caseId will be delivered from the page, and will be used to query for additional Case data. The Map<Id, CaseWrapper> will be used for multiple reasons. We want to ensure that we're displaying a unique list of Cases to the user, so storing the CaseWrappers in a Map and using the Case ID as the key will prevent duplicate instances of the wrapper for the same case, even if multiple channel notifications are received in a short time frame.

Add a method to query for the required Case data, based on the caseId attribute supplied from the page, and put an instance of the CaseWrapper class in the Map with the Case ID as the key value.

```
public void addCaseId(){
        Case tmpCase = [SELECT Id, caseNumber, status, priority,
owner.name, account.name, contact.name,
                    (SELECT Id, commentBody, createdBy.Name,
createdDate
                    FROM CaseComments
                    ORDER BY CreatedDate desc
                    LIMIT 5)
            FROM Case
                WHERE Id = :caseId];
        CaseWrapper cw = new CaseWrapper();
        cw.c = tmpCase;
        cw.ts = system.now();
        mCaseWrappers.put(cw.c.Id, cw);
```

Understanding that a keyset in a Map cannot retain a particular order, we'll put the Comparable interface to work to return the list of CaseWrappers to the page in the sequence we desire. Add another method that returns a list of CaseWrappers from the Map values. The CaseWrapper list returned by the Map values can be sorted, and then returned to the page.

```
public List<CaseWrapper> getCases(){
        List<CaseWrapper> cases = mCaseWrappers.values();
        cases.sort();
        return cases;
    }
```

In order to support the Visualforce pie charts, we need to add another class wrapper that will store the queried summary data from the system based on Case Priority and Case Status. This simple class wrapper contains a string and integer member variables. Instances of this class wrapper will hold the name of a case attribute, and the integer will represent how many Cases reflect that attribute. Add the following code:

```
public class CaseData{
        public string value {get;private set;}
        public integer nRecs {get;private set;}

        public CaseData(string val, integer n){
            value = val;
            nRecs = n;
        }
    }
```

Using Case Status as an example, we can expect to see data similar to the table below:

| Status | nRecs |
|--------|-------|
| New | 4 |
| Working | 12 |
| Escalated | 1 |

We need to add two methods that return a list of CaseData wrappers to the page. We'll use an AggregateResult query in each to quickly group on Case Status and Priority, with the count of records in each group. For more information on AggregateResults, please refer to the Apex documentation. Add the following code to your controller.

```
public List<CaseData> getStatusData(){
        List<CaseData> statusData = new List<CaseData>();
        List<AggregateResult> arStatuses = [SELECT status status,
COUNT(Id) nRecs
                                        FROM Case
                                        WHERE isClosed = false
                                    GROUP BY status];
        for(AggregateResult ar : arStatuses){
            statusData.add(new CaseData((string)ar.get('status'),
                                (integer)ar.get('nRecs')));
        }
        return statusData;
    }

    public List<CaseData> getPriorityData(){
        List<CaseData> priorityData = new List<CaseData>();
        List<AggregateResult> arPriorities = [SELECT priority
priority,
COUNT(Id) nRecs
                                        FROM Case
                                        WHERE isClosed = false
                                        GROUP BY priority];
        for(AggregateResult ar : arPriorities){
            priorityData.add(new CaseData((string)
ar.get('priority'),
  (integer)ar.get('nRecs')));
        }
        return priorityData;
    }
```

We have completed the controller and can now move on to the Visualforce page. Create a new Visualforce page named "ActionFunctionCaseNotifications" with the same <apex:page> tag attributes and <apex:includeScript > tags as the previous examples. Similar to the other examples, we'll need to add a JavaScript block to subscribe to the channel notifications, and pass the delivered messages to our ActionFunction. Add the following JavaScript to your page below your IncludeScript tags:

```
<script type="text/javascript">
        var j$ = jQuery.noConflict();
    j$(document).ready(function() {
            // Connect to the CometD endpoint

            j$.cometd.init({
                url: window.location.protocol+'//'+window.location.
hostname+'/cometd/28.0/',
                requestHeaders: { Authorization: 'OAuth {!$Api.
Session_ID}' }
            });

            j$.cometd.subscribe('/topic/CaseNotifications',
function(message) {
                findCaseDetails(message.data.sobject.Id);
            });

        });
</script>
```

Notice the findCaseDetails method invocation within the subscribe method. This method will call out to the ActionFunction, which will be created after adding a few more components to the page.

The page will be segmented into two major sections: the left panel with the pie charts, and the right panel with the Case details and comments. In order to achieve this presentation, we'll use an <apex:panelGrid> with two small style classes for the columns. These classes instruct the panels on their width, and to align with the top of their containing elements. Add the following styles:

```
<style>
    .panelLeft {
        width: 25%;
        vertical-align: top;
    }
.panelRight {
        width: 75%;
        vertical-align: top;
    }
</style>
```

Now add a sectionHeader and form to the page.

```
<apex:sectionHeader title="Action Function" subTitle="Case
Notifications" />
<apex:form id="form">
</apex:form>
```

Add an <apex:panelGrid> tag as a direct child to the form with two columns, spanning the entire width of the page, and reflecting the styleClasses defined from above.

```
<apex:panelGrid columns="2" width="100%"
columnClasses="panelLeft,panelRight">

</apex:panelGrid>
```

Create a grouping for the pie charts by adding an <apex:panelGroup> tag inside the PanelGrid as the content for the first column,. Add the following code inside the PanelGroup to reflect the AggregateResult data returned for the pie charts from the controller.

```
<apex:panelGroup >
<apex:pageBlock title="Case Status">

            <apex:chart data="{!statusData}" height="200" width="250"
                                    background="#F5F5F5">
                <apex:legend position="bottom"/>
            <apex:pieSeries labelField="value" dataField="nRecs"
donut="50">
                        <apex:chartLabel display="middle"
orientation="vertical"

                                            font="bold 12px Helvetica"/>
            </apex:pieSeries>
            </apex:chart>


    </apex:pageBlock>
    <apex:pageBlock title="Case Priority">

<apex:chart data="{!priorityData}" height="200" width="250"
                    background="#F5F5F5">
<apex:legend position="bottom"/>
                <apex:pieSeries labelField="value" dataField="nRecs"
donut="50">
                        <apex:chartLabel display="middle"
orientation="vertical"

                                            font="bold 12px Helvetica"/>
            </apex:pieSeries>
            </apex:chart>


    </apex:pageBlock>
  </apex:panelGroup>
```

This will create two donut-style pie charts representing the number of Cases by Status and Priority. Any additional elements added to this PanelGroup will appear in the narrow column on the left.

The content for the column on the right is Case detail information and related comments. Add an <apex:pageBlock> tag after the closing </apex:panelGroup> tag. All content added to this component will appear in the wide column on the right. The content in this column is generated by an <apex:repeat> tag that creates PageBlockSections for each instance of a CaseWrapper returned by the getCases method in the controller. The first PageBlockSection contains Case Detail information, and the second contains a PageBlockTable to display any comments that have been created on this case. Each wrapper in the list will have both PageBlockSections to display content. Notice that the repeat tag is wrapped with an <apex:outputPanel> with styles to handle content overflow. This helps create a clean page in two ways. First, it prevents the content in the column on the right from growing exceedingly long and cumbersome looking. Second, and more importantly, regardless of how long the content becomes, the pie charts will hold a static position on the page relative to any scrolling occurring in the column on the right.

```
<apex:pageBlock title="Recent Case Updates">
<apex:outputPanel layout="block" style="height:500px;overflow-y:scroll;">
      <apex:repeat value="{!cases}" var="cw">
              <apex:pageBlockSection title="{!cw.c.caseNumber}" columns="2">
                      <apex:outputField value="{!cw.c.caseNumber}"/>
                      <apex:outputField value="{!cw.c.status}"/>
                      <apex:outputField value="{!cw.c.priority}"/>
                      <apex:pageBlockSectionItem >
                              <apex:outputLabel value="Owner Name"/>
                              <apex:outputField value="{!cw.c.owner.name}"/>
                      </apex:pageBlockSectionItem>
                      <apex:pageBlockSectionItem >
                              <apex:outputLabel value="Account Name"/>
                              <apex:outputField value="{!cw.c.account.name}"/>
                      </apex:pageBlockSectionItem>
                      <apex:pageBlockSectionItem >
                              <apex:outputLabel value="Contact Name"/>
                              <apex:outputField value="{!cw.c.contact.name}"/>
                      </apex:pageBlockSectionItem>
              </apex:pageBlockSection>
              <apex:pageBlockSection columns="1">
                      <apex:pageBlockTable value="{!cw.c.CaseComments}" var="cc"
                              rendered="{!cw.c.CaseComments.size > 0}">
                              <apex:column value="{!cc.createdBy.Name}"/>
                              <apex:column value="{!cc.createdDate}"/>
                              <apex:column value="{!cc.commentBody}"/>
                      </apex:pageBlockTable>
                      <apex:outputText value="There are no comments on
  this case." rendered="{!cw.c.CaseComments.size == 0}" style="font-
  weight:bold"/>
              </apex:pageBlockSection>
      </apex:repeat>
</apex:outputPanel>
</apex:pageBlock>
```

The final and most important tag that we need to add is the <apex:actionFunction>. This tag will generate JavaScript upon page load that acts as a conduit between the client JavaScript and the controller. Add the following code directly after the closing </apex:panelGrid> tag, but still inside the form:

```
<apex:actionFunction action="{!addCaseId}" name="findCaseDetails"
rerender="form">
<apex:param name="caseId" assignTo="{!caseId}" value="" />
</apex:actionFunction>
```

The ActionFunction tag is analogous to a method declaration in JavaScript. By creating this ActionFunction, we are essentially adding another JavaScript method that can be called upon and interacted with as any other. In our example, the child tag <apex:param> is analogous to the method parameters, expecting a string value to be passed when calling this method. Review the JavaScript block that was created earlier in this example; the subscribe method is calling the findCaseDetails method and passing the ID of the Case provided in the channel notification. When the ActionFunction is invoked, it calls the controller method addCaseId and rerenders the form to reflect the latest data from the server.

Test this page as you have with the other examples. You should see case details appear alongside the charts as you update cases.

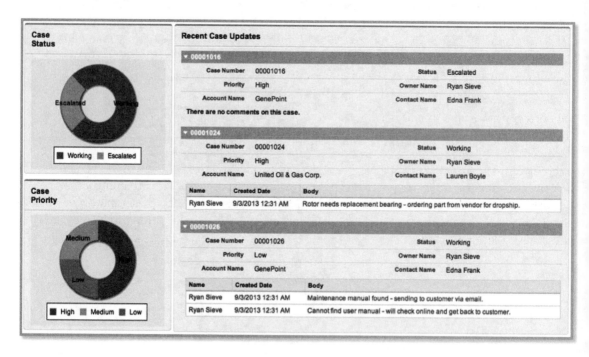

Generally speaking, the performance of an ActionFunction is not as fast as a RemoteAction. This page typically returned results within ~750 ms of a channel notification, despite the additional queries and processing. Following the model in the second example, two pages were benchmarked with RemoteAction and ActionFunction. The RemoteAction page consistently outperformed the ActionFunction by at least ~100-150 ms. Again, this difference is nominal, but must be considered in extending functionality in these design patterns.

# Summary

The examples in this chapter are intended to help illustrate the various ways to implement the Streaming API in a Visualforce page. In the first example, there is no server-side logic, and everything is handled in the page upon receipt of the channel notification. If the page is using data delivered within a channel notification for informational purposes only, this can be a quick and clean way to deliver the information to the end user. If additional data is needed from the database for display on the page or user interaction, RemoteAction and ActionFunction methods can be invoked upon receipt of a channel notification. This allows the page to receive and display data in a near real-time fashion, while still having access to the controller, view state, or other vital pieces of Apex code. Ultimately, RemoteAction and ActionFunction implementations interact with the CometD framework via JavaScript to bridge the gap between a channel notification, and meaningful interaction with the user on a page. RemoteAction is typically faster, requires more JavaScript, and has greater flexibility in managing pages than Visualforce AJAX components. On the other hand, ActionFunction is typically easier to implement, requires little to no JavaScript, and allows you to rerender other Visualforce components.

When designing a solution that utilizes the Streaming API, consider which objects are supported, what events should issue notifications so Limits are not exceeded, and how timely the notifications and interactions should be with the user. Your Push Topic queries should only consider the information that is needed, rather than issuing notifications for every record that's committed for a particular object. It's also important to choose the implementation that scales best over time. If you expect to have your page grow in complexity while maintaining quick performance, then design your initial solution with RemoteActions. If the page is moderately simple or response time is not of the utmost importance, then ActionFunction can be the simplest and fastest solution to implement.

# Chapter 9
# Creating Reusable Page Templates

- Reusing Visualforce Pages
- Creating Page Templates
- Including Visualforce pages within a Page
- Creating Compositions
- Building a Console With Templates
- Custom Components

The concept of reusable page templates should be familiar to anyone who has worked with web development tools like Dreamweaver or Content Management Systems like Joomla or Drupal. Templates are often used to store static elements like headers, footers, logos, menus and so on. From that perspective reusable templates make it convenient to make changes from code in one centralized location, thus enabling it to be easily maintained.

Templates can be used in other ways, such as to customize UI and UX for specific browsers and devices. Finally, they can allow you to extract common functionality and logic, and create and place them in custom components that can be reused across different applications. To summarize, Visualforce allows you to create elements that can be reused in three ways:

1.  Including existing Visualforce pages using <apex:include>

2.  Defining Templates <apex:composition>

3.  Defining Custom Components

This chapter looks at the different methods for reusing Visualforce pages and components, then focuses on creating page templates using the `<apex:composition>` element. To show how templates can be useful, this chapter builds a simple application that serves as a simple content manager.

## Including a Visualforce Page

One very simple way to reuse Visualforce pages is to create generic content in one page and simply include it in other pages. This has the advantage of allowing you to update static content from a single page. For example, let's create a quick template that greets the user and includes a custom logo on every page.

You can include one page within another using <apex:include>. For example, consider a form that you use in other pages. Rather than recreating the form on other pages, simply include it one page. For example, the following listing, called myForm creates a simple form that prompts the user for a name, then saves that name:

```
<apex:page standardController="Article__c" >
<apex:form>
    <apex:outputLabel value="Name: " for="nameField"/>
    <apex:inputText id="nameField" value="{!nameField}"/>
    <apex:commandButton action="{!save}" value="Save"
id="saveButton"/>
</apex:form>

</apex:page>
```

Now that we have this form we can include it other pages like this:

```
<apex:page standardController="Article__c" >
    <!-- do something...
... -->
    <apex:include pageName="myForm"/>
    <!-- do something else...
... -->

</apex:page>
```

## Working with <apex:composition>

Compositions allow you to create a main page that inserts content that's defined in a template. You create page compositions using the <apex:composition> element. You can include other components within this element, but it looks for one subelement, <apex:define>, that defines the content that will be templated. The Define element maps to an <apex:insert> element in the Visualforce page template. Here's a summary of the composition element:

| | Name | Required | Description |
| --- | --- | --- | --- |
| Element | composition | | Used in the main Visualforce page. |
| Attributes | template | yes | Specifies the name of the Visualforce page containing the template markup. |
| Subelements | define | yes | Defines the section in the main page that will be templated. Takes a string attribute that is mapped to the corresponding insert element in the template page. |
| related elements | insert | yes | Contains the Visualforce components and content to be inserted. |

The code fragment below shows the basic structure for the page.

```
<apex:composition template="my_Visualforce_Template">
    ...
    <apex:define name="header">
        ...
    <apex:define name="header">
    ...
</apex:composition>
```

`<apex:composition>` takes two attributes:

| Attribute Name | Description |
|---|---|
| rendered | Used when you want to conditionally display an `<apex:component>`. You must be wrap it inside a `<apex:outputPanel>` component, and add the conditional expression to its rendered attribute. |
| template | The template page used for this component. For this value, specify the name of the Visualforce page or use merge-field syntax to reference a page or PageReference. |

`<apex:define>` has has one attribute:

| Attribute Name | Description |
|---|---|
| name | The name of the insert component into which the content of this define component should be inserted. |

`<apex:insert>`

| Attribute Name | Description |
|---|---|
| name | The name of the matching define tag that provides the content to be inserted into this Visualforce page. |

# Building a Content Manager

The following example was inspired by a need to manage content on the Developer Force web site at developer.salesforce.com. The original idea was to create a database that tracks authors in a database and manages the articles written by these authors. Because the database could potentially be used to publish content we wanted to store the manuscripts and their revisions, and manage the workflow associated with the edit-review cycles. We also needed a way to relate content by topic so that we could, for example, list all articles that were related to Visualforce, or display a list of authors who had written blogs covering Apex Code.

I'll use a simplified version of that example here to demonstrate how Visualforce pages can be reused. Like all of the examples in this book, this example assumes you are familiar with declarative development, and know how to create objects and fields. So I'm not going to walk through the declarative steps for creating these objects. However, the chapter provides sufficient explanation so that if you want to follow along, you can build these objects and their related fields in 20 to 30 minutes.

In this scenario there are three custom objects:

- Articles

- Authors

- Tags

Articles are related to Authors through a master-detail relationship. In addition Articles are related to tags through a second master detail relationship. The Articles object contains the following custom fields and relationships:

| Custom Fields & Relationships | | New | Field Dependencies | |
|---|---|---|---|
| **Action** | **Field Label** | **API Name** | **Data Type** |
| Edit \| Del | Article Body | codeNS__Article_Body__c | Rich Text Area(32768) |
| Edit \| Del | Author | codeNS__Author__c | Lookup(Author) |
| Edit \| Del | Deck | codeNS__Deck__c | Text(255) |
| Edit \| Del | Head | codeNS__Head__c | Text(255) |
| Edit \| Del | Link to Article | codeNS__Link_to_Article__c | URL(255) |
| Edit \| Del | Publish Date | codeNS__Publish_Date__c | Date |
| Edit \| Del | Received | codeNS__Received__c | Date |
| Edit \| Del \| Replace | Status | codeNS__Status__c | Picklist |
| Edit \| Del | Tag | codeNS__Tag__c | Master-Detail(Tag) |

*Figure 9-1. Custom fields and relationships for the Articles custom object.*

Note that for the purposes of this example Authors is created as a custom object. In actual development we could have just as easily renamed the standard Contacts object and utilized its extensive features. By creating a custom object, we'll have to implement many of those features. Consider reusing standard objects whenever possible.

**Custom Fields & Relationships** New | Field Dependencies | Set Hist

| Action | Field Label | API Name | Data Type |
|---|---|---|---|
| Edit \| Del | Addess | codeNS__Addess__c | Text Area(255) |
| Edit \| Del | biography | codeNS__biography__c | Text(255) |
| Edit \| Del | Cell | codeNS__Cell__c | Phone |
| Edit \| Del | email (default) | codeNS__email_default__c | Email (Unique) |
| Edit \| Del | email (other) | codeNS__email_other__c | Email (Unique) |
| Edit \| Del | wiki link | codeNS__wiki_link__c | URL(255) |
| Edit \| Del | Work Phone | codeNS__Work_Phone__c | Phone |

*Figure 9-2. Custom fields and relationships for the Authors custom object.*

**Custom Fields & Relationships** New | Field Dependencie

| Action | Field Label | API Name | Data Type |
|---|---|---|---|
| Edit \| Del | Parent | codeNS__Parent__c | Text(254) |

*Figure 9-3. Custom fields and relationships for the Tags custom object.*

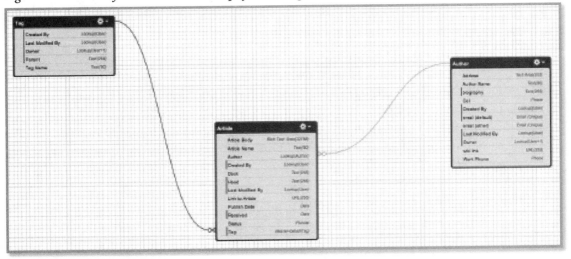

As you might have guessed, the Tags custom object allows us to tag content. This simple tag manager lets us tag articles by topic, thus allowing us to display related articles. Tag contains just one custom field, Parent, which allows us to create hierarchical relationships. For example, we can create a hierarchy that recognizes that "controller extensions" is a subcategory under "Visualforce" that falls under the main category of "User Interfaces." In addition we could also tag "controller extensions" with "Apex" which falls under "Application logic." In this way we can create multiple inheritance hierarchies to find and display related content.

With just three objects, we are able to create a powerful application that tracks articles and authors, and related content. With just a few modifications, one could add workflows to manage the editing process and approvals handle submitting content for publishing. However, the user interface currently requires the user to jump from one screen to another in order to view and edit authors, articles and their tags. That's where Visualforce comes in.

## Creating a Console Using Templates

To show how templates can be useful, this example shows how to create a console that will allow you to display and edit articles, authors and related tags all from one convenient screen. The console also lets editors select a topic tag and view all articles related to that topic. Alternatively, the editor can list all articles authored by a particular writer. By creating a template we are able to provide these different views using a consistent structure, thus ensuring the editor has a consistent look and feel across pages.

Creating and using templates requires three steps:

- Create the template page using `<apex:define>` to describe your reusable content.

- Create your composition. This is a Visualforce page instance. `<apex:composition>` is used to describe the data to be rendered, and you will use `<apex:insert>` elements to insert the content defined by the `<apex:define>` in the template.

- Invoke your page.

### Step 1. Defining the Template

Now let's put this together into a working example. The first step is to create the template that we can reuse. In this case, the template page has been named "contentTemplate."

```
<apex:page >
    <!--Create the Header portion of page -->
    <apex:outputPanel layout="none">
        <apex:insert name="Header"/>
        <apex:pageMessages />
    </apex:outputPanel>

    <!--Console panel portion of page using a PanelGrid with 3
columns -->
    <apex:panelGrid Columns="3">
        <!--Column 1-->
```

```
    <apex:outputPanel >
        <apex:insert name="ArticleInfo" />
    </apex:outputPanel>

    <!--Column 2-->
    <apex:outputPanel >
        <apex:insert name="AuthorInfo" />
    </apex:outputPanel>

<!--Column 3-->
    <apex:insert name="TagInfo"/>
    </apex:panelGrid>
</apex:page>
```

This template defines the overall structure, which consists of two regions: One area for the header of the page; and second for the body of the page. The page header adds a greeting to the user and utilizes <apex:pageMessages /> to display validation errors in the event a user misses a required field or inputs invalid data.

The body is broken up into three columns using the panelGrid component. Each panel reports on one of three custom objects. Each panel contains an <apex:insert name="*some_ identifier*"> where *some_identifier* is the name of the component we want to insert. This identifier references a corresponding <apex:define> element in the main Visualforce page we are about to create.

## STEP 2. BUILDING THE CONSOLE

Now that we have a template we can create a specific view that allows us to view and edit related sObjects. For clarity, this example utilizes a standardController as described in Chapter 3. Here's the page definition:

```
<apex:page standardController="Article__c" >
...
</apex:page>
```

Next, it's useful to create variables so we don't have to enter lengthy names object references throughout the code.

```
        <apex:variable value="{!Article__c.author__r}" var="auth"/>
        <apex:variable value="{!Article__c.tag__r}" var="tagit"/>
```

For the template, create an <apex:composition> element and within it insert an <apex:define> element that references the header in the template page, like this:

```
<apex:composition template="VFPageTemplate">
        <apex:define name="Header">
            <apex:sectionHeader title="Author"/>
        </apex:define>
...
</apex:composition>
```

When Visualforce sees the <apex:define> element it looks to the value of the template attribute to locate the template page, and associates the name attribute (*name="Header"*) with the corresponding <apex:insert> element in the template.

Now let's create the instances for the panel. Place the following define element within your composition (without the ellipses).

```
<apex:define name="ArticleInfo">
  . . .
</apex:define>
```

Within this <apex:define>, create a form to contain the first panel, like so:

```
<apex:form >
    <apex:pageBlock mode="detail" >
        <apex:pageBlockButtons location="top">
            <apex:commandButton action="{!edit}"
value="Edit"/>
            <apex:commandButton action="{!delete}"
value="Delete"/>
        </apex:pageBlockButtons>
        <apex:pageBlockSection columns="1" title="Article
Information">
            <apex:outputField value="{!Article__c.
Name}"/>
            <apex:outputField value="{!Article__c.
Author__c}"/>
            <apex:outputField value="{!Article__c.
Status__c}"/>
            <apex:outputField value="{!Article__c.
Publish_Date__c}"/>
            <apex:pageBlockSectionItem >
                <apex:outputLabel value="Last Modified
By"/>
                <apex:outputText >
                    <apex:outputField
value="{!Article__c.LastModifiedById}"/>,  
                    <apex:outputField
value="{!Article__c.LastModifiedDate}"/>
                </apex:outputText>
            </apex:pageBlockSectionItem>
        </apex:pageBlockSection>
    </apex:pageBlock>
</apex:form>
```

So far we've created a form that displays details about an article including it's title, author and status. We've also added command buttons that allow us to go to the edit page, or to delete the article.

Now, follow the same pattern to create the second form to display the author related to this article:

```
<apex:define name="AuthorInfo">
            <apex:form >
                <apex:pageBlock mode="detail" tabStyle="Author__c" >
                    <apex:pageBlockButtons location="top" >
                        <apex:commandButton value="Edit"
action="{!URLFOR($Action.Author__c.edit,Article__c.Author__c)}"/>
                    </apex:pageBlockButtons>
                    <apex:pageBlockSection columns="1" title="Author
Information">
                        <apex:pageBlockSectionItem >
                            <apex:outputLabel value="Name"/>
                            <apex:outputField value="{!Article__c.
Author__c}"/>
                        </apex:pageBlockSectionItem>
                        <apex:pageBlockSectionItem >
                            <apex:outputField value="{!auth.Name}"/>
                        </apex:pageBlockSectionItem>

                        <apex:outputField value="{!auth.Cell__c}"/>
                        <apex:outputField value="{!auth.email_
default__c}"/>
                        <apex:outputField value="{!auth.email_
other__c}"/>
                        <apex:outputField value="{!auth.Work_Phone_
_c}"/>
                        <apex:outputField value="{!auth.wiki_link_
_c}"/>
                    </apex:pageBlockSection>
                    <!-- apex:pageblockSection >
                        <apex:pageBlockSectionItem >
                        <apex:outputField value="{!auth.
biography__c}"/>
                        </apex:pageBlockSectionItem>

                    </apex:pageblockSection -->
                </apex:pageBlock>
            </apex:form>
</apex:define>
```

Note the use of the URLFOR() action in command buttons for these last two forms. The trained eye may be wondering why this wasn't required in the first form. The reason is that this page is linked to the Articles__c standard controller. So, actions implicitly reference Articles__c without requiring the full object notation. However, actions referencing other objects must name those objects explicitly. The URLFOR() action is described in detail in Chapter 3.

Finally, here's the third form to display the related tags.

```
<apex:define name="TagInfo">
    <apex:form >
        <apex:pageBlock mode="detail" tabStyle="Tag__c" >
            <apex:pageBlockButtons location="top" >
                <apex:commandButton value="Edit"
action="{!URLFOR($Action.Author__c.edit,Article__c.Tag__c)}"/>
            </apex:pageBlockButtons>
            <apex:pageBlockSection columns="1" title="Tag
Information">
                <apex:outputField value="{!Article__c.
Tag__c}"/>
            </apex:pageBlockSection>
        </apex:pageBlock>
    </apex:form>
```

Step 3. Override the default layout to use this Visualforce page.

The resulting page is shown in Figure 9-5:

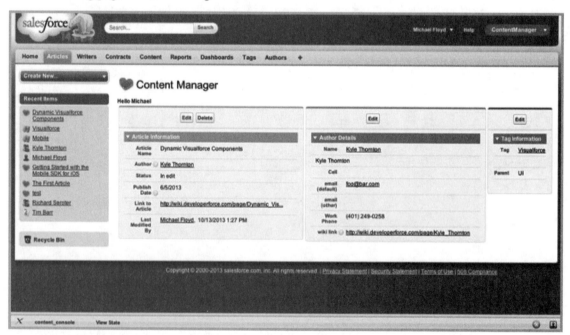

*Figure 5. Resulting Page from Listing 1.*

Template Pages can be useful in serving different renderings of a page based on the device making the request. For example, you could customize pages for different browsers, mobile devices and even eReaders. In fact, we'll use this approach in Chapter 11 where we discuss Mobile app development.

# Reuse Through Custom Components

You may have noticed that in our example we created three forms, all of which have the same basic structure encapsulated in an `<apex:form>` element. Now that we have a working Console, we might want to tidy up our code and create a custom component that simplify our markup.

That's where custom components come in. Custom components are components you define and they allow you to encapsulate a common design pattern and then reuse that component in one or more Visualforce pages.

Unlike page templates, which also enable developers to reuse markup, custom components provide more power and flexibility. Custom components allow developers to define attributes that (much like the new `<apex:input>` element) can be passed into each component. The value of an attribute can then change the way the markup is displayed on the final page, and the controller-based logic that executes for that instance of the component. This behavior differs from that of templates, which do not have a way of passing information from the page that uses a template to the template's definition itself.

Another consideration is that custom component descriptions are displayed in the application's component tree (and in the reference dialog alongside standard component descriptions). Template descriptions, on the other hand, can only be referenced through the Setup area of Salesforce because they are defined as pages.

You define them like this:

```
<apex:component>
    <apex:attribute name="myattribute" type="String"
description="Stuff I can do"/>
...
</apex:component>
```

For example:

```
<apex:component>
<apex:attribute name="record" description="The type of record we are
viewing."
type="Object" required="true"/>
<apex:pageBlock title="Viewing {!record}">
<apex:detail />
</apex:pageBlock>
</apex:component>
```

Then you use them like this.

```
<apex:page >
    <c:myCustomComponentPage record="Account" />
</apex:page>
```

Here's our new example

```
<apex:component>
    <apex:attribute name="objName" type="Object" required="true"/>
```

```
        <apex:attribute name="Field1" type="Object" required="true"/>
        <apex:attribute name="Field2" type="Object" required="true"/>
        <apex:attribute name="Field3" type="Object" required="true"/>
            <apex:form >
                <apex:pageBlock mode="detail" >
                    <apex:pageBlockButtons location="top">
                        <apex:commandButton action="{!edit}"
value="Edit"/>
                        <apex:commandButton action="{!delete}"
value="Delete"/>
                    </apex:pageBlockButtons>
                    <apex:pageBlockSection columns="1" title="Article
Information">
                        <apex:outputField value="{!Article__c.Name}"/>
                        <apex:outputField value="{!Article__c.
Author__c}"/>
                        <apex:outputField value="{!Article__c.
Status__c}"/>
                        <apex:outputField value="{!Article__c.Publish_
Date__c}"/>
                        <apex:outputField value="{!Article__c.Link_to_
Article__c}"/>
                        <apex:pageBlockSectionItem >
                            <apex:outputLabel value="Last Modified By"/>
                            <apex:outputText >
                                <apex:outputField value="{!Article__c.
LastModifiedById}"/>,  
                                <apex:outputField value="{!Article__c.
LastModifiedDate}"/>
                            </apex:outputText>
                        </apex:pageBlockSectionItem>
                    </apex:pageBlockSection>
                </apex:pageBlock>
            </apex:form>
</apex:component>
```

## Summary

Visualforce allows you to create elements that can be resued in three ways:

- Include an existing VF Page using `<apex:include>`
- Defining Templates `<apex:composition>`
- Defining Custom Components

As you'll see in the chapter 12, which covers on Mobile Design Templates, Page Templates can be used to great adavantage. In fact, each method of resuability  has its benefits and drawbacks. For example, custom Components and page templates can both cause your component tree to grow in size. Be sure to review Chapter 14 regarding performance issues as you design your applications.

# Chapter 10
# Using JavaScript with Visualforce

- Including JavaScript in Visualforce Pages

- Referencing Components from JavaScript

- Using actionFunction to Call Apex Methods from JavaScript

- JavaScript Remoting

- Building a Spreadsheet Interface to Access Force.com Data

- Accessing the Analytics API Using ForceTK

Because Visualforce accepts free-form HTML inline within a page, you can stuff pretty much anything into Visualforce that you can place in any HTML document so long as it is well-formed. That includes JavaScript.

JavaScript in HTML is often reserved for simple client-side handling of UI elements, but it opens a huge door filled with options for creating feature-rich applications with elaborate UI's including responsive design for mobile devices. There are countless JavaScript libraries designed for everything from string manipulation to data visualization and animation. In fact the Salesforce Mobile Packs presented in Chapter 15 are extensive examples that make use of JavaScript libraries like jQuery Mobile, Backbone, Angular, Xamarin, Sencha and others.

In addition to including JavaScript in your pages, Visualforce components also support AJAX requests through Action tags like `<apex:actionFunction>` and `<apex:actionSupport>`. These components provide a simplified way to call Apex methods stored in controllers and controller extensions. This has the effect of moving processing off the client and onto the server (since controllers run on the server), which has many benefits including better performance, behaved execution of code and fewer round trips to service client requests.

Another powerful feature, called JavaScript Remoting, also enables you to call Apex methods written in your controllers and controller extensions directly from JavaScript on your Visualforce page. Later in this chapter, we'll show how you can use JavaScript Remoting to create a spreadsheet-like interface for entering data in a Force.com database.

Let's start with the basics of getting JavaScript into your Visualforce pages and binding functions to components.

## Including JavaScript in Visualforce Pages

You can, of course add Javascript functions directly into your Visualforce pages using the HTML `<script>` tag. While this may be appropriate for small functions in single pages, it's generally a better practice to store larger scripts as libraries in a centralized location and make them universally available to all of your pages. You can do this by placing your JavaScript in a static resource, and calling it by referencing the static resource using an `<apex:includeScript>`.

For example, to reference a JavaScript file called myJSlib.js, go to **Setup | App Setup | Develop** and click on **Static Resources**. From there, click **New** and follow the prompts to name your static resource (e.g., myJSlib) and upload myJSfunctions.js. You can then include your file using the `<apex:includeScript>` element, like this:

```
<apex:page>
      <apex:includeScript value="{!$Resource.myJSlib}"/>
</apex:page>
```

This references the `$Resource` global variable and instantiates it with the name of your JavaScript file.

You can also use `<apex:includeScript>` to reference externally-hosted JavaScript files. The following example shows how to include the jQuery framework from a globally hosted CDN network.

```
<apex:page>
 <apex:includeScript value="//cdnjs.cloudflare.com/ajax/libs/
jquery/2.0.3/jquery.js"/>
</apex:page>
```

Check your CDN for the latest deployment. Here's a more complete example that uses a `StandardController` and references a `recordsetVar` that can be used to list articles in a database.

```
<apex:page standardStylesheets="false" showHeader="false"
sidebar="false" standardController="Article__c"
recordsetVar="articles">
  <apex:stylesheet value="https://ajax.aspnetcdn.com/ajax/jquery.
mobile/1.1.0/jquery.mobile-1.1.0.min.css" />
  <apex:includeScript value="https://ajax.aspnetcdn.com/ajax/jQuery/
jquery-1.7.2.min.js"/>
  <apex:includeScript value="https://ajax.aspnetcdn.com/ajax/jquery.
mobile/1.1.0/jquery.mobile-1.1.0.min.js"/>
   <h1>Article Inventory</h1>
</apex:page>
```

Note the addition of `<apex:stylesheet>` to include CSS that can be used to style the page. This differs from `<apex:includeScript>` even though both are static resources. We've also added mobile support by including a second reference jQuery Mobile.

## Referencing Components from JavaScript

The magic that enables us to bind HTML elements, Visualforce components and JavaScript is a humble identifier attribute. All Visualforce tags include an id attribute that can be used by HTML tags, scripts and Visualforce components to bind them together. In Chapter 12 we used the `name` attribute to bind `<apex:define>` in a template to `<apex:insert>`. The `id` attribute can be used in a similar manner.

To refer to a Visualforce component in JavaScript, you must specify a value for the `id` attribute for that component. When the page is parsed, a DOM ID is constructed from a combination of the component's `id` attribute and the ID attributes of all components that contain the element. For instance, the `<apex:outputLabel>` tag's `for` attribute can be used with the `<apex:inputField>` tag's `id` attribute.

In Chapter 12, we showed how to create a page template that displays three outputPanels. The example allowed you to view and update an article, author or related tags from a single page. This example adds a simple feature to the console that allows viewers to increase the font size for readability. It uses a JavaScript function to stylize each of the panels.

```
<script>
  function changeFont(input, textid) {
   if(input.checked) {
     document.getElementById(textid).style.fontSize = "larger";
     alert("Font size changed");
     }
   else {
     document.getElementById(textid).style.fontWeight = "normal";
     }
   }
</script>
```

With the script complete, here's the modfications to the first outputPanel, which calls the function, passing in the checkbox itself, and the DOM ID of the target component.

```
<apex:outputPanel id="thePanel" layout="block">
    <apex:insert name="Header"/>
    <apex:pageMessages />
    <label for="checkbox">Hello {!$User.FirstName}</label>
      <input id="checkbox" type="checkbox"
onclick="changeFont(this,'{!$Component.thePanel}');" />
  </apex:outputPanel>
```

Note the use of `{!$Component.thePanel}` expression, which obtains the DOM ID of the HTML element generated by the `<apex:outputPanel id="thePanel">` component. `$Component` is a global variable that simplifies the referencing of the DOM ID generated for the Visualforce component (a panel in the case). To reference a specific Visualforce component's DOM ID, you can add a component path specifier to $Component, using dot notation to separate each level in the component hierarchy of the page. For example, use $Component.itemId to reference a component at the same level in the Visualforce component hierarchy, or use $Component.grandparentId.parentId.itemId to specify a more complete component path.

A $Component path specifier is matched against the component hierarchy:

- At the current level of the component hierarchy where $Component is used; and then
- At each successive higher level in the component hierarchy, until a match is found, or the top-level of the component hierarchy is reached.

There is no backtracking, so if the ID you're trying to match requires a traversal up and then back down, it won't match.

Returning to our example, the following outputPanel is the target, and contains text that will be changed.

```
    <apex:outputPanel id="thePanel" layout="block">
        Change my font weight!          .
    </apex:outputPanel>
</apex:page>
```

## Using the <apex:actionFunction> Component

This standard Visualforce component provides a simple way to invoke an Apex controller action method directly from JavaScript code. The benefit here is that you can invoke server-side logic written in your Apex controller or controller extension directly from JavaScript code on the Visualforce page. In addition to providing an easy way to call Apex methods, <apes:actionFunction> supports AJAX and the ability to specify a rerender target. This allows you to refresh a portion of your Visualforce page based on the response from the server.

The <apex:actionFunction> element takes the following form:

```
<apex:actionFunction action="{!methodInApexController}"
name="methodInJavascript" rerender="showstate">
....
<script type="text/javascript">
    methodInJavascript();
<script>
```

| Attribute Name | Attribute Type | Description |
|---|---|---|
| action | ApexPages.Action | The action method invoked when the actionFunction is called by a DOM event elsewhere in the page markup. Use merge-field syntax to reference the method. For example, action="{!save}" references the save method in the controller. If an action is not specified, the page simply refreshes. |
| focus | String | The ID of the component that is in focus after the AJAX request completes. |
| id | String | An identifier that allows the actionFunction component to be referenced by other components in the page. |
| immediate | Boolean | A Boolean value that specifies whether the action associated with this component should happen immediately, without processing any validation rules associated with the fields on the page. If set to true, the action happens immediately and validation rules are skipped. If not specified, this value defaults to false. |
| name | String | The name of the JavaScript function that, when invoked elsewhere in the page markup, causes the method specified by the action attribute to execute. When the action method completes, the components specified by the reRender attribute are refreshed. |
| onbeforedomupdate | String | The JavaScript invoked when the onbeforedomupdate event occurs--that is, when the AJAX request has been processed, but before the browser's DOM is updated. |
| oncomplete | String | The JavaScript invoked when the result of an AJAX update request completes on the client. |
| rendered | Boolean | A Boolean value that specifies whether the component is rendered on the page. If not specified, this value defaults to true. |
| reRender | Object | The ID of one or more components that are redrawn when the result of the action method returns to the client. This value can be a single ID, a comma-separated list of IDs, or a merge field expression for a list or collection of IDs. |
| status | String | The ID of an associated component that displays the status of an AJAX update request. See the actionStatus component. |
| timeout | Integer | The amount of time (in milliseconds) before an AJAX update request should time out. |

The one drawback is that the Apex controller or controller extension cannot return data back to the invoking JavaScript code. Another consideration is the AJAX request will include the page's view state, which can affect performance.

## JavaScript Remoting

JavaScript remoting in Visualforce lets you call methods in Apex controllers from JavaScript, enabling you to create pages with complex, dynamic behavior that isn't possible with the standard Visualforce AJAX components. Like the `<apex:actionFunction>`, JavaScript Remoting lets you invoke methods in your Apex controller through JavaScript. Generally, JavaScript Remoting is a more flexible and performant option when compared to `<apex:actionFunction>`, because it allows you to pass parameters and return types into the Apex controller method (with automatic mapping between Apex and JavaScript types), and allows for asynchronous processing through a callback. Unlike `<apex:actionFunction>`, the AJAX request does not include the view state for the Visualforce page, thus resulting in a faster round-trip. The one drawback is that JavaScript Remoting requires a little more work.

There are three steps to JavaScript remoting:

1.  Create a remote method definition in your Apex controller class. You'll need to add an annotation to this definition. For example:

```
//Apex Controller code
@RemoteAction
global static String getItemId(String objectName) { ... }
```

2.  Add the JavaScript to your Visualforce page that calls the remote method.

3.  Create a response handler callback function written in JavaScript.

The following example creates a Visualforce page that presents the user with a dialog box that takes the name of an account. The script then calls the Apex controller, which looks up the account and reports the results.

Listing 1 presents the controller.

```
global with sharing class AccountRemoter {
    public String accountName { get; set; }
    public static Account account { get; set; }
    public AccountRemoter() { } // empty constructor

    @RemoteAction
    global static Account getAccount(String accountName) {
    account = [SELECT Id, Name, Phone, Type, NumberOfEmployees
                FROM Account WHERE Name = :accountName];
        return account;
    }
}
```

*Listing 10-1—This Apex controller performs a lookup and returns fields from the Account object.*

Listing 10-2 shows code for the Visualforce page with the remote method call and callback handler:

```
<apex:page controller="AccountRemoter">
    <script type="text/javascript">
    function getRemoteAccount() {
        var accountName = document.getElementById('acctSearch').value;

        Visualforce.remoting.Manager.invokeAction(
            '{!$RemoteAction.AccountRemoter.getAccount}',
            accountName,
            function(result, event){
                if (event.status) {
                    // Get DOM IDs for HTML and Visualforce elements
like this
                    document.getElementById('remoteAcctId').innerHTML
= result.Id
                    document.getElementById(
                        "{!$Component.block.blockSection.secondItem.
acctNumEmployees}"
                        ).innerHTML = result.NumberOfEmployees;
                } else if (event.type === 'exception') {
                    document.getElementById("responseErrors").innerHTML =
                        event.message + "<br/>\n<pre>" + event.where
+ "</pre>";
                } else {
                    document.getElementById("responseErrors").
innerHTML = event.message;
                }
            },
            {escape: true}
        );
    }
    </script>

    <input id="acctSearch" type="text"/>
    <button onclick="getRemoteAccount()">Get Account</button>
    <div id="responseErrors"></div>

    <apex:pageBlock id="block">
        <apex:pageBlockSection id="blockSection" columns="2">
            <apex:pageBlockSectionItem id="firstItem">
                <span id="remoteAcctId"/>
            </apex:pageBlockSectionItem>
            <apex:pageBlockSectionItem id="secondItem">
                <apex:outputText id="acctNumEmployees"/>
            </apex:pageBlockSectionItem>
        </apex:pageBlockSection>
    </apex:pageBlock>
</apex:page>
```

*Listing 10-2—Visualforce markup calling the AccountRemoter controller written in Apex.*

## Building a Spreadsheet Using JavaScript Remoting

The following example implements a prototype spreadsheet on the Force.com platform. With this prototype, data can be entered into the Salesforce database in a spreadsheet manner. It will allow the users to change multiple records at one time, view subtotals of a group of records, and see programmed formula values change as they input their data. This allows the user to keep the benefits that comes with a spreadsheet, without having to worry about security or lost data. Once they save this, they will be able to collaborate on a record through its Chatter feed, make reports out of the data, or communicate this data with their partners through Communities.

The example uses a plugin called ParamQuery (http://paramquery.com), which is a jQuery plugin that allows users to display and manage their data in a tabular way. As you'll see, we're using JavaScript Remoting to access Salesforce data and display it in a spreadsheet manner. In this scenario, Tthe spreadsheet allows users to input values for a planned resource quantity and an actual resource quantity to be delivered to corporate accounts each month. The report helps them forecast the resource demand for the following months. Each Salesforce record is represented as one row.

The example queries records through JavaScript remoting, which is placed in a custom Javascript object. Each object is stored in an array to be sent to the ParamQuery grid. The code here is abbreviated to for clarity. However, you can install the package in your Salesforce org by going to `https://login.salesforce.com/packaging/installPackage.apexp?p0=04t30000001AFfR`. Listing 10-3 contains the Visualforce page.

```
<apex:page ...>
    function getGridData(){
            Visualforce.remoting.Manager.
invokeAction('{!$RemoteAction.SpreadsheetController.
queryDemandPlan}',
            $('.fiscal-year').val(), $('.product-type').val(),
                    function(result){
                      var gridData = [];
                      $(result).each(function (i) {
//other process
                            gridData.push(createArrayElement(this,
false));
                      });
                      gridCallback(gridData);
            GridObj.dataModel = { data: gridData};
$grid = $("#grid-array").pqGrid(GridObj);
}//end callback function
        );   //end vf remoting
}//end function getGridData
```

*Listing 10-3—Visualforce page containing the JavaScript function.*

Listing 10-4 shows the `@RemoteAction` used in the Apex controller.

```
@RemoteAction
```

```
        global static List<DemandPlanning__c> queryDemandPlan(String
year, String pt){
        return [select Id, Name, Plan10__c, Diff10__c, Result10__c,
Plan11__c, Diff11__c, Result11__c,
            Plan12__c, Diff12__c, Result12__c, Plan1__c, Diff1__c,
Result1__c, Plan2__c, Diff2__c, Result2__c,
                Plan3__c, Diff3__c, Result3__c, Plan4__c,
Diff4__c, Result4__c, Plan5__c, Diff5__c, Result5__c,
            Plan6__c, Diff6__c, Result6__c, Plan7__c, Diff7__c,
Result7__c, Plan8__c, Diff8__c, Result8__c,
                Plan9__c, Diff9__c, Result9__c, DPAccountName__c,
DPAccountName__r.Name, FiscalYear__c, ProductType__c
        from DemandPlanning__c where
                FiscalYear__c = :year and ProductType__c = :pt
order by DPAccountName__c];
        }
...
</apex:page>
```

*Listing 10-4—Code fragment containing the @RemoteAction annotation.*

The resulting spreadsheet is shown in *Figure 10-1.*

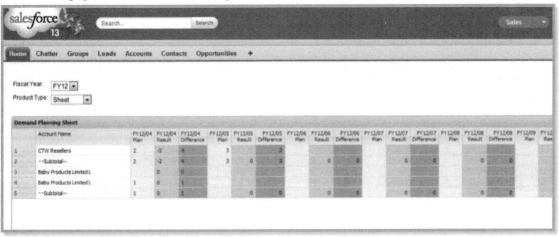

*Figure 10-1: Viewing the spreadsheet created*

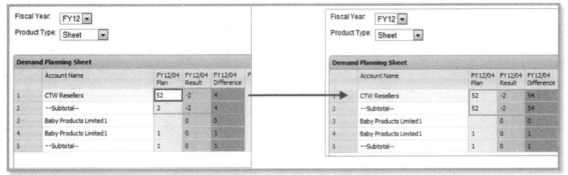

*Figure 10-2: Cell values are recomputed when values are updated.*

ParamQuery has a "cellSave" API that allows you to implement a callback method when a cell is edited. This lets us recompute subtotals when values are changed.

We also needed a way to let the user easily choose which account a record is related to. ParamQuery has the perfect solution for this. It allows you to append an HTML select element to a cell in its grid. This will show the user a drop-down list of accounts whenever they edit the cell.

```
var dropDownEditor = function (ui, accountArr) {
        var $cell = ui.$cell, data = ui.data, rowIndx =
ui.rowIndxPage, colIndx = ui.colIndx;
        var dataCell = $.trim(data[rowIndx][colIndx]);
        var str = "";
        for (var i = 0; i < accountArr.length; i++) {
str += "<option data-id='" + accountArr[i].Id + "' " + (dataCell ==
accountArr[i] ? "selected" : "") + " >" + accountArr[i].
Name + "</option>";
        }
        var $sel = $("<select>" + str + "</select>").appendTo($cell);
    }
```

*Listing 10-5— Appending an HTML select element to a cell in its grid in order to show the user a drop-down list of accounts.*

Figure 10-3 shows the result.

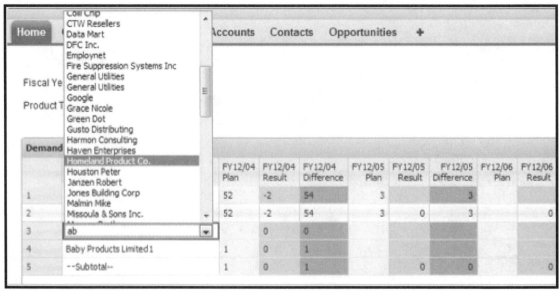

*Figure 10-3: The dropdown list created in Listing Five.*

To save the data back to Salesforce, Lisitng Six iterates through the grid and places each row in a JavaScript object that matches the Salesforce object. Then, Listing Six creates an array of the custom object that can be passed to the controller using JavaScript Remoting.

```
for(var i=0; i<gridData.length; i++){
            if(!gridData[i][1]){    //if it is not a subtotal row
                demandPlanList.push(
    createObjectFromArray(gridData[i], fiscalYear, productType) );
                }
        }
        Visualforce.remoting.Manager.invokeAction('{!$RemoteAction.
SpreadsheetController.saveRecords}', demandPlanList,
            function(result){
        //other process
            }
        );
```

*Listing 10-6. Iterating through the grid.*

```
@RemoteAction
    global static void saveRecords(DemandPlanning__c[]
demandPlanList){
        upsert demandPlanList;
    }
```

*Listing 10-7—The Apex Method servicing the JavaScript call.*

This could have been done Apex and straight Visualforce, albeit with more complexity. You also get the performance boost by limiting the view state.

## JavaScript REST Toolkit

The JavaScript REST Toolkit, or ForceTK, created by Principal Developer Evangelist Pat Patterson was originally designed to work around what's known as the "same origin policy." ForceTK's main job is to wrap the Force.com REST API with a JavaScript interface, so you can call methods such as `create()` and `upsert()` rather than dealing directly with `XmlHttpRequest` or `jQuery.ajax()`. It also exposes its own low-level `ForceTK.ajax()` method, which accepts a partial URL path, HTTP method, payload, and so on. It has the distinct advantage of saving you from having to deal with OAuth tokens. ForceTK.`ajax()` is the key to calling REST APIs such as the new (as of Winter '14) Analytics API without any heavy lifting. You can find ForceTK on Github at `https://github.com/developerforce/Force.com-JavaScript-REST-Toolkit`.

This final example was originally published in Pat's blog on Developer Force and utilizes ForceTK get access the Force.com Analytics API. The Analytics REST API itself is new in the Winter '14 release, and it's worth mentioning that the longer term plan is to provide similar functionality in an Apex API, in the same way that the Chatter REST API preceded Chatter in Apex. Having said that, though, right now, the Analytics REST API is the only supported mechanism for loading Report data, and it shows how ForceTK can be used in a real-world example.

After defining some CSS, we include the jQuery, ForceTK and Google API Loader (JSAPI) JavaScript libraries. We'll use JSAPI to dynamically load the Google Charts library.

```
<apex:includeScript value="{!$Resource.jquery}" />
<apex:includeScript value="{!$Resource.forcetk}" />
<apex:includeScript value="https://www.google.com/jsapi" />
```

Skipping down to the `$(document).ready()` handler, the first thing we do is read a Report ID from a query parameter. Passing `reportId` to the page makes it much more versatile.

```
// When the DOM is ready...
$(document).ready(function() {
    // Pass in the report ID like so:
    // https://c.prerelna1.visual.pre.force.com/apex/
AnalyticsDemo?reportId=00Ox0000000fX7XEAU
    var reportId = '{!$CurrentPage.parameters.reportId}';
```

If we successfully found a Report ID, we initialize ForceTK and define a variable to hold the Report data:

```
if (reportId) {
    // Get an instance of the REST API client and set the session ID
    var client = new forcetk.Client();
    client.setSessionToken('{!$Api.Session_ID}');

    // We'll keep the report data around for the life of the page
    var report = null;
```

Now we can go ahead and call `ForceTK.ajax()` to run the report synchronously. Notice that the URL path is relative to `/services/data`:

```
client.ajax("/v29.0/analytics/
reports/"+reportId+"?includeDetails=true", function(response){
```

In the anonymous callback, the first thing we do is save the report data in the report variable, then write it to a <pre> element on the page. You wouldn't do this in production, but it's essential for development – you really want to be able to see the raw report data.

```
// Save the report data
report = response;

// For debugging
$("#output").text(JSON.stringify(report, null, ' '));
```

In this example, I'm using one of the standard example reports included in Developer Edition: 'Opportunities by Type'. In the regular report view, this tells us the total amount, expected revenue and age of our Opportunities, broken out by their Type—See Figure 13-4.

What I want to do is show a Pie Chart of a single column of that data, and let the user switch between columns via a drop-down list, like the one shown in Figure 13-5.

So the first thing we need to do is populate that drop-down from the list of aggregate columns in the report metadata. The Analytics API documentation discusses the Report data format in some detail, suffice to say here that I'm iterating through the aggregate columns in the report, extracting the column labels:

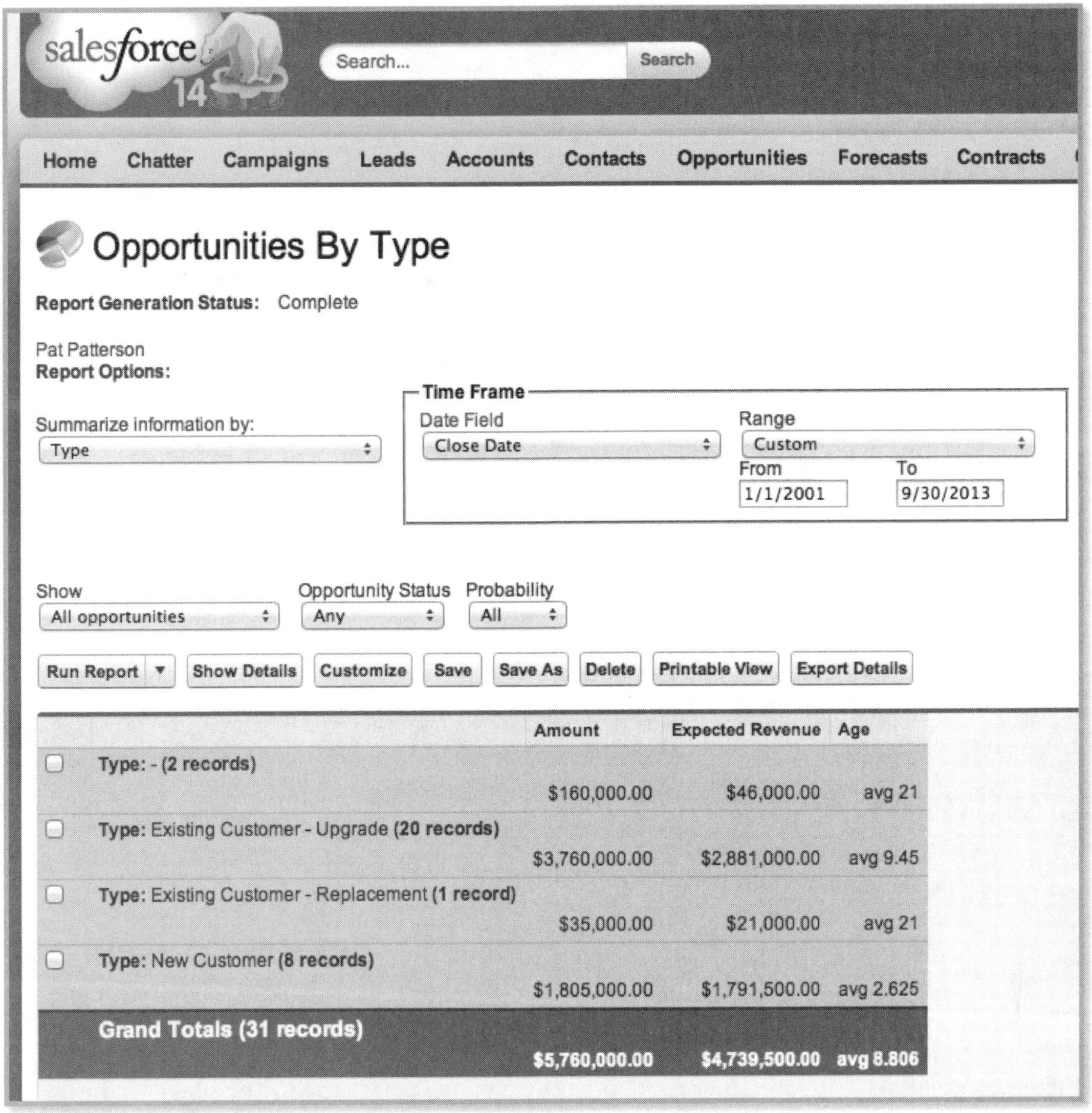

*Figure 10-4. Report view showing Opportunities by Type.*

```
// Grab the aggregate metadata and load it into a <select>
$.each(report.reportMetadata.aggregates, function(index, agg) {
    $("#selectAgg").append('<option value="'+index+'">'+
        report.reportExtendedMetadata.aggregateColumnInfo[agg].label+
    '</option>');
});
```

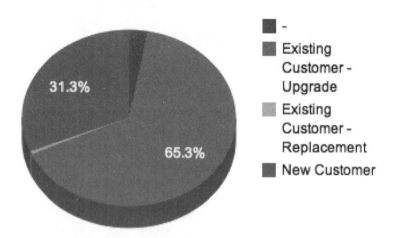

*Figure 10-5: Example of the chart we'd like to display utilizing data acquired using the Analytics API.*

Now we can render the pie chart. We break this out into its own function, `renderPieChart()`, so we can call it both after the data loads, and when the user selects an aggregate column in the drop-down. After setting a default column, `renderPieChart()` loads the Google Chart library:

```
google.load("visualization", "1", {packages:["corechart"], 'callback'
: function() {
```

Once the library has loaded, we can extract labels for the grouping and aggregate columns. The first entry in the data array that we pass to the Google Charts library has to contain metadata, rather than the data itself, even though it's not shown on the pie chart. Still, we populate the array with the actual labels, rather than dummy strings, in case we want to reuse the code in a different context.

```
// Metadata for the aggregate column
var columnInfo = report.reportExtendedMetadata.
aggregateColumnInfo[report.reportMetadata.aggregates[column]];

// Legends (not shown on pie chart)
var dataArray = [[
    report.reportExtendedMetadata.groupingColumnInfo[report.
reportMetadata.groupingsDown[0].name].label,
    columnInfo.label
]];
```

Now we can iterate through the report summary data and create the DataTable object that the Charts API uses:

```
$.each(report.groupingsDown.groupings, function(index, grouping) {
    dataArray.push([grouping.label, report.factMap[index.
toString()+"!T"].aggregates[column].value]);
});

var data = google.visualization.arrayToDataTable(dataArray);
```

We want to label the chart according to the data being shown, and format the data appropriately when we're showing currency fields:

```
var options = {
    title: report.attributes.reportName + ": " + columnInfo.label,
    is3D: true,
};

if (columnInfo.dataType === "currency") {
    var formatter = new google.visualization.NumberFormat({
        prefix: '$' // This is just sample code - should really
determine the correct currency symbol!
    });
    formatter.format(data, 1);
}
```

Now, at last, we can create the chart, and pass in the options and data:

```
// Create and draw the chart
var chart = new google.visualization.PieChart(document.
getElementById('piechart_3d'));
chart.draw(data, options);
```

And the finished result is shown in Figure 10-6. Again, you wouldn't show the raw JSON report data to users, but it's essential during development for understanding the report structure:

This example showed JavaScript calling the API from a Visualforce page, but the great thing about ForceTK is that you can use exactly the same code from a page hosted anywhere – even in a hybrid mobile app – by just tweaking the initial call to pass a session ID to the ForceTK client.

The Salesforce Analytics REST API unlocks analytics data for developers, and the ability to call the API from JavaScript on Visualforce pages and elsewhere enables a whole new world of dynamic apps leveraging the Salesforce Platform.

## Summary

There a multitude of things you can do utilizing JavaScript in Visualforce. Indeed, an entire book could be dedicated to this topic. In this chapter we examined methods for inserting JavaScript into Visualforce pages that included embedding JavaScript directly into your page, and by importing it using the <apex:includeScript> tag. This opens the door to JavaScript libraries like jQuery, Dojo, Angular, Backbone and many others.

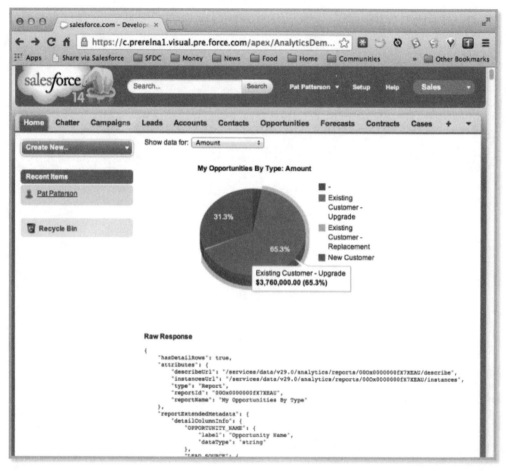

*Figure 10-5. The final chart*

The chapter also showed how you can call Apex methods inside of controllers and controller extensions using <apex:actionFunction>, and presented examples utilizing JavaScript Remoting. We ended with an example that makes use of Pat Patterson's ForceTK library, which simplifies JavaScript Remoting and OAuth authentication. All of the source code can be found on the Developer Force web site at http://developer.salesfoce.com.

# Chapter 11
# Building Mobile Apps Using Visualforce, JavaScript, and HTML5

There was a time when large organizations shunned the use of personal BYOD (bring your own device). But as large enterprise organizations grappled with and solved issues like security, enterprise mobile app development has become one of the more exciting areas in software development at the moment. Indeed Salesforce Platform's security model and OAuth 2 support allow you to build mobile apps that can access cloud data securely.

Chapter 10 offered a nice segue into mobile development because many of the techniques presented will now be used to build mobile apps that can access Force.com data. In particular we'll use JavaScript Remoting, and ForceTK in a mobile context. But first, let's look at how to enable your Force.com app to support mobile development.

We'll also take advantage of some of the tutorials presented on Developer Force. Specifically the Warehouse App, which is presented in the Force.com Workbook tutorial. If you've worked through that tutorial, this section will show you how to enable that app for mobile.

- Design Considerations
- Enabling Connected Apps
- REST versus JavaScript Remoting
- Extending the Warehouse App to Mobile
- Refactoring Force.com Apps for Mobile

## Design Considerations

For simple applications where all you need is for the same Visualforce page to display well across different form factors, a responsive design approach is an attractive option.

Responsive design uses CCS3 media queries to dynamically reformat a page to fit the form factor of the client browser. You could even use a responsive design framework like Twitter Bootstrap to achieve this. Another option is to design multiple Visualforce pages, each optimized for a specific form factor and then redirect users to the appropriate page using one of the strategies described in the previous section. Note that having separate Visualforce pages does not, and should not, imply code functionality duplication. A well architected solution can maximize code reuse both on the client-side (by using Visualforce strategies like Components, Templates etc.) as well as the server-side (e.g., encapsulating common business logic in an Apex class that gets called by multiple page controllers).

Chapter 12 examined method for reusing code within Visualforce pages, and one of those methods was Template Pages. This offers a good use case for templates whereby code and logic common to the overall app could be stored in a template page. Pages optimized for say, a tablet and an smart phone, could be optimized for presentation on that device. Figure 1 provdes a conceptual overview.

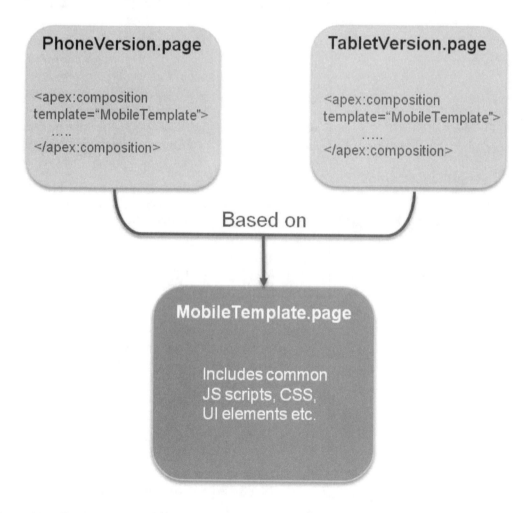

*Figure 11-1. Designing a Visulaforce tremplate page to act as the mobile template.*

# Enabling your Salesforce app

There are many ways to connect to the Salesforce Platform. One is by using APIs such as the Force.com REST API. The other is through Visualforce using a controller that responds to requests from your mobile application. You should also know that the Mobile SDK provides a container that for converting your pure HTML5 Visualforce app into a hybris app that can access many of the same features of a native mobile application. However, this book focuses on Visualforce and discussion of the Mobile SDK to is beyond the scope of this book. Please refer to the Salesforce 1 Mobile Developerment Guide on http://developer.salesforce.com for more information.

Which ever method you choose you wil stille need to set up a connected app, which tells =Force.com that the connecting mobile app is an external app. The role of this app is to make this identification to the platform and provide a consumer key that will be negotiated when your mobile app connects to the platform.

## CREATING THE CONNECTED APP

1. Log into your Force.com instance.

2. In Setup, navigate to Create > Apps.

3. Under Connected Apps, click New.

4. For Connected App Name, enter a name, such as Test Client

5. Under Developer Name, enter your developer ID.

6. For Callback URL, enter sfdc://success

**Note:** The Callback URL does not have to be a valid URL; it only has to match what the app expects in this field. You can use any custom prefix, such as sfdc://.

7. For Contact Email, enter your email address.

8. For Selected OAuth Scopes, choose the permissions settings for your app. For descriptions, see Scope Parameter Values.

9. Click Save.

**Note:** After you create a new connected app, wait a few minutes for the token to propagate before running your app.

**Tip:** The detail page for your connected app displays a consumer key. It's a good idea to copy the key, as you'll need it later.

# Extending the Force.com  Warehouse App to Mobile

Not all apps are built from scratch. Indeed, many readers will find themselves in sutuations where they have an existing Force.com app that they need to enable for mobile devices. Building on what we already know, this first example walks you through a similar process by extending the "Warehouse App" that's used in the *Force.com Platform Workbook* on `http://developer.force.com/workbooks`. In fact, we suggest to download the tutorial and use it to set up your own Warehous app by going through the first three tutorials. From there tou will be able to follow along. Complete source is also presented on GitHub—See resources below.

## REST vs Remoting

This first example avoids the complexities of using OAuth by utilizing the JavaScript Remoting technique described in the previous chapter. This will serve as our data transport mechanism to push and pull data from @RemoteAction methods in an Apex controller class. An added advantage of this approach over using the REST services layer, is that we don't have an API call limit to deal with. However, one trade-off is that we can't leverage the Connected Apps feature of the Platform Mobile Services.

There are two similar JavaScript libraries that have been made available on GitHub. Forcetk, which was also presented in the previous chapter uses REST and OAuth. The other library, Remotetk.js uses JavaScript Remoting and Apex, and we'll use the latter. Keep in mind that our web-based mobile application will be very simple, and that the basic user interface, although attractive and styled for a mobile form factor, will not be very robust. Our effort will be a "just enough" exercise; just enough to give you a taste of what kind of apps you can build with a mobile web approach.

Also keep in mind that there are a number of considerations with taking the HTML5 mobile web approach. The first is that a mobile web touch experience still does not quite match the performance and feel of a true native app, but it continues to get closer and closer. Another key point is that JavaScript will almost always be an integral part of the package.

While JavaScript is a powerful, extensible and challenging programming language to master, there are numerous libraries and frameworks evolving that provide both structure and leverage to the language to help prevent your complex business logic from devolving into a pile of unstructured, unmanageable and brittle code. See Chapter 14 for information on performance and best practices.

We'll use the Force.com Remotetk.js library for our Force.com data transport layer with Apex, and some simple custom JavaScript code to reside between our HTML markup and the Remotetk. js generic JavaScript library that will connect to the remoting engine on the Force.com platform. It may not be as elegant an overall solution, but this less abstract approach may allow you to better visualize how the various moving parts of a mobile web app all hook together.

## Getting Started

We're going to build out the application from the bottom up. We will assume you have completed the Force.com Tutorial #1, and have the Merchandise__c custom object configured and loaded with some sample data in a working Force.com org. We'll start our app implementation with the Apex controller and its unit tests, and build out the components based on the dependencies between them.

Our Code Is In Github: If you'd like to follow along, you can cut and past the Apex and Visualforce code snippets from a GitHub repository at https://github.com/forcementor/MobiWare and slowly build up the application with the following parts shown in Table 1.

| RemoteTKController.cls | an Apex class with supporting @RemoteAction CRUD methods. |
|---|---|
| TestRemoteTKController.cls: | an Apex class providing unit test coverage for the controller. |
| RemoteTK.component | a Visualforce component containing a JavaScript utility library for Remoting access to the Controller methods. |
| MobiWareApp.component | a Visualforce component containing the app's custom JavaScript code. |
| MobiWareView.component | a Visualforce component containing the markup for the three mobile pages. |
| MobiWare.pag | : a single Visualforce page that will host your app. |

*Table 11-1. Libraries and componets you'll find usefull in this example.*

As we add these six components to your org, we'll review what they do and a little bit about how they work; the key is to quickly get you a working app that you can then dissect and explore on your own.

The completed code resides in the repo at https://github.com/forcementor/MobiWare where you have the options of cloning the repository to your hard drive, or simply navigating to it in a browser, and by selecting the 'Raw' link in the upper right corner of the code panel. You can do a 'Select 'All' and 'Copy', and then 'Paste' it into your Force.com code editor. All of the code is under the /src folder, and positioned in the appropriate classes, components, and pages subdirectories that match the structure of a Force.com metadata package.

By the way, if you are not yet familiar with Git and Github, now's as good a time as any to learn. It has quickly become a new standard as a source code repository, and you will quickly come up to speed on its use, as well as become addicted to it as a source code repository. Here's a link to a great presentation that will explain how Git works, and another link to the Top 10 learning resources to help you quickly ramp up.

## Develop In The Cloud

You can choose to build out the components of our app in the Force.com development environment of your choice. You can use the UI editors under the Setup->Develop area, the Developer Console Repository, or the Eclipse Force.com IDE; any of these will do just fine. The manner in which Apex classes, pages and components are named upon creation varies from devenv to devenv. For example, you must first name the class if in the Force.com IDE or Developer Console, but in the UI editor, just pasting the class code into the code window will establish the class name when the code is saved.

It's generally a better practice to build out an application one piece at a time, in an incremental approach, testing first and then adding more and more functionality with each iteration to insure that everything is working well before adding too much complexity. For simplicity, this example focuses on the Viusalforce and runs through the steps of creating each component from the code base in the Git repository, and we'll test when we're all done. The one exception will be running the Apex unit tests after creating the controller and its test class.

## Some JavaScript Caveats

Before we get started, I want to share some words of caution to those of you not too familiar (yet) with JavaScript:

First: unlike Apex, JavaScript is case sensitive, and also very sensitive about matching block delimiters (those funny curly braces '{}' ) and semi-colon statement terminators. You're mostly going to be pasting completed code, but if you decide to experiment and change that code, (and I heartily recommend you should!) you'll have to remember to be very careful. Later, down the road, you can (and should) ramp-up on JavaScript Unit Testing practices with frameworks and tools such as Jasmine to help you avoid and manage any regression related bugs. You can go here to find out more.

Second: JavaScript typically 'fails silently.' In other words, you won't necessarily see errors appearing in the user interface if there are problems with your code at run-time, and you will have to rely on your browser's developer tools to visualize what's going on behind the scenes to inspect errors and the HTTP data stream. You can use the developer tools that come with Safari, or whatever other browser you're using, to monitor console output and to examine your requests and responses.

### STEP 1: BUILD THE APEX CONTROLLER

Navigate to the src\classes directory and copy the code for the RemoteTKController.cls

Create a new Apex class, which will be named RemoteTKController, and paste the copied apex code from the Git repository to overwrite the class template code. Make sure that your code saves properly and that there are no compilation errors.

Let's take a closer look at one of the @RemoteAction methods, there's one for each CRUD operation including UPSERT and for both SOQL queries and SOSL searches. The method arguments typically include the string name of the sObject, an Id (if applicable to the operation,) and a field list. Below is the UPDATE method named updat() to avoid use of the reserved word. This class is a good example of dynamic Apex, as it is designed to handle any sObject type generically by iterating on the fields collection parsed from the JSON packet, deserializing the sObject in memory and executing the DML operation. Notice the substantial amount of error handling logic, as errors must be handed back gracefully to the mobile client.

```
@remoteAction
public static String updat(String objtype, String id, String fields) {
    Schema.SObjectType targetType = Schema.getGlobalDescribe().
get(objtype);
    if (targetType == null) {
        return makeError('The requested resource does not exist',
'NOT_FOUND');
    }

    SObject obj = targetType.newSObject(id);

    Map<String, Object> fieldMap = null;
    try {
```

```
        fieldMap = (Map<String, Object>)JSON.
deserializeUntyped(fields);
    } catch (JSONException je) {
        return makeError(je.getMessage(), 'JSON_PARSER_ERROR');
    }

    try {
        for (String key : fieldMap.keySet()) {
            obj.put(key, fieldMap.get(key));
        }
    } catch (SObjectException soe) {
        return makeError(soe.getMessage(), 'INVALID_FIELD');
    }

    try {
        update obj;
    } catch (DMLException dmle) {
        String fieldNames = '';
        for (String field : dmle.getDmlFieldNames(0)) {
            if (fieldNames.length() > 0) {
                fieldNames += ',';
            }
            fieldNames += '"'+field+'"';
        }
        return '[{"fields":['+fieldNames+'],"message":"'+dmle.
getDmlMessage(0)+'","errorCode":"'+dmle.getDmlType(0).name()+'"}]';
    }

    return null;
}
```

## Step 2: Add The Apex Controller Test Class

Navigate back to the src\classes directory in the Git repository and copy the code for the TestRemoteTKController.cls

Create a new Apex class, which will be named TestRemoteTKController, and paste the copied apex code from the Git repository to overwrite the class template code. Make sure that your code saves properly and that there are no compilation errors.

Now run the tests; the exact manner in which you run them will depend on where you're doing your development. If you just created the test class in the UI Editor, you can click the 'Run Test' button at the top of the page.

Verify that all of your tests pass.

We're not going to dive into the test class, but simply remind you that it would of course be needed to deploy your Apex controller into a production org.

## STEP 3: ADD THE REMOTETK.COMPONENT

Navigate to the src\components directory and copy the code for the RemoteTK.component.

Create a new Visualforce component, set the name (and Label if in the UI Editor) as RemoteTK and paste the copied Visualforce code from the Git repository to overwrite the component template code. Make sure that your code saves properly and that there are no compilation errors.

We're using a custom Visualforce component to host this JavaScript library which manages our generic sObject data transport between our mobile web client and the Apex controller. It's a bit unusual to host JavaScript in this manner, as usually our JavaScript libraries are stored as static resources. However, while the latter approach provides the additional benefits of caching and compression, this practice is very useful when in a learning or development mode when you want to have easy access to your JavaScript code.

This library was designed to provide generic CRUD and query operations using JavaScript Remoting rather than the REST API, and you'll find a JavaScript method for each of the public @ RemoteAction methods on the Apex controller. For example, below is the CREATE method that calls the @RemoteAction creat() method in Apex:

```
/*
  * Creates a new record of the given type.
  * @param objtype object type; e.g. "Account"
  * @param fields an object containing initial field names and values
for
  *               the record, e.g. {Name: "salesforce.com",
TickerSymbol:
  *               "CRM"}
  * @param callback function to which response will be passed
  * @param [error=null] function to which jqXHR will be passed in
case of error
  */
 remotetk.Client.prototype.create = function(objtype, fields,
callback, error) {
     Visualforce.remoting.Manager.invokeAction('{!$RemoteAction.
RemoteTKController.create}', objtype, JSON.stringify(fields),
function(result){
         handleResult(result, callback, error);
     }, {
         escape: false
     });
 }
```

*Listing 11-2. Creates a new report of a given type.*

Notice the call to the Visualforce.remoting.Manager.invokeAction(), the reference to the mated controller action, and the callback method which returns a response object with results from the Apex method containing either data or messages.

## Step 4: Add The MobiWareApp.component

Navigate to the src\components directory and copy the code for the MobiWareApp.component.

Create a new Visualforce component, set the name (and Label if you are using a UI Editor) as MobiWareApp and paste the copied Visualforce code from the Git repository to overwrite the component template code.

Make sure that your code saves properly and that there are no compilation errors.

This is custom JavaScript code to manage our application logic, handle the display and mobile page transitions, and process application user events. Once again, we are hosting it in a custom Visualforce component as above.

Here is some code from the function that loads the main list view. Notice the call to the client.query() method to fetch the data; the client object is an instance of a Remotetk class from the library. This call is quite complex, and includes setting up a click handler on each item in the populated list with a callback method that will both load the detail form with data from the selected record, and transition the user to the form page to display the data.

```javascript
//Populate the record list and set up list item click handling.
function getRecords(callback) {
    $j('#lstMerchandise').empty();
    client.query("SELECT Id, Name, Description__c, Price__c, Total_
Inventory__c FROM Merchandise__c ORDER BY Name LIMIT 20"
    ,
    function(response) {
        $j.each(response.records,
        function() {
            var id = this.Id;
            $j('<li style="height:45px;"></li>')
            .hide()
            .append('<a href="#"><b>' + this.Name + '</b></a>')
            .click(function(e) {
                e.preventDefault();
                    $j.mobile.loading( 'show' );

                    // We could do this more efficiently by adding
these fields to the fields in the SELECT,
                    // but we want to show dynamic use of the
retrieve function.
                    client.retrieve("Merchandise__c", id,
"Name,Id,Description__c,Price__c,Total_Inventory__c"
                    ,
                    function(response) {
                        //Load the inputs on the form with the
field values from the reponse object
                        //passed back from the apex controller
retrieve method.
                        $j('#Name').val(response.Name);
```

```
                          $j('#Description__c').val(response.
Description__c);

                          $j('#Price__c').val(response.Price__c);
                          $j('#Total_Inventory__c').val(response.Total_
Inventory__c);

                                  $j('#Id').val(response.Id);

                          //Refresh the page.
                                  $j.mobile.loading( 'show' );
                          $j.mobile.changePage('#pagDetail', "slide",
false, true);

                          }, errorCallback);
                      })
                      .appendTo('#lstMerchandise')
                      .show();
                  });

                  //Refresh the list.
                  $j('#lstMerchandise').listview('refresh');

                  if (typeof callback != 'undefined' && callback !=
null) {
                      callback();
                  }
              }, errorCallback);
          }
```

*Listing 11-2.. Loading the live main list view*

Notice also how the returned response object is parsed and used to populate the various input controls on the appropriate form. You'll see similar patterns through out this component which has been left intentionally verbose. Much of the logic could be re-factored into a more generic pattern which would result in less code to write and maintain, but that's a more sophisticated topic for a later post.

## STEP 5: ADD THE MOBIWAREVIEW.COMPONENT

Navigate to the src\components directory and copy the code for the MobiWareView.component.

Create a new Visualforce component, set the name (and Label if in the UI Editor) as MobiWareView and paste the copied Visualforce code from the Git repository to overwrite the component template code. Make sure that your code saves properly and that there are no compilation errors.

Let's take a closer look at how the HTML5 markup is broken out into three sets of DIV tags, each one representing a different page in the mobile UI: the List View, the Detail View, and the Edit View. It is the data-role attribute that binds the DIV in the jQuery framework, which is then responsible for rendering the DIV in a touch form factor. Notice also the two HTML FORMS and the standard HTML inputs that we will bind to the fields from our sObject, and notice that the Detail View form has its fields set as ReadOnly.

```
<apex:component >
<!-- Merchandise List Page -->
<div data-role="page" id="pagList" data-theme="b" data-
title="Merchandise" >

    <div data-role="header" data-position='fixed' >
        <h1>Merchandise List</h1>
        <a href="#" id="btnNew" class="ui-btn-right" data-theme="b"
data-icon="plus">New</a>
    </div>
    <div data-role="content">
        <ul id="lstMerchandise" data-role="listview" data-theme="c"
data-filter="true" data-autodividers="true">
        </ul>
    </div>
    <div data-role="footer" data-position="fixed">
        <h4>MobiWare</h4>
    </div>
</div>

<!-- Merchandise Detail Page -->
<div data-role="page" data-theme="b" id="pagDetail">

    <div data-role="header" data-position="fixed">
        <a href="#pagList" data-iconpos="left" data-icon="back" data-
rel="back">Back</a>
        <h1>Merchandise Detail</h1>
        <a href="#" data-iconpos="left" data-icon="check" class="ui-
btn-right" id="btnEdit" data-theme="b" >Edit</a>
    </div>

    <div data-role="content">
        <form action="" method="post" id="frmDetail">
            <input type="hidden" name="Id" id="Id" />
            <label for="Name">Merchandise Name:</label>
                <input type="text" name="Name" id="Name" value=""
readonly="readonly" style="background-color:lightgrey;"/>
            <label for="Description__c">Description:</label>
            <input type="text" name="Description__c" id="Description__c"
value="" readonly="readonly" style="background-color:lightgrey;"/>
            <label for="Price__c">Price:</label>
            <input type="text" name="Price__c" id="Price__c" value=""
readonly="readonly" style="background-color:lightgrey;"/>
            <label for="Total_Inventory__c">Total Inventory:</label>
            <input type="text" name="Total_Inventory__c" id="Total_
Inventory__c" value="" readonly="readonly" style="background-
color:lightgrey;"/>
        </form>
```

```
        </div>
        <div data-role="footer" data-position="fixed" >
            <a href="#" class="ui-btn-left" data-icon="delete"
id="btnDelete" data-theme="a">Delete</a>
            <h4>MobiWare</h4>
        </div>
</div>


<!-- Merchandise Edit Page -->
<div data-role="page" data-theme="b" id="pagEdit">

    <div data-role="header">
        <a href="#pagList" data-iconpos="left" data-icon="back" data-
rel="back">Cancel</a>
            <h1>Merchandise Detail</h1>
            <button data-role="button" id="btnSave" data-iconpos="left"
data-icon="check" data-theme="b">Save</button>
        </div>

    <div data-role="content">
            <form action="" method="post" id="frmEdit">
                <input type="hidden" name="Id" id="Id" />
                <label for="Name">Merchandise Name:</label>
                    <input type="text" name="Name" id="Name" value="" />
                <label for="Description__c">Description:</label>
                <input type="text" name="Description__c" id="Description__c"
value="" />
                <label for="Price__c">Price:</label>
                <input type="text" name="Price__c" id="Price__c" value=""
step="0.01"/>
                    <label for="Total_Inventory__c">Total Inventory:</label>
                <input type="text" name="Total_Inventory__c" id="Total_
Inventory__c" value="" step="0" />
            </form>
        </div>

    <div data-role="footer" data-position="fixed">
            <h4>MobiWare</h4>
        </div>

</div>

</apex:component>
```

Listing 11-4. Using HTML <DIV> tags to establish different page views on the mobile device.

## Step 6: Add The MobiWare.page

Navigate to the src\pages directory and copy the code for the MobiWare.page. Create a new Visualforce page, set the name (and Label if in the UI Editor) as MobiWare and paste the copied Visualforce code from the Git repository to overwrite the component template code. Make sure that your code saves properly and that there are no compilation errors.

Let's take a closer look at this last piece of our app, the Visualforce page. It acts primarily as a host container for our modular Visualforce components, as well as for the links to any remote libraries. There's really not much here, but take note of the attributes in the apex:page tag to set the doctype for HTML5, and to turn off the standard Salesforce.com look and feel.

Note the embedded Visualforce component references, and the jQuery bootstrapping logic. You also must take care to manage the dependent order of the components and JavaScript library links, insuring that they are loaded on the page in the correct sequence. Finally, while you'll notice that we include links to hosted jQuery libraries, you can of course host your own libraries as static resources.

```
<apex:page docType="html-5.0"
           showHeader="false"
           sidebar="false"
           standardStyleSheets="false"
           contentType="text/html"
>


<!--
Use the RemoteTK component with all necessary JavaScript to connect
with the
Apex controller @RemoteAction methods for secure CRUD operations.
-->
<c:RemoteTK />


<!--
Load the custom application JavaScript that will manage all client
side application logic.
-->
<c:MobiWareApp />


<html>
    <head>
        <title>MobiWare</title>

        <!-- Set Content type for the HTML -->
        <meta http-equiv="Content-Type" content="text/html;
charset=UTF-8" />

        <!-- Set a viewport to insure that the target device properly
sets the form factor perspective -->
```

```
        <!-- <meta name="viewport" content="width=device-width,
initial-scale=1" />  -->
          <meta name="viewport" content="width=device-width, initial-
scale=1.0, maximum-scale=1.0" />

        <!-- We will use the cloud based jQuery libs to avoid loading
them as static
        resources. You can of course download them and maintain your
own versions as
        static resource. Take note to BE CAREFUL to correctly control
ordering of the
        JS includes! Testing in a desktop webkit browser such as
Safari will work fine,
        BUT Chrome will not load insecure content libraries without
clicking on the
        'Load Anyway' shield link in the URL bar!
        -->
        <link rel="stylesheet" href="http://code.jquery.com/
mobile/1.2.0/jquery.mobile-1.2.0.min.css" />
        <script src="http://code.jquery.com/jquery-1.8.2.min.js"></
script>
        <script src="http://code.jquery.com/mobile/1.2.0/jquery.
mobile-1.2.0.min.js"></script>

        <!-- This is the bootstrapping JavaScript code -->
        <script type="application/javascript">

            //Get a reference to jQuery that we can work with -
Salesforce.com also uses jQuery!
            $j = jQuery.noConflict();

            //Create the RemoteTK client.
            var client = new remotetk.Client();

               //Pass it the Visualforce session id so it can handle
all CRUD
               //operations using JavaScript Remoting calls rather
than the REST API.
            client.setSessionToken('{!$Api.Session_ID}');

            //Kick things off...
            $j(document).ready(function(){

                //Set up the listerners for the button clicks.
                addClickListeners();

                //Display a loading animated icon.
                $j.mobile.loading( 'show', {
```

```
                    text: 'MobiWare...',
                    textVisible: true,
                    theme: 'z',
            });

            //Load the main page with data.
            getRecords(function(){
                    $j.mobile.loading('hide');
            });

        });

    </script>

  </head>

  <body>
        <!-- MobiWare main view -->
        <c:MobiWareView />
  </body>
</html>
</apex:page>
```

Listing 11-5. Adding the Visualforce components and the boostrapping logic.

## STEP 7: LAUNCH THE APPLICATION

You should now be able to launch the MobiWare application, and we'll see if everything works as planned. I suggest that you run your desktop tests in a Safari browser for two reasons. The first, is that in addition to being a WebKit based browser, (it can render a touch style user interface and emulate multiple Apple device form factors,) it also has no problem loading unsecured content linked to across the web. Since we're linking to our jQuery libraries residing on an unsecured server, we don't want the browser blocking those calls, and Safari won't.

*Figure 11-1 (previous page). The resulting screen also allows you to drill down to the Detail View for an item.*

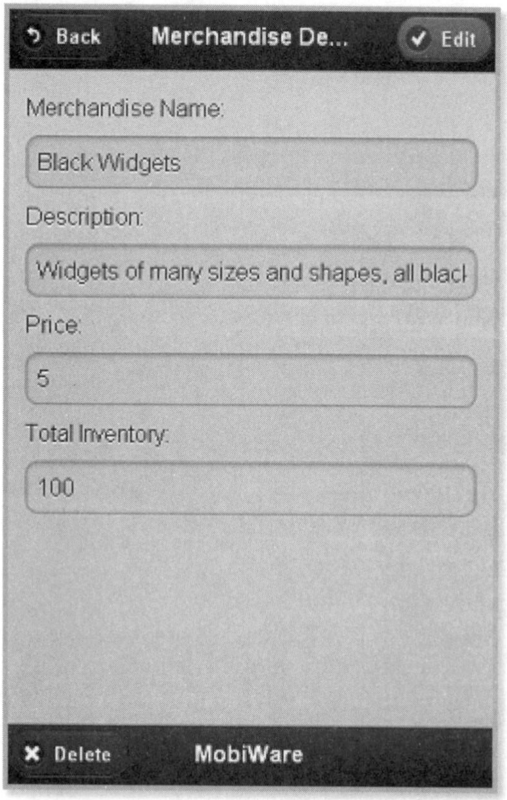

*Figure 11-2. The drill down page ti view the Detail View for an item.*

You can also use Chrome, but you will have to configure it to show the unsecured content each time you launch the mobile page, or configure it to launch with a special flag to turn off the security check. That's one extra step I think you'd rather avoid, as the fewer moving parts the better. The second reason is the available developer tools to monitor our JavaScript execution and our data transport, and the Safari developer tools work great for those tasks.

So, launch your browser and login to your org. To launch your mobile page, modify your URL address to include only the salesforce.com service instance and add '/apex/MobiWare' and then press enter. You should see the MobiWare application load in your browser with a display of up to twenty Merchandise records from your database.

```
https://c.{SERVER_NAME}.visual.force.com/apex/MobiWare
```

You can do the same thing on a mobile device, logging into your development application as usual. Of course, Salesforce.com will display in a very small presentation, but once logged in, you can change the URL to add the name of the Apex page.

When you're ready to put a mobile web application into production, it can be launched through a Force.com Site, exposing mobile Visualforce pages in a secure and sensible manner. Your users will simply need to navigate to a custom domain that you can be configured with your company name, and keep in mind that a mobile Visualforce application can also be used to create a mobile website for your company.

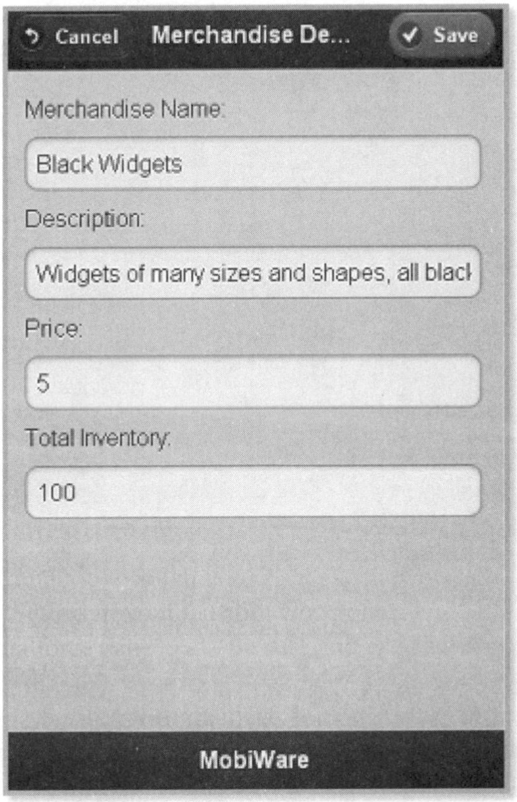

*Figure 11-3 (previous page). The Edit View, which you can from the previous screen.*

On an iPhone, once displayed, users can save the link on their device home screen to launch at the click of an icon. There are even open source JavaScript libraries that you can add to your app that will cause a popup bubble message to prompt users to 'Add to Home.' You might try adding one such library to the MobiWare app as an exercise. You will find one such popular library from cubiq.org here.

You will need to download their JavaScript library and add it to the MobiWare project as either a static resource or embedded in a Visualforce component. As mentioned above, I've kept the JavaScript for this project in Visualforce components for easy access to the code from the UI editor or Developer Console, but you are of course free to move it all into static JavaScript library files.

## Refactoring Force.com Apps for Mobile

One common use case I see is 'trapped' business logic in Apex. For example, code supporting business rules or data processing is often written directly into the main body of a method on a controller class, rather than being deliberately isolated and implemented in a modular fashion as part of a layered architecture. Such code in a controller or extension class might be bound to a Visualforce page called from

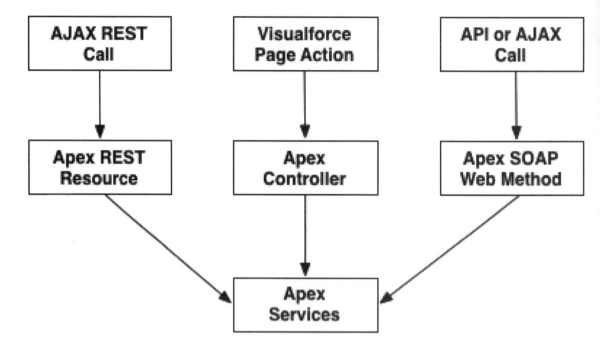

*Figure 11-4. MVC and Separation of Concerns.*

a custom button or link embedded in a standard page layout of an sObject.

In order to leverage the contained business logic, we have to find a way to separate these two different concerns. The proper approach is to refactor the code, extracting the business logic from the controller method and placing it inside its own static method in a public service class. This allows it to be easily invoked from any particular entry point, including the Apex controller class where it originally resided.

If you have not already been down this road, it's time to come up to speed on the concept of Separation of Concerns (SOC), and other related software design patterns, that you can apply to your Apex code base to provide flexibility, scalability, consistency and maintainability. This set of articles, Apex Enterprise Patterns - Separation of Concerns by Andrew Fawcett of FinancialForce. com, provides an excellent and comprehensive overview and primer to the concepts. I highly recommend that you read them in depth, as they present these time tested patterns in an Apex context, and they speak to our immediate purpose around refactoring for mobile. In particular you will want to read the post on the Service Layer.

These patterns promote a modular approach when designing Apex classes that manage business application logic, and describe the deliberate organization of such code into a predefined collection of layers that follow established best practices, providing multiple benefits as a result.

In the following diagram, you can see that logic in a service class can be accessible from multiple entry points. Service methods can be invoked from a controller, a REST resource, or a SOAP web method.

As an aside, you could also access such logic from a trigger, however trigger handler logic is often considered a different layer, and is typically isolated into domain specific classes rather than services. For more information read the SOC article on the Domain Layer.

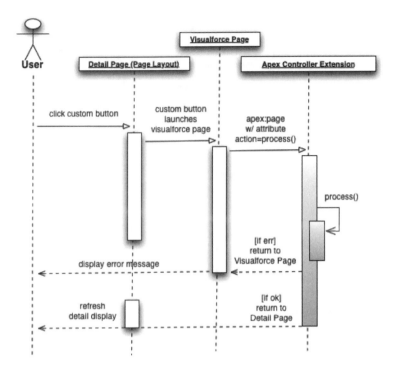

*Figure 11-5. UML sequence diagram showing the interaction.*

But don't get hung up on the potential complexities. While our legacy code may not have originally been architected in such a manner, our immediate task is simply to migrate our custom business logic from the Apex controller extension class into it's own service class and method, so that it may be invoked from multiple entry points.

Returning to our example of code in a controller that is bound to a Visualforce page, let's explore for a minute the logic flow and user experience of this common pattern. When the custom button is pressed, the user is redirected to the Visualforce page which shares the current record's context and StandardController, but is extended with a custom Apex controller extension class. When the Visualforce page is invoked, it delegates on load to an action on the controller extension class by way of the <apex:Page> 'action' attribute. The action method on the class is immediately invoked, and the contained logic is processed.

Upon successful processing, the action method redirects the user back to a refreshed instance of the original detail page from which the custom action was originally executed, and the Visualforce page is never visibly rendered. In the event of an exception case, when an error occurs during the processing, the action method will handle the exception, add a message to the page's <apex:PageMessages> collection, and subsequently return a null value to redirect the user back to the custom page to see the message. The following UML sequence diagram shows the interaction; note the shaded process logic area under the life line of the controller extension class:

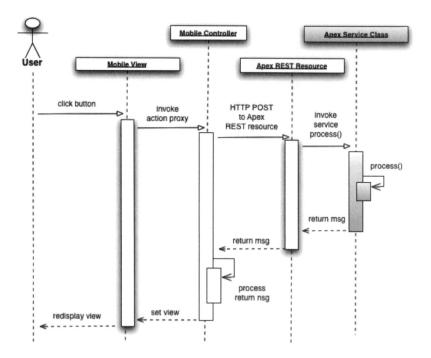

*Figure 11-6. UML sequence diagram*

The challenge arises when designing a mobile application serving up this same record in a mobile view, with a design that calls for a similar action to invoke the exact same logic built into the pre-existing Apex controller extension. The problem is that the controller extension class and its action method cannot be directly accessed by the mobile app.

To refactor this, we will access it from both the original controller extension, and from a new Apex REST resource class.

Here is a modified UML diagram to illustrate the change from the perspective of the interaction with the custom Visualforce page. You can see where we have added one more swim lane to represent the service class and its method for a call from the controller class:

## SOC is for Testing Too

An added benefit of this approach is that a new test class can be constructed whose sole responsibility is for testing the custom processes in the service class. Any unit tests previously testing the method in the controller extension class can be migrated to the new test class.

Adding additional processes to the new service class requires only isolated changes to that class and its related test class. You will no longer need to touch the controller class and its tests, thus reducing risk and the potential for inadvertently breaking them.

Unit tests for the controller extension will now only be required to test the immediate controller functionality, and such tests no longer have to include logical assertions against the service logic.

You can see that the Separation of Concerns pattern trickles down into the testing layer, and promotes a cleaner, more focused, decoupled, simplified and structured testing approach. So, let's look at how we will refactor our code to apply this modular approach.

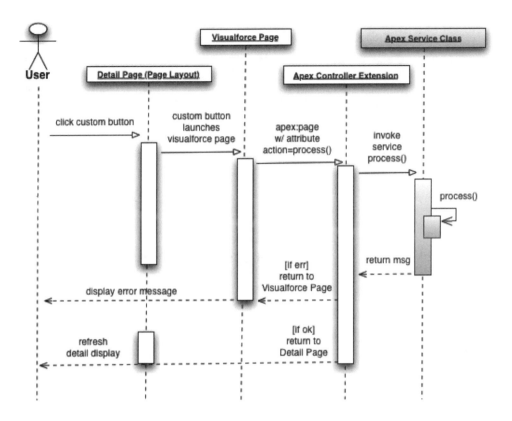

*Figure 11-7. UML sequence diagram*

# Building a Service Class

Many of the examples you'll see in the MobilePak reference apps will show you how to fetch one or more records and perform CRUD operations on them, but there's not too much on how to launch actions from any particular record's context. A specific REST request is typically needed from any mobile client to invoke such a process in Salesforce. Actions can be easily invoked from mobile applications, but require a custom Apex action API built into your salesforce org. There are two general approaches to access your custom API.

If you're using a REST approach from either a native mobile app or a mobile web app using Ajax for its REST service calls, you will need to create a custom Apex REST resource to invoke your action on an HTTP POST request from the client. The Apex REST pattern allows you to build such resources very easily, and invoke them through the Apex REST Service API. However, if you're leveraging JavaScript Remoting from a mobile web app hosted in a Visualforce page, then you'll require a client side Ajax method to call a global @RemoteAction method on an Apex class.

Regardless of the approach you decide on to make the action request from your mobile app, the primary task at hand will be to refactor the existing Apex business logic needing to be invoked, so that it may be accessed from alternate entry points. First we'll build a new class and a public static service method. You should make the names of both the class and method self-documenting of course, but in this case we'll use generic names.

```
public class MyCustomService{

    public static string MyCustomProcess(ID recordId){

        //Custom process logic gets moved to here from
controller...
        ...

        //Set up the message and return it.
        return message;

    }

}
```

Our service method will expect only the ID of the record as a parameter, and the method will be responsible for fetching the object as needed from the data layer for processing. It is a best coding practice to simplify the signatures and parameter collections of the service methods as much as practical, however it's your design decision how to best define the inputs to your methods.

Keep in mind that there are some data type limitations when working with web services, and you will benefit from any effort to decouple the logic of your classes. In this example, the calling routines need not concern themselves with anything other than providing the identity of the record to act upon; they need to know absolutely nothing about the state of the object, or how it will be processed by the service.

Once the record has been fetched, the method will process the data based on the logic extracted from the original method in the controller class, and then, based on success or failure, will pass back an appropriate message.

## Refactoring the Controller Action Method

Next we'll change the action method in the controller class, removing the original business logic and calling the new service method. We must refactor to evaluate the returned message which will be used to determine subsequent feedback and navigation for the user.

```
public class MyControllerExtension{

    private ApexPages.StandardController controller;

    //Constructor for the extension.
    public MyControllerExtension(ApexPages.StandardController
pController{

        controller = pController;

    }

    //Action method called from the 'action' attribute on the
apex:page tag.
    public PageReference MyCustomAutoRunAction(){
```

```
                //Call the new service static method and return the
message.
            string resultMessage = MyCustomService.
MyCustomProcess(controller.getId());

            //Determine appropriate user feedback and navigation based
on the message returned.
            ...

    }

}
```

Note that we're simply passing to the service method the record's ID as derived from the StandardController. This controller action method will still require logic to determine how to respond with the appropriate user feedback and navigation based on the message returned from the service.

## Build an Apex REST Resource API

Now that we have the service method in place, we can build a simple Apex REST resource that will provide an external API to the service from an HTTP request from our mobile app or any other REST based application that needs to call it.

Our Apex resource class method simply wraps a call to the service class method, and passes back the resulting message. Depending on the signature of the service class method, the Apex REST resource will need to support whatever parameters are required to invoke it. In our sample case, it simply needs to pass along the record ID.

```
@RestResource(urlMapping='/MobileActions/*')
global with sharing class MobileActions {

    @HttpPost
    global static String doMobileAction(String recordId, String
action) {

        if(action == 'MyCustomAction') {

            //Invoke the new service static method and return the
message.
            ID tempId = (ID)recordId;
            return MyCustomService.MyCustomProcess(tempId);

        } else {

            return 'Unknown action: ' + action;

        }

    }

}
```

n the revised diagram below, you can see the interaction from a mobile app via the Apex REST resource class, which can now invoke our custom business logic from its new home in our service class.

## Also Works With JavaScript Remoting

The REST API works great if we're connected to the org using OAuth, making calls through the REST API. However, if we're using a mobile web approach with our mobile client hosted inside a Visualforce page, we will have an Apex controller class that handles the action with an @ RemoteAction method called from Ajax. That Apex controller method would look something like this, simply passing back the resulting message to the calling routine:

```
global class MyController{

    //Action method called from the Ajax 'action'.
    @RemoteAction
    global static String MyCustomRemotingAction(string recordId){

        //Call the new service static method and return the
message.
        ID tempId = (ID)recordId;
        return MyCustomService.MyCustomProcess(tempId);

    }

}
```

Our final diagram below shows the interaction from the mobile web app now hosted in a Visualforce page, invoking the service logic via a call from client side Ajax to an @RemoteAction method on an Apex class.

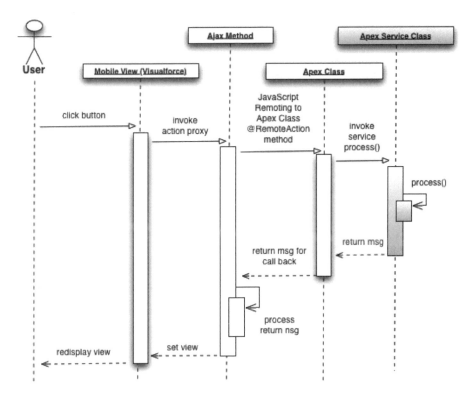

*Figure 11-8. The resulting UML diagram sequence.*

## Summary

As you can see, you gain tremendous flexibility when refactoring Apex into a more modular architecture. This approach allows previously 'trapped' custom business logic to be called as a service from any entry point, both internal or external to the org.

The same pattern can be applied to similar scenarios, perhaps where a custom button calls a JavaScript stub, using the Ajax Toolkit to invoke a SOAP Apex web method. Once again, the key is to extract and isolate the business logic contained in the SOAP web method into a separate service class, so that it can be called via the SOAP API as well as from a REST service or any Apex code elsewhere in your org.

Adopting a SOC approach provides maximum flexibility with just a bit of effort to build out a more structured architecture. You can incrementally refactor your existing code base in bite size chunks as needed, delivering constant and incremental improvement to your application while exposing valuable functionality to your shiny new mobile apps.

So...what are you waiting for? Go do it.

# Chapter 12
# Building Mobile Apps with Mobile Design Templates

Mobile Design Templates are an open-source project envisioned by Developer Evangelist Sandeep Bhanot to help Salesforce Developers quickly build mobile apps with mobile optimized UIs. Mobile Design Templates are an open-source library of 22 mobile-optimized that combine HTML5 and CSS3 markup into Visualforce pages and address many of the common mobile use cases for interacting with Salesforce data.

The library includes templates to view and edit customer data, view backend reports, find nearby records, and much more. Developers can customize and reuse these templates at will to meet their specific UI/UX requirements. Being able to use these open-source templates as a starting point for their UI/UX design should dramatically shorten the time it takes to develop a great looking web/hybrid app on the Salesforce Platform. Here are some other important tidbits about the design templates.

You can combine these static templates with a JavaScript library like ForceTk or one of the Mobile Packs for Backbone, Angular or Knockout to provide live data bindings with any Salesforce backend.

Since they utilize standard web technologies like HTML5, CSS3 and JavaScript, your apps will benefit from the cross-platform support these standrads provide, and your UI will be optimized for the phone form factor.

## Getting Started

The best way to get started with the Mobile Design Templates is visit Templates interactive home page on the Salesforce Mobile Services site at http://www2.developerforce.com/en/mobile/services/mobile-templates. The page is designed as an interactive walkthrough to the 22 templates. I say interactive because as you scroll down the page, you'll see each template broken down into its constituent HTML5/CSS3 components. The phone image on the right shows the results of adding code in realtime. That is, it will update with each template/section making the whole learning process more visual and easier to follow.

The templates are modular, customizable, open-source CSS3 and HTML5 markup that can be modified at will to meet your specific UI/UX requirements. Here are some other features:

- You can combine these static templates with a JavaScript library like ForceTk or one of the Mobile Packs for Backbone, Angular or Knockout to provide live data bindings with any Salesforce backend.

- The templates provide cross-platform (iOS, Android etc.) support, courtesy of the use of standard Web technologies like HTML5, CSS3 and JavaScript.

- All templates are optimized for the phone form factor.

The base HTML5/CSS3 can be modified to work with any Salesforce object (standard or custom) in the context of any mobile use case. There are templates to view and edit customer data, view backend reports, find nearby records, and much more. These starting points for UI and UX design should dramatically shorten the time it takes to develop a great looking Web or hybrid app on the Salesforce Platform. Thereafter, you can customize and reuse these templates at will to meet the specific requirements of your mobile app.

## Uses Cases

Mobile templates cover the following popular use cases:

| Template | Description |
| --- | --- |
| List View Templates List View | Provides different visual representations for showing a list of standard or custom Salesforce records. |
| Detail View Templates Detail View | Provides various read-only views of a standard or custom data record. Typically, users will navigate to one of these detail views by clicking a record in a List View. |
| Data Input Templates Data Input | Used to capture user input from a phone. The different form elements included in these templates (phone, date, number, text, etc.) can be used in any mobile app that requires users to add or update Salesforce data |

| Template | Description |
|---|---|
| Map View Templates Map View | Provides Google Map-based designs for implementing the common ' Find Nearby' functionality on a mobile device. These templates can be combined with the Geolocation custom field in Salesforce, and its corresponding SOQL companion, to add geolocation functionality to any Web or hybrid mobile app. |
| Calendar View Templates Calendar | Provides mobile optimized views of a user' s Salesforce calendar (Tasks and Events). |
| Report and Dashboard Templates Report and Dashboard | Provides mobile optimized report views of Salesforce data. These templates are developed using the open-Source charting library and developers can combine them with the Salesforce Analytics API to add reporting capabilities to their mobile apps |
| Miscellaneous | Use these templates as a starting point to add a Settings, Splash or About screen to your mobile app. |

*Table 13-1. Overview of Mobile Templates.*

## Sample App Use Case

The following exampe is a simple mobile web app in written in Visualforce using the Picture List View template to view Contact records in Salesforce. List View templates provide different visual representations for showing a list of Standard or Custom Salesforce records and the Picture List View template in particular can be used to display any data that has a picture associated with it (Contact, User, Product, etc.). The template also has an optional feature whereby a swipe-right on any image in the list reveals some 'Quick Action' icons. The user can then perform these quick actions (like emailing or calling the Contact) directly from this view (versus from a drill-down detail view). Here's a screenshot of the completed Visualforce page. You can also peruse the entire codebase for this sample app in the Sample Apps directory of the GitHub repo.

I'll build on this basic app over the next couple of blog posts and show you how to combine multiple templates into an end-to-end, fully featured mobile app. Note also that while the Picture List View template and this sample app uses Contacts as an example, every mobile design template is use case agnostic and can be modified and reused with any Salesforce object (Standard or Custom) in the context of any mobile use case.

## Using Mobile Design Templates in Visualforce

Lets start with how you can use any of the templates in a mobile optimized Visualforce page. The first step is to download the templates project from GitHub. You can do so by executing the following from the command line.

```
git clone https://github.com/developerforce/Mobile-Design-
Templates.git
```

If you don't have Git installed, you can also click on the 'Download ZIP' icon on the right of the repo home page and download the project as a zip file. Next, upload the templates zip file as a Static Resource in your DE Org. Finally, lets look at our Visualforce page skeleton that imports the necessary JavaScript and CSS from the templates Static Resource zip.

```
<apex:page docType="html-5.0"
           showHeader="false"
           sidebar="false"
           standardStylesheets="false"
           standardController="Contact"
           extensions="Contacts_Ext">
    <head>
        <meta charset="utf-8"/>
        <meta name="viewport" content="width=device-width, initial-
scale=1,
                    minimum-scale=1, maximum-scale=1, user-
scalable=no"/>
        <apex:stylesheet value="{!URLFOR($Resource.Mobile_Design_
Templates,
            'Mobile-Design-Templates-master/common/css/app.min.
css')}"/>
        <apex:includeScript value="{!URLFOR($Resource.Mobile_Design_
Templates,
          'Mobile-Design-Templates-master/common/js/jQuery2.0.2.min.
js')}"/>
        <apex:includeScript value=
         "{!URLFOR($Resource.Mobile_Design_Templates,.
        'Mobile-Design-Templates-master/common/js/jquery.touchwipe.min.
js')}"/>
        <apex:includeScript value=
                "{!URLFOR($Resource.Mobile_Design_Templates,
                 'Mobile-Design-Templates-master/common/js/main.min.
js')}"/>
    </head>
    <body>
        <div id="mainContainer"/>
    </body>
</apex:page>
```

The two most important imports for using the mobile templates in a web page are app.min.css and main.min.js (note that the GitHub project also has the uncompressed versions of these files for easier review). These two files respectively define the CSS and minimal JavaScript required to render the templates. In addition to these two files, the templates also require jQuery 2.0.2 (for basic DOM manipulation in main.min.js). The Picture List View Template used in this sample also requires a small JS library (jquery.touchwipe.min.js) to enable touch gestures in the List View.

In addition to the JS and CSS imports, note the use of the HTML5 doctype and the disabling of the standard stylesheets, header and sidebar in the Visualforce page. This is a way to make the page mobile optimized and load faster on a mobile device.

## Data Binding with the Mobile Design Templates

All Mobile Design Templates in the GitHub repo use static/hard-coded data for illustrative purposes. This helps a new developer quickly review the overall UI/UX offered by a template and determine if its a good starting point for their own mobile use case/app. However, in order to use a template in an actual mobile app, the HTML5/CSS3 markup has to be populated with live data from Salesforce. In the case of this sample app, we need to query a list of Contact records from Salesforce and then build out the appropriate page markup. There are several options for a developer to bind these mobile web templates to Salesforce data.

- JavaScript Remoting when the templates are used in a Visualforce page
- JavaScript wrapper for the REST API (aka ForceTK) to perform CRUD access to Salesforce data from a template Visualforce or web page
- Mobile Packs for Backbone, Angular or Knockout when the templates are used in an app built using one of those MV* frameworks.

In the interest of keeping things simple, this example uses JavaScript Remoting in this sample to query the list of Contact records. Before I dive deeper into the data binding code, lets quickly review how I store the Contact pics in Salesforce. Since the Contact Standard Object does not have a native picture field, I created a Rich Text Custom Field (Contact_Pic__c) and used it to upload thumbnail images to Contact records. You can also upload images as Attachment or Chatter Files and then use a combination of Formula Fields and trigger/API logic to store and display the images.

Next, lets review how to query and display a dynamic list of Contact records using the Picture List View Template.

## Using JavaScript Remoting to Query Contact Records

The following markup shows how I use JavaScript Remoting to provide the data binding for the page.

```
var contactRecs = new Array();
var compiledListViewTempl = _.template($("#listView").html());

$(document).ready(function() {
    getAllContacts();
});

function getAllContacts(){
    Visualforce.remoting.Manager.invokeAction(
            '{!$RemoteAction.Contacts_Ext.getContactRecs}',
            function(records, e) {
                    showContacts(records);},
                    {escape:false});
}

function showContacts(records) {
```

```
        contactRecs.length = 0;
        for(var i = 0; i < records.length; i++) {
                records[i].Pic = '{!URLFOR($Resource.BlankAvatar)}';
                if (typeof records[i].Contact_Pic__c != "undefined"){
                    records[i].Pic = $(records[i].Contact_Pic__c).
attr('src');
                }
                contactRecs[records[i].Id] = records[i];
        }

        $('#mainContainer').empty();
        $('#mainContainer').append(compiledListViewTempl({contacts :
records}));
        $(document).trigger('onTemplateReady');
    }
```

The getAllContacts JavaScript method invokes the getContactRecs function on the Contacts_
Ext Extension class via JavaScript Remoting. The method returns a list of Contact records which
are then processed in the showContacts callback method. There, we iterate thr. the Contact
records and assign a default 'blank avatar' image to any Contact record that doesn't have an
associated image in the Contact_Pic__c Rich Text Custom Field (lines 18-24). Finally, we insert
the list of Contacts into the page DOM (lines 2, 27) using the Underscore utility library (more on
this later).

Note the triggering of the onTemplateReady custom JavaScript event on line 28. As mentioned
earlier, the templates use a minimal amount of JavaScript (main.min.js) to enable basic user
interactivity. The main.min.js script listens for the onTemplateReady event before executing
some initialization logic and you're therefore required to fire that event once the template markup
has been inserted into the page DOM.

## Using Underscore to generate the template markup

The real action in the VF page happens in the Underscore template that generates the dynamic list
of Contacts using markup from the the Picture List View Template.

```
<script type="text/html" id='listView'>
    <div class="app-wrapper">

        <nav class="main-menu">
            <a href="#">Accounts</a>
            <a href="#">Opportunities</a>
        </nav>

        <header>
            <div class="main-menu-button main-menu-button-left"><a
class="menu"> </a></div>
            <h1>Contacts</h1>
        </header>
```

```
<div class="app-content">
    <ul id="cList" class="list-view with-swipe left-thumbs right-
one-icons">
        <% for(var i = 0; i < contacts.length; i++){ %>
          <li>
            <div class="thumbs">
              <% if (typeof(contacts[i].Phone) != "undefined") { %>
                <a href="tel:<%= contacts[i].Phone %>"
class="thumb thumb-1">
                    <img class="thumb" src="{!URLFOR($Resource.
Mobile_Design_Templates,
                    'Mobile-Design-Templates-master/common/
images/icons/tile-phone.png')}"/>
                </a>
              <% } %>

              <% if (typeof(contacts[i].Email) != "undefined") {%>
                <a href="mailto:<%= contacts[i].Email %>"
class="thumb thumb-2">
                    <img class="thumb" src="{!URLFOR($Resource.
Mobile_Design_Templates,
                    'Mobile-Design-Templates-master/common/images/
icons/tile-email.png')}"/>
                </a>
              <% } %>
              <img class="thumb thumb-3" src="<%= contacts[i].Pic
%>"/>
            </div>
            <a href="#/contact/<%= contacts[i].Id %>"
class="content">
                <h2><%= contacts[i].Name %></h2>
                <%= contacts[i].Title %>
                <div class="list-view-icons">
                    <span class="icon-right-arrow"> </span>
                </div>
            </a>
          </li>
        <% } %>
    </ul>
  </div>
</div>
</script>
```

This is our first glimpse of the Mobile Design Templates in action. I simply copy pasted this markup from the Picture List View Template in GitHub (minus the dynamic binding part). I then made a couple of minor tweaks to the markup to suit my specific use case. For example, removing the gear icon from the header and updating the menu list (under the <nav class="main-menu"> section).

As is evident from the above markup, all templates use plain-vanilla HTML5 with CSS3 styling to generate a mobile-optimized view. They have no dependency on external frameworks like jQuery Mobile, Twitter Bootstrap etc. The template markup and CSS is also very modular and composable. Adding a list item in the Picture List View Template is as simple as adding a <ul> tag with the list-view with-swipe left-thumbs right-one-icons CSS styles applied to it (line 15). Adding a Quick Action icon (revealed when the user does a swipe-right on the thumbnail) is simply a matter of applying the thumb CSS style to the <img> tag (lines 21, 28). As so on. For a more detailed breakdown of the different components of the Picture List View and other templates, simply scroll down through the interactive home page and see the templates come to life.

Remember also that the templates are not a all-or-nothing monolith. You can and should pick and choose components of a particular template that fit your specific use case and requirements. Don't want the Contact title to show in your list view? Just drop the respective markup from the page. Don't need the Quick Action on-swipe component? Simply drop the entire <div class="thumbs"> tag.

## Customizing the Look and Feel of the Templates

In addition to being modular and composable, the templates are also completely customizable in terms of their look and feel. Simply modify app.css to implement your unique styling and UX requirements. Lets take a very simple example to see this in action. Lets say I wanted to display a red border around the Contact image when the user does a swipe-right to reveal the Quick Action icons. All I have to do is to change the respective style class in app.css to the following:

```
ul.list-view li.swiped .thumb-3 {
    left: 115px;
    border:2px solid red;
}
```

And voila, the list view looks a little different. The CSS used in the templates was generated from Saas and so if you're more comfortable in a tool like Compass, you can modify the Saas files instead.

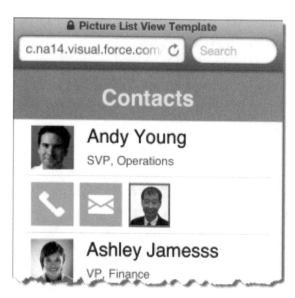

*Figure 12-1. Customizing the template look and feel with simple CSS3 adjustments.*

## Using the Templates: CalendarView Quick Example

The following example, created bt Developer Evangelist Josh Birk, presents a simple calendar app that hooks into Salesforce events via the REST API.

## Introducing SObjectData.js

One thing we wanted with our recent additions and updates to the Mobile Packs was to be able to support the new SmartSync framework. While the original examples for SmartSync included Backbone.js as a framework, we also wanted to be able to use SmartSync with lower level libraries like jQuery Mobile. The Mobile Design Templates also require some jQuery to work their magic. For the jQuery Mobile Pack, and libraries like the Mobile Design Templates, I wrote a new library to abstract SmartSync without requiring an MVC style library like Backbone or Angular: SObjectData. This library runs on top of ForceTK (or RemoteTK) and SmartSync to provide easy data access and handling.

This application will use a very small portion of SObjectData. Al it does is fetch data and accesses it. This application will be designed for a local hybrid application, designed to work with our Mobile SDK handle authentication. So with that, and the Mobile Design Template, and SObjectData—Table 13-2 shows the Prerequisites: :

| Mobile SDK | For the Salesforce OAuth plugin as well as the SmartSync framework. |
| Mobile Design Templates | For our user interface. This will also bring in jQuery and Underscore. |
| SObjectData | Data access and manipulation against SmartSync. |

*Table 13-2. Prerequisites.*

## Authentication

Since this is a local hybrid app – we'll leverage the Mobile SDK for authentication. This will require setting up a Connected App, and setting the keys correctly using either forcedroid or forceios to generate a sample application. From there, you can pretty much keep bootconfig. json from the www directory and replace the rest with our sample from github. If this is new to you, check out the Mobile SDK documentation to get up and running.

## Querying Data

Accessing your data with SObjectData is done via the fetch method of an SObjectData instance. Just give it three parameters: type (SOSL or SOQL), query and callback. For our calendar app, we'll query based on a time span (either TODAY or THIS_WEEK) and then divide all the events into different arrays we can association with our template. First we instantiate our SObjectData. This object will be associated with a specific set of data (in this case our events), knows the SObjectType and fields associated with that data set and makes it easy to access and manipulate the data:

```
var Events = new SObjectData();
```

Now in this instance, we don't need to define either the SObjectType or fields – SObjectData will infer all of that based on the result of our query:

```
function refreshData(span) {
  Events.fetch('soql','Select Id, Subject, StartDateTime,
ActivityDate, ActivityDateTime, DurationInMinutes, Description,
Location from Event WHERE ActivityDate = '+span+' ORDER BY
StartDateTime ASC',divideEvents);
}
```

## Using the Calendar View Template

The Calendar View has two main sections – the first sets up the dates on the left side and a visual indicator as to the number of events (and/or tasks) associated with the date, and the right side which will show the full details for a specific day. The application has taken the records from our query and divided them into arrays for each day of the week, and then associated all of those into one array (along with a couple of other convenient arrays like days of the week). We can now bind these to an underscore template:

```
<div class="content">
 <div class="span-50 padding-right-gutter-half">
   <h1 class="padding-bottom-gutter"></h1>
   <ul id="week-planner" class="week-planner">
   <script id='events-template' type='text/template'>
   <% for(var i = 0; i < 7; i++){
   %>
   <%
   if(Week_Dates[i] != null) {
   %>
     <li data-date="<%=Week_Dates[i]%>">
     <div class="date"><B><%=Days_of_Week[i]%></B><BR /><%=Week_
Dates[i]%></div>
     <ul class="week-planner-items">
       <% for(var x = 0; x < Week_Events[i].length; x++) {%>
       <li class="event"></li>
       <%}%>
     </ul>
     </li>
   <%
     }
     } %>
   </script>
   </ul>

   <!-- .week-planner -->
 </div><!-- .span-50 -->
 <div id="days-events" class="span-50 padding-left-gutter-half">
```

```
<script id='days-template' type='text/template'>
  <%
  for(var i = 0; i < 7; i++){
  %>
  <%
  if(Week_Dates[i] != null) {
  %>
    <div class="date-content" id="date-content-<%=Week_Dates[i]%>">
    <h1 class="event">Events</h1>
    <div class="events">
    <% for(var x = 0; x < Week_Events[i].length; x++) {%>
     <h3><%=Week_Events[i][x].Subject%></h3>
     <P><%=activityTimeSpan(Week_Events[i][x])%></P>
     <P><%=Week_Events[i][x].Location%></P>
     <P><%=Week_Events[i][x].Description%></P>
    <%}%>
  </div>
 </div>
 <%
 }
 } %>
</script>

</div><!--.span-50-->
</div><!-- .content -->
```

With a little jQuery:

```
$('#week-planner').empty();
$('#days-events').empty();

$('#week-planner').append(eventsTmpl({
 Week_Dates : Week_Dates,
 Week_Events : Week_Events
}));
$('#days-events').append(daysTmpl({
 Week_Dates : Week_Dates,
 Week_Events : Week_Events
}));
calendarObj.init();
```

Note the calendarObj.init call. This is an alternative to the onTemplateReady event that Sandeep used in his tutorial if we want to refresh only a specific view out of the the Mobile Design Templates

## Adding the Tabbed View Template

For a little variety, the application can switch between events for Today and events for This Week. For simplicity, we'll call back to the API's for each button press – but in a future iteration we'll make better use of a local cache and refresh mechanism. To make our application a tabbed one, we just add the HTML from the template:

```
<div id="tabbed-list-view-nav" class="tabbed-list-view-nav">
 <a id="today-tab" class="span-50 on">Today</a>
 <a id="week-tab" class="span-50">Week</a>
 <div id="tabbed-list-view-nav-arrow" class="tabbed-list-view-nav-
arrow"> </div>
</div>
```

And then bind some events with jQuery:

```
$('#today-tab').click(function() {
   refreshData('TODAY');
});

$('#week-tab').click(function() {
   refreshData('THIS_WEEK');
});
```

## ActivityDateTime to Date

Those of us who have dabbled with Apex Date formats and JavaScript in the past have learned that the two don't always get along. As part of this app, I've got a simple function to take an event record, pull the ActivityDateTime and then convert it to a proper JavaScript date in UTC (to keep time zone shifts correct):

```
function activityToDateTime(record){
    activity_string = record.ActivityDateTime;
    activity_array = activity_string.split("T");
    date_array = activity_array[0].split("-");
    time_array = activity_array[1].split(".")[0].split(":");
    activity_month = parseInt(date_array[1])-1;
    return new Date(Date.UTC(date_array[0],activity_month,date_
array[2],time_array[0],time_array[1]));
  }
```

## Summary

This last example presented a simple calendar application. You can see how libraries like SObjectData, and the Mobile Design Templates make it easy to get the basics up and running. And while we've just glossed over the Mobile SDK, you can quickly turn your Visualfore mobile apps into hybrid apps once you've installed the Mobile SDK. You'll find information on using this and many other technologies in the Salesforve Mobile App Development Guide on http://developer.salesforce.com

This chapter also introduced the Mobile Design Templates and presented a second app that allows you to access Contact records and display them on a mobile device. By combining Mobile design temapltes with the techniques presented in Chapter 10, you will be well on your way to building sophisticated enterprise mobile apps that can access data securely in the cloud.

# Chapter 13
# Visualforce Performance and Best Practices Rapidfire Rendering of Visualforce Pages

- Sources of Performance Issues

- Optimizing in the Requirements Phase

- Optimizing with Efficient Page and Controller Design

- Optimizing Visualforce and Apex Code

- Optimizing Using Web Development Best Practices

Going back to Chapter 1, Thinking in Visualforce, the entire platform enforces the MVC paradigm. So while the programmatic features of the Force.com platform make it easy to customize functionality, you should use standard objects and declarative features whenever possible. Standard objects and declarative features—such as approval processes, visual flows, and workflows—are highly optimized already and don't count against most governor limits. They typically simplify data models and reduce the number of Visualforce pages necessary for business processes, making them a best practice.

In fact, this entire book is filled with best practices for developing UIs using Visualforce. However, there will be times when you find that pages render slowly. Visualforce allows you to build applications that make use of a broad array of cloud-based services, such as the Apex Code, Salesforce data services, the Chatter-based social enterprise, and so on. Although the Force.com platform scales to handle billions of transactions, that's not an invitation to ignore web application best practices. This chapter explains a number of considerations and best practices for ensuring that your Visualforce pages and applications perform well for the people who use them.

## Investigating Visualforce Performance Issues

Let's assume you are reading this chapter because something is slow right now. The first place to begin your quest towards effective optimization is to investigate the possible sources of your performance issues and identify the source. Here are some suggestions.

## Is the problem with your Visualforce page?

Before diving into your Visualforce code, verify that Visualforce is the problem. For example, if you are experiencing slow load times, ensure they are not the result of a network issue by checking the load time of other Salesforce pages. If they are also slow, it can be the result of bandwidth or latency issues related to Salesforce. To check on the status of the Salesforce servers, visit trust. salesforce.com.

You should also check the status of your network connections and ensure they are functioning properly. Check other, nearby computers to be sure it is not actually a network issue, and compare the results to response times from a completely different internet connection.

In working with a User, make sure a simpler problem is not the cause. Have them reboot their computer and try again. Be sure they try your Visualforce page with different browsers: Occasionally browser updates can cause unforeseen difficulties.

## Use the Developer Console to Isolate Performance Bottlenecks

The Force.com Developer Console is a great tool for investigating the performance of your Visualforce markup and other Force.com features on the page. The Force.com Developer Console includes an easy-to-use graphical timeline view to help you understand where your Visualforce pages are spending their time processing.

Reviewing the timeline and debug log for slow requests should be your first step in solving performance problems with Visualforce pages. The debug log details the performance of requests as the server processes them. The details show every execution step for methods, queries, workflows, callouts, DML, validations, triggers, and pages by type and time. This information allows you to see what's consuming system resources and helps you identify issues in your code. From the Timeline tab you will be able to see exactly which processes in your page take the most time.

The Force.com Developer Console provides detailed insight into the performance of requests as they are processed on the server, but that is only one factor in the performance experienced by those using your Visualforce pages. In particular, browser-embedded tools can provide insight into network latency and load times, the efficiency of JavaScript code, and so on. Describing these tools is beyond the scope of this book. However, some tools you may consider include:

## BROWSER PROFILING AND DEBUGGING TOOLS

| Tool | Description |
|------|-------------|
| Chrome Dev Tools | The Developer Tools, bundled and available in Chrome, allows web developers and programmers deep access into the internals of the browser and their web application. |
| Firebug | Firebug integrates with Firefox to put a wealth of web development tools at your fingertips while you browse. You can edit, debug, and monitor CSS, HTML, and JavaScript live in any web page. |
| YSlow | YSlow analyzes web page performance by examining all the components on the page, including components dynamically created by JavaScript. It measures the page's performance and offers suggestions for improvement. YSlow provides grade, components, and statistics views for the page. |
| webpagetest.org | A web site that wroks well for mobile browser testing. |

## TESTING TOOLS AND CONSIDERATIONS

- Use automated testing. Testing complex flows in an application can be tedious and produce inconsistent results. Leverage tools like LoadRunner and Selenium to automate testing. Automated tests can click on links, enter and retrieve data, and record execution times. Automation tools may uncover bottlenecks and defects missed by manual testing.

- Perform cross-browser testing. Test with as many browsers and versions as possible

- Test with large data volumes. You may have designed your pages to avoid unbounded data, implement pagination, and to filter and display only relevant data. You should still test with large data volumes. You may encounter scenarios with data skews where particular users have access to a larger number of records than anticipated. The Developer Force site includes several excellent articles covering Large Data Volumes including "Best Practices for Deployments with Large Data Volumes" at http://wiki.developerforce.com/page/Best_Practices_for_Deployments_with_Large_Data_Volumes

Adding automated testing to your development process can test for and help you prevent performance regressions.

# Perform Separate Mobile Testing

Be sure to review performance in all contexts where your Visualforce pages will be used. Mobile browsers have very different performance characteristics than desktop browsers, including slower processors, less memory, and network latency and bandwidth limitations.

The Salesforce Mobile app launches Visualforce Mobile pages in an embedded browser, and browser capabilities vary across manufacturers, devices, and versions. Depending on the embedded browser's JavaScript support, you may experience performance issues. Testing with a mobile device can uncover performance issues that are hidden to developer machines. You can use tools like webpagetest.org for initial mobile browser testing, but there is no substitute for testing on the actual hardware in use by your organization and customers.

Refer to the chapters on developing for mobile devices for additional information and mobile development best practices.

## Optimizing During the Requirements Phase

The largest gains in Visualforce performance are achieved during the requirements phase, before you write a single line of code. Putting every possible feature on a few " kitchen sink" -style pages invariably results in reduced performance. Be proactive and push back on requirements that may have a negative impact on performance. This section outlines things to consider on your way to designing effective Visualforce pages that perform well.

Quite often, developers build Visualforce pages containing unbounded data; a large number of components, rows, and fields; or include features that aren't vital steps in their business processes. These " kitchen sink" pages may not be usable, won't perform well, and risk reaching governor limits (view state, heap size, record limits, and total page size). If in doubt, build a prototype to validate a concern. You want to avoid the situation of rolling out your pages with all the features implemented only to have it be unusable.

Here are some specific things to consider as you are creating the requirements for your Visualforce pages:

| Best Practice | Description |
|---|---|
| **Utilize standard features versus custom code** | As described in the introduction of this chapter, utilize declarative features whenever possible. |
| **Design task-centric pages** | Design focused pages that concentrate on individual task flows, not pages with every possible feature. Probably the most common Visualforce performance problem customers experience has to do with overloading a page, trying to make one or a few pages hold all of the features they need to manage their business. We recommend instead that pages be designed with specific tasks, with a sensible workflow and navigation paths between tasks. |
| **Prioritize the user experience** | Prioritize by building your pages around a user experience story and limiting non-essential features. Balance additional features to a page against usability and business requirements. Overloaded pages go against many of the concepts in this document and performance only gets worse as your business grows. |

| Best Practice | Description |
|---|---|
| **Design list view pages to use pagination** | Pages that show lists of records should never be "unbounded." That is, the code should always limit to a maximum the number of records displayed. Unbounded pages will result in longer load times, approach governor limits, and become unusable as your organization grows and has more data. Rather than display an unbounded list of records, use pagination to allow access to records beyond the first screen. Pagination is a standard user interface pattern for list views, and support for it is built into the StandardSetController available to Visualforce pages. |
| **Reduce the number of records** | Reduce the number of records displayed on a page by limiting the data retrieved through SOQL. A good rule of thumb is 100 records. |
| Use SOQL OFFSET | SOQL OFFSET also allows you to paginate to a specific subset of results within SOQL, using your own pagination logic. |
| **Avoid "data grid" pages** | A specific subset of list view pages is the "data grid" page, where many records are displayed with their fields available for editing. Multiply the number of records by the number of fields per record to display, and you can quickly reach thousands of input fields, especially for lists without pagination. Thousands of input components on a page will potentially overflow the maximum view state size, and will result in a Visualforce component tree that is slow to process. |
| Custom Data Grids | Custom data grids encapsulate many of the potential performance issues in Visualforce. You should consider the types of users as some may have access to a much larger number of records. Leverage pagination and filters and, where possible, make data |
| **Read-only to reduce view state** | Consider displaying only the essential data for a given record and provide a link for an Ajax-based details box, or even a separate page, to view the rest. |

## Efficient Page and Controller Design

Efficient Visualforce pages start with good page design, and make appropriate use of additional Force.com platform technologies. Knowing when and where to leverage features of the platform can take a system design from good to great. This section describes a few things to consider when designing your custom application's pages, and includes source code examples of how to implement them.

- Use pagination and filtering to reduce the number of records displayed on a single page.
- Use the `with sharing` keywords to display only those records the user is allowed to see.
- Use lazy loading to reduce or delay expensive calculations or data loading.
- Offload expensive processing using asynchronous tasks when that processing is secondary to the purpose of the page.

## Reduce the Number of Records Displayed on a Single Page

Large page sizes directly affects load times. Use pagination and filtering to reduce the number of records displayed on a page. The built-in StandardSetController makes pagination simple to implement, and adding filtering is straightforward. You can also use SOQL OFFSET to write your own custom pagination logic. In all cases Visualforce pages must be under the standard response limit of 15 MB.

### Pagination Using StandardSetController

Take advantage of pagination with a list controller to present fewer records per page.

### Pagination Using SOQL OFFSET

Use the SOQL OFFSET clause to write logic that paginates to a specific subset of results within SOQL In addition, avoid using data grids, which display many records with editable fields. Data grids frequently expand to thousands of input components on a page and exceed the maximum view state size, resulting in a Visualforce component tree that's slow to process.

If your Visualforce page needs a data grid:

- Use pagination and filters.
- Where possible, make data read-only to reduce the view state size.
- Only display essential data for a given record, and provide a link for an Ajax-based details box or separate page to view the rest.

### Filtering

Limit the data coming back from SOQL calls in your Apex controllers. For example, using AND statements in your WHERE clause, or removing null results. See online help for details on constructing clauses.

## Limit Records Displayed Using with Sharing

Another strategy for reducing the number of records being displayed at once is to use the with sharing keyword when creating your Apex controllers. This limits the records returned to those to which the user has access rights, instead of all records in your organization. with sharing may also be an important aspect of any security or information access limitations you need to build into your system.

## Optimizing Visualforce and Apex Code

Writing efficient code for Visualforce pages involves writing good Apex and SOQL, in addition to the Visualforce markup. Following are some techniques you can use to write code that performs well, methods you can use to diagnose existing pages that aren' t performing well, and ways you can optimize them.

## View State

Managing, optimizing, and reducing the view state is often the number one task developers need to do to get their Visualforce pages to perform as desired. To maintain state in a Visualforce page, the Force.com platform includes the state of components, field values, and controller state in a hidden form element. This encrypted string is referred to as the view state  and has a limit of 135KB. Large view states required longer processing times for each request, including serializing and de-serializing, and encryption and decryption. By reducing your view state size, your pages can load quicker and stall less often.

Under **Setup | My Personal Information | Personal Information** in your org, be sure you have checked off both the **Development Mode** and **Show View State in Development Mode** boxes. This will now allow you to explore your page's View State in unencrypted mode to examine exactly what is being stored.

You can monitor view state performance through the View State tab in the development mode footer and take the following actions:

- Use the `<apex:actionRegion>` tag to submit form data from specific sections of the Visualforce page.

- Use the transient keyword in your Apex controllers for variables that aren't essential for maintaining state and aren't necessary during page refreshes.

- If you notice that a large percentage of your view state comes from objects used in controllers or controller extensions, consider refining your SOQL calls to return only data that's relevant to the Visualforce page.

- If your view state is affected by a large component tree, try reducing the number of components your page depends on.

Even though View State is now stored on the server (since API Version 29.0), it is still important to manage what is stored there, and keep its size to a minimum – in all events it must be less that the 135K maximum size.  Use the transient key word in APEX to remove items from View State.

Another way to reduce View State size is to use "stateless" commands. For example, instead of using `<apex:commandButton>` or `<apex:commandLink>` components (which need to be inside a `<apex:form>` component) to invoke an action, use an `<apex:outputLink>` or other stateless display method instead and implement the action through an `<apex:page>` action attribute if it works for your page. Stateless display methods include:

```
<apex:dataList>
<apex:dataTable>
<apex:panelGrid>
<apex:panelLink>
<apex:outputPanel>
<apex:outputText>
```

There are other stateless display methods, as well. The key here is that they are not required to be set within `<apex:form>` tags, and therefore do not increase View State on your page.

When you are listing out information, can you get by with Read Only information? If so, use the `@ReadOnly` designation, and display the information with `<apex:outputText>` components instead of `<apex:inputField>`, or other tag requiring the `<apex:form>` tag area. In the case of records lists, utilize the StandardListController, or the StandardSetController for the page, or the `<apex:EnhancedList>` or `<apex:ListView>` components to let the Visualforce page maintain the data, and control the paging, freeing up your code and View State for other tasks. Maybe list the records out ahead of time, and provide a separate Edit button for the User to make changes later, or let them use the in-line editing feature, if available.

## Consider Custom State Management for Your Page

If View State is still an issue, consider bypassing some of it altogether by doing your own state management. For example, use an HTML `<form>` instead of `<apex:form>`. If your page is to be displayed on mobile devices, this is also a way to reduce the size for their embedded browsers.

## Refine SOQL Queries in Controllers / Extensions

Are the page SOQL or SOSL queries taking a long time? Time to get surgical: use WHERE clause conditions to zero in on exactly the records you are looking for, and then only the specific fields you need. Including unnecessary records and fields not only takes extra time, it also likely consumes extra View State storage. If it is a query utilized in other areas, consider if an additional index on a particular field would speed things up. If so, and you have one of the three External IDs permitted on each sObject available, consider designating it an External ID, and use the new index in your SOQL query.

## Use a Custom Index to Speed Queries

Previously, we were not able to index formula fields nor include null values in an Index. This effectively meant that a query on either formula field, or for null values required a full-table scan. As of Winter '12, Custom Indexes are available on formulas and nulls to make your SOQL query run faster. Some specifics apply – contact Salesforce.com Customer Support to set them up.

Did you remember to use "with sharing" on your Custom Controllers and Extensions? If not, you are likely packing back extra data that the User shouldn't be seeing anyway. Be sure and honor any sharing rules in place. Also, perform calculations on the server, next to the data. It's more efficient there anyway, and means you will have less data to bring back to calculate locally, just the final result to display. You may utilize formula or Roll Up Summary fields to accomplish this, or simply use calculations in producing aggregate results in the query itself.

Regarding calculations, optimize the logic by putting "easy out" clauses first. For example, suppose you are going to look up a Zip Code object to verify address input, but only when the "batch input" flag is not checked. In the Validation Rule, or formula calculation, check the batch input flag first so the system isn't looking up the Zip Code object each time, only to find out it wasn't necessary. Make use of aggregate queries to avoid additional processing of the returned results, and don't forget to use the ascending or descending clause to sort the result set ahead of time.

## Efficient Getter Methods and Lazy Load

It's an odd thing, but when you look through your page's debug log, you are likely to notice that the Properties and Getters / Setters in your Custom Controllers and Extensions are often called multiple times during a Visualforce page load. Be sure and use Lazy Loading techniques to prevent multiple look-ups of the same record. For example, the following getter code snippet returns the Account record associated with the page, but only looks it up the first time when the field is null. On subsequent calls, it simply returns the stored value, saving an additional SELECT query each time:

```
Account MyAccount;
public Account getMyAccount() {
    if (MyAccount == null) {
        MyAccount = [SELECT name, annualRevenue FROM Account
WHERE
                id = :ApexPages.currentPage().getParameters().
get('id')];
    }
    return MyAccount;
}
```

In another form of Lazy Loading, consider that the user can only view a certain number of rows at a time on the screen. If there is only room for ten or twenty rows, why are you waiting to get thousands back during the initial load? Instead, request a QueryMore construct, or use the SOQL Offset for future calls, and use the LIMIT clause to only fetch the number of rows that can be shown at a time. Then your page does not have to wait while the entire collection is assembled at once.

## Large Component Tree?

How are you using components on your page? Artful combinations of components within components displayed in a grid component can be intriguing, but take extra load time. Take a moment to reduce the number and depth of any hierarchical components on your page. Flat component structures load much faster than deep, complex, hierarchical component structures.

## Avoid Over-Design and Deep Component Hierarchies

Don't over-engineer your custom components, and in particular, avoid deep component hierarchies, that is, components that embed components that embed components. Visualforce pages are optimized but large or deep hierarchies increase processing time. Each level in the hierarchy creates overhead in the processing of the page, requiring Visualforce to maintain state information for each level. Traversing up and down the hierarchy can increase processing time and memory consumed, which in addition to being slow can cause pages to hit heap size governor limits.

Here is a page containing nested custom components:

```
<apex:page standardController="Account"
extensions="MyConForTextArea">
<apex:form>
<c:mycomponent/>
</apex:form>
</apex:page>
<apex:component id="mycomponent">
<script type="text/JavaScript">
...
</script>
<c:mycomponent2/>
</apex:component>
<apex:component id="mycomponent2">
<apex:inputField value="{!Account.Name}"/>
<apex:inputText value="{!mTextArea}"/>
<apex:commandButton value="Save" action="{!mySave}"/>
</apex:component>
```

The component tree for this design looks something like this:

- Root Component
    - ◊ Page Component
        - Form Component
            - c:mycomponent
                - c:mycomponent2
                    - InputField Component
                    - HTML Component
                    - InputText Component
                    - HTML Component
                    - CommandButton Component

As you add more components and HTML, the component tree grows and increases server-side management. The highest processing costs are incurred by deeply nested components as context must be provided at each level and maintained throughout the entire request. Leverage custom components only when that logic is intended for re-use or are part of a package. Flat component structures process faster, so limit nesting custom components to logically organize functionality.

## Reduce Multiple Concurrent Requests

Concurrent requests are long running tasks that can block other pending tasks. You can reduce these delays whenever possible by utilizing several techniques, including Action Polling, the Streaming API, Asynchronous Tasks, Caching data in Custom Settings, and JavaScript Remoting.

## Action Polling

Action Polling can be an excellent choice for periodic updates. Instead of holding up the initial page load, you can render the initial information right away, then check periodically for updates later. However, be sure its action is lightweight, and avoid performing DML, external service calls, and other resource-intensive operations in its action methods. Extend the interval of the polling as long as you can get away with: instead of every five seconds, can you wait fifteen seconds, or even thirty, for the next poll?

Keep in mind that the nature of polling is like the proverbial kids in the backseat, constantly asking "Are we there yet?" Similarly, the <apex:ActionPoller> component often generates more distraction than results. Consider utilizing the Streaming API to refactor it, effectively just getting the final result when it's ready.

## Streaming API

When your application is polling SOAP or REST APIs to detect changes, consider refactoring to utilize the Streaming API. Effectively, it is the equivalent of just telling the kids "We're here!" one time, without all the intervening "Are we there yet?" requests. The Streaming API allows you to set up PushTopics in advance, and receive specific information back as it occurs, utilizing a publish / subscribe model to greatly reduce resource consumption.

## Offload Processing to Asynchronous Tasks

What is the solution to a Visualforce page with lots to do? Delegate! Handoff the hard, slow stuff to other tasks. Here we are talking about asynchronous logic. The delegated tasks will come back in near-real time, we are just not going to hold up our page rendering on them. Several possibilities fit this bill: you can use the AJAX Toolkit, JavaScript Remoting, or create an @future call in your Custom Controller or Extension. Action polling and use of the Streaming API also fit into this category. An added benefit is that the separate process gets its own set of Governor Limits, and depending on how it's defined, that may be the larger, batch version of the Governor Limits.

## JavaScript Remoting

The AJAX Toolkit and JavaScript Remoting provide similar functionality. Of the two, you will find that JavaScript Remoting is lighter weight, and easier to set up and get running, so use it if you don't otherwise have a preference. There are three steps to setting up JavaScript Remoting:

1. Use APEX to write your remote method, and mark it with `@RemoteAction`

2. In JavaScript set up the call to the "remote" method on your Visualforce page

3. Write a JavaScript callback function for your Visualforce page to handle the results

## New in Winter '14—Deferred Loading of JavaScript Resources

In previous iterations of Salesforce Platform there were problems with JavaScript resources delaying the load of your Visualforce page. The page would wait until all of the JavaScript code returned before displaying the page. As of Winter '14, deferred loading of JavaScript Resources is provided in the `<apex:includeScript>` component. This component has a new attribute, loadOnReady. When set to "true", the page will load as soon as its DOM is constructed, and then the JavaScript will be run. The result is that most of your page loads immediately, and the remainder shows up when it's available. It's not a panacea, however. If your JavaScript is needed before the page is fully loaded, you will not be able to use this technique in full, but you may at least force the JavaScript to wait until child frames, images, and other external resources start loading before consuming time.

For other JavaScript, consider moving it outside of the `<apex:includeScript>` tag and placing it into a `<script>` tag right before your closing `<apex:page>` tag. The `<apex:includeScript>` tag places JavaScript right before the closing `<head>` element. Therefore, Visualforce loads the JavaScript before any other content on the page. A similar caution applies here: You should only move JavaScript to the bottom of the page if you're certain it will not have any adverse effects on the page. For example, JavaScript which requires document.write or event handlers should remain in the `<head>` element.

## Cache Global Data in Custom Settings

Utilizing AJAX, JavaScript Remoting, and asynchronous tasks can solve a lot of problems, but where do you store the results for further use? One area for consideration is the Custom Settings area. Two types of storage are available, List and Hierarchical. If you are accessing the information only via Apex code or the APIs, either is fine. If the results need to be available to Approval Processes, Formula Fields, Workflow, or Validation Rules, only Hierarchical will work.

One advantage to using Custom Settings for asynchronous results is that it can be accessible by declarative logic. It is cached locally, so it does not require a SOQL `SELECT` statement to retrieve. Another option is to create an sObject to store results. However, you'll need to implement SELECT and DML operations to maintain it.

Another, often overlooked, option is to store pertinent information in the Visualforce pages themselves. Each Visualforce page maintains a map of parameter values which are accessed in Key / Value pairs. In the Lazy Loading example above, we retrieved the record ID associated with our Visualforce page by calling:

```
SELECT name, annualRevenue FROM Account WHERE
              id = :ApexPages.currentPage().getParameters().
  get('id')
```

Note at the end of the SELECT statement that we access the parameter Map construct on a given Visualforce page by looking into the collection of Visualforce pages, finding the current page, getting the Parameters Map, and looking up the value for the ID key.

You can also 'put' your own custom string values into this map. For example,

```
ApexPages.currentPage().getParameters().set('PurchaseOrder',
  '123456');
```

will store that Purchase Order value in the map of the current page. Accessing the Map on other pages simply requires knowing the name of the Visualforce page you want to access: Use the name of the specific page, and get its parameters, for example, OtherPage. getParameters().set('PurchaseOrder', '123456'). Similarly, you can reference Maps on other pages to retrieve information by using the get method: OtherPage.getParameters(). get('PurchaseOrder').

## Optimizing Web Best Practices

Depending on the content type you've declared, Visualforce allows you to embed everything from XML, HTML and other content directly in your code. Most commonly this is HTML, which contains anything you can embed in an HTML page including JavaScript, CSS, and AJAX.

So the first tip is to optimize your Visualforce page HTML for efficient processing, both on the server side where Visualforce validates it for correctness, and on the client side where it makes performance more responsive in the user's browser.

Next, review the HTML that Visualforce components generate. Visualforce pages require valid HTML and may correct invalid HTML during compilation, causing your HTML to render in ways you don't intend. For example, if you have a <head> or <body> tag inside of your <apex:page> tag, the Visualforce page removes it at runtime.

Likewise, you should review any Ajax code. During an AJAX request, the server validates and corrects inbound HTML to ensure that the response properly fits back into the DOM. This process is quick if your Visualforce page contains valid markup and if corrections are unnecessary.

It is always a good practice to reduce HTML bloat as much as is practical. Although the browser caches HTML and compiled Visualforce tags, retrieving them from the cache impacts performance. Unnecessary HTML also increases the size of the component tree and the processing time for AJAX requests.

Are you using any iFrames on your page? Remember that each iFrame is importing content from an outside server. This involves more wait time for your page while the external servers are accessed for their content to complete your page. Consider using an <apex:Include> tag instead, to include a separate Visualforce page with similar content, or use an internal process to re-create like results on your page. One caveat: re-creating the content yourself may push your page into Governor Limit problems, in which case you may need to stick with the original iFrame.

Since the iFrame content is produced elsewhere, it does not count against your Visualforce page Governor Limits.

If you must include content from another Internet source, consider imbedding a link in your Visualforce page that the User will click when they want to see that content. That way, there is no waiting on the external content during the initial page load. Another option here is to look into using Canvas. Canvas will permit your users to not only look at the external content, but also to interact with it without leaving your Visualforce page.

## Optimizing CSS

While CSS styles can improve the appearance of Visualforce pages, they might also add significant weight. Follow these tips to optimize your Visualforce page CSS for efficient delivery to the client, improve caching, and accelerate page display in the browser.

Whenever possible consider externalizing stylesheets, which means taking styles out of the page itself and placing them in separate CSS files. This practice can increase the number of initial HTTP requests, but it reduces the size of individual pages. So when possible combine all CSS files into one or two cascading sheets to reduce the number of HTTP requests. This also allows you to manage your CSS styles from a centralized location. After the browser caches the stylesheets, the overall request size decreases.

Other steps you can take are to:

- Remove comments and whitespace (spaces, newlines, and tabs), and compress the resulting file for faster downloads.

- Use static resources to serve CSS files, as well as images, JavaScript, and other non-changing files. Stylesheets and other assets served this way benefit from the caching and content distribution network (CDN) built into Salesforce.

- For pages that don't use Salesforce CSS files, set the <apex:page> tag's showHeaders and standardStylesheets attributes to false. This practice excludes the standard Salesforce CSS files from the generated page header.

**Tip:** For Javascript and CSS, it might be burdensome during development to make a change, process and package it, and deploy. Consider automating this process through a script.

## Optimizing JavaScript

Optimize your JavaScript to ensure efficient delivery to the client, improve caching, and accelerate page display in the browser.

Consider externalizing JavaScript files. This process increases the number of initial HTTP requests, but it also reduces the size of individual pages and takes advantage of browser caching.

- Build custom versions of JavaScript libraries with only the functions you need. Many open-source JavaScript libraries, such as jQuery, provide this option, which significantly reduces the file size.

- Combine all JavaScript files into a single file to reduce HTTP requests, and remove duplicate functions as they might result in more than one HTTP request and waste JavaScript execution.

- Remove comments and whitespace (spaces, newlines, and tabs), and compress the resulting file for faster downloads.

- Put scripts at the bottom of the page. By loading scripts just before the closing </body> tag, the page can download other components first and render the page progressively.

**Note:** Only move JavaScript to the bottom of the page if you're certain it doesn't have any adverse effects on your page. For example, do not move JavaScript code snippets requiring document.write or event handlers from the <head> element.

- Consider including JavaScript files using a standard HTML <script> tag right before your closing </apex:page> tag instead of using <apex:includeScript>. The <apex:includeScript> tag places JavaScript right before the closing </head> element, causing the browser to attempt to load the JavaScript before rendering any other content on the page.

- Use static resources to serve JavaScript files, as well as images, CSS, and other non-changing files. JavaScript and other assets served this way benefit from the caching and content distribution network (CDN) built into Salesforce.

**Tip:** For Javascript and CSS, it might be burdensome during development to make a change, process and package it, and deploy. Consider automating this process through a script.

## Summary

Optimizing Visualforce page speed involves a plethora of options, yet there are excellent tools at our disposal to speed the pathway to success. To summarize best practices, consider:

- Design your Visualforce pages according to some general guidelines.
- Use standard objects and declarative features.
- Limit the amount of data that your Visualforce pages display.
- Delay expensive calculations or data loading.
- Offload processing to asynchronous tasks.
- Cache global data in custom settings.

When it comes to efficiency your options look at your Apex Code, SOQL, and Getter methods. Look for ways to optimize:

- View state
- Component hierarchies
- Polling
- HTML
- CSS
- JavaScript
- Image usage
- Pages for Internet Explorer

As you work your way through optimizing your Visualforce page load time and efficiency, we strongly recommend utilizing A/B testing to be sure that any "enhancements" you apply actually result in a faster page. For example, if you add an index to speed SOQL or SOSL queries, be sure and examine your before (B), and after (A) timeframes. Don't forget: When your Users are happy, you'll be happy too!